ISLAMIC THOUGHT
GROWTH AND DEVELOPMENT

ENCYCLOPAEDIC SURVEY OF ISLAMIC CULTURE SERIES

ISLAMIC THOUGHT
Growth and Development

Edited by
MOHAMED TAHER

ANMOL PUBLICATIONS PVT. LTD.
NEW DELHI-110 002 (INDIA)

ANMOL PUBLICATIONS PVT. LTD.
4374/4B, Ansari Road, Daryaganj
New Delhi-110 002

Islamic Thought: Growth and Development

First Edition 1998
ISBN 81-7488-946-9

PRINTED IN INDIA

Published by J.L. Kumar for Anmol Publications Pvt. Ltd., New Delhi-110 002 and Printed at Mehra Offset Press, Delhi.

Contents

Preface

The *Encyclopaedic Survey of Islamic Culture* is a unique reference source. This series seeks to anthologise the most important primary and secondary materials on a wide variety of topics and writers of Islamic culture and civilisation. The scholar, the student and the layman will find in various volumes not only a generous selection of reprinted articles, but original essays, bibliographies, and other materials brought for the first time in a comprehensive and exhaustive fashion.

The need for this collation grew out of our awareness that there is no comprehensive source of information for the study and research of the field. Other published works are too specialised in the topics discussed or neglect the institutional as well the individual role which the Islamic system plays. Few encyclopaedic works do exist, and few anthologies also have appeared. Fewer books, again, have systematically covered such topics as Islam in Africa, Islamic sociology, Islamic polity, Islamic thought, etc. Although these topics have been addressed separately, no attempt has been made to discuss them as part of a united treatment of the literature of the field.

Islam brought a total change in all spheres of life. It revolutionised many societies, both in the east and the west. But this is not always accepted and acknowledged. To quote Major Arthur Leonard from his work: Islam; her moral and spiritual value:

"Never to this day has Europe acknowledged in an honest and whole hearted manner the great and everlasting debt she owes to Islamic culture and civilisation. Only in a lukewarm and perfunctory way has she recognised that when, during the dark ages, her people were sunk in feudalism and ignorance, Muslim civilisation under the Arabs reached a high standard of social and scientific splendour that kept the flickering members of European society from utter decadence.

"Do not we, who now consider ourselves on the top most pinnacle ever reached by culture and civilisation, recognise that, had it not been for the high culture, the civilisation and intellectual, as well as the social splendours of the Arabs and soundness of their school system, Europe would to this day have remained sunk in the darkness of ignorance. Have we forgotten that the Muslim maxim was that, the real learning of a man is of more public importance than any particular religious opinions he may entertain, that Muslim liberality was in striking contrast with the then intolerant state of Europe? Does the magnificent valour of the Arabs, inspired as it was by a theism as lofty as it was pure, not appeal to us? Does not the moderation and comparative toleration shown by them to the conquered, notwithstanding the fierce and burning ardour to regenerate mankind that impelled them onward to conquest, also appeal to us? Does it not all the more appeal to us when we contrast this with the bitterness of the attitude of the Christian sects towards one another? Especially when we consider that in Christendom, as it was then constituted, extortion, tyranny and imperial centralisation, combining with ecclesiastical despotism and persecution, had practically extinguished patriotism, by substitution in its place schismatic and degenerate Church?"

Further the same writer continues to say:

> "Is it possible that Europe is unmindful of, and has the ingratitude to ignore the splendid services of the scientists and philosophers of Arabic? Are the names of Assamh, Abu Othman, Alberuni, Albeithar, Abu Ali Ibn Sina (Avicenna) the great physician and philosopher, Ibn Rushd (Anempace) besides a host of others but dead letters? Is the great work that they have done and the fame they have left behind them in their books to be consigned to the limbo of oblivion, by an ungrateful but antipathetic Europe?

"It cannot be that already we have lost sight of the amazing intellectual activity of the Muslim world during the earlier part of the `Abbaside' period more especially. It cannot be that we have quite forgotten the irrecoverable loss that was inflicted on Arabian literature, and on the world at large, by the wanton destruction of thousands of books that was promoted by Christian bigotry and fanaticism? It cannot be surely said of Christian Europe that for centuries now she has done her best to hide obligations to the Arabs; yet most assuredly, obligations such as these, are far too sacred to lie much linger hidden."

This is one side of the story. The other side is that the West has definitely absorbed much of the Islamic contributions and is "unaware." To quote Marcus Marby and William Underhill "Bold new visions from ancient landscapes" (*Newsweek*, May 29, 1995): Christian and Islamic civilizations have been in conflict for most of their history. But as often as they have clashed, they have enriched each other. In this ninth century, Moors brought advanced architecture, astronomy and medicine to occupied Spain. While Europe lingered in the Dark Ages, courtly poetry from Persia inspired the troubadours, whose verse evolved into the literature of the early French Renaissance. Even whiling away hours over coffee and conversation—the basis for the cafe—came from Arab culture... France's most popular dish today is not escargots but couscous. French slang is peppered with Arab words like kif-kif (50-50) and Insha Allah (God willing). The hottest new music is Arab-inspired rai" (p. 28). The list of Arabic borrowed words in English and Western usages are many more, not mere algebra, alchemy, azimuth, albatross, timbal, zenith, etc.

There is, in short, a lot of misinformation and incorrect representation about Islam. And more so there is a need today to describe and interpret the issues and express in clear terms what this thought actually deals with. Due to social and cultural changes, the salient aspects of the field require examination. The post cold war era has left the world with a unipolar political system. Islam is a system which promises the world that if applied in toto it would solve the multi-dimensional problems of the modern era. But is there any one who wishes to test this module and try it in a space and time to see the truth of the statement?

The primary purpose of this encyclopaedic survey is to serve as a basic handbook on significant topics of Islamic culture. To facilitate an understanding of the field, the series presents a survey and an analysis of the various socio-cultural forces that shape both the structure and functions of the field as well as by the way this society has changed. We also analyse the larger forces outside the community, such as assimilation and acculturation, and forces inside the community, like, role of the leadership, role of the social and cultural groups and the so much alleged 'imbalance' in the theory and practice of the faith.

We are confident that this work will make a permanent and significant contribution to the study of Islam. Its style is simple, and it is presented in a style accessible to a wide audience. Its target audience is faculty, students, and all concerned with the understanding of the faith of the second largest following in the world. While it has scholarly materials, it is nevertheless also of use to those who have no knowledge of the field, as well as to those who are working in related and allied fields. Most important, we hope that this series will be useful in teaching and learning as an educational resource in the academic world.

The series is planned to be both, multi-volume and multi-faceted set, which will run into hundreds of numbers. The compilation of such a huge set is a gigantic task and requires the support and encouragement of all concerned. It requires feed-back and also support from the literary market place and literary circles all over.

A collection of articles, or an anthology, has many benefits, like, it renews our acquaintance with literature which we have neglected, it reveals to us material of which we were ignorant, and it exposes relationships where we did not suppose them to exist. This is the ultimate purpose of our efforts and we wish and pray that this is fulfilled.

A word of acknowledgement is due to the inspiration of the idea of a comprehensive, commulative and compact set of literary works on the Islamic culture. These inspirers are from all walks of life and their efforts must be acknowledged which includes contributors, authors and editors, as well as the publishers who have graciously contributed to this project and we duly acknowledge their cooperation. The well wishers are many more and listing all the concerned by names is impossible here. Each must be duly rewarded for this gesture, and this is our sincere prayer.

—Editor

1

The Religion of Islam: An Introduction

AHMAD A GALWASH

(Abstract: Islam, the way of submission, has definitely a relation with modern civilization, and Islam has been benefcial to humanity in geneal and it has an everlasting influence on the development of human character).

The diffusion of knowledge over the world and the spread of civilisation have very largely lessened the difference between one nation and another and have almost subdued the flames of animosity kindled in men's bosoms by blind fanaticism evoked by religion or creed. History relates many awful wars waged in the name of religion.

Today, however, people are largely imbued with the sprit of toleration and love of truth and liberty. The more enlightened do respect the doctrines and principles of others, however widely they differ from their own. The followers of different religion make earnest endeavours to spread their own faith and to plant their standards even farther afield. It is left to reason to examine and judge the respective merits of each. Christian missionaries in the Orient may be heard loudly preaching Christianity to followers of Moses and Mohammad without the least apprehension of any unlawful opposition on the part of their hearts.

From time to time, we read of some, distinguished person who has abandoned the religion of his forefathers to adopt a different persuasion, which, in the light of reason he has found more acceptable. Further the spirit of intelligent curiosity has been so fully developed in human beings by education, that books are eagerly read which deal with the dogmas and tenets of different nations. The widest possible knowledge of these is sought and at times an attachment to new beliefs is not hidden, nor a readiness to adopt them.

On the other hand, the more highly a nation is civilised, the more it is inclined to make known its customs, habits and national or religious character.

Although some vague knowledge of the laws and tenets of Islam may be obtained from treatises and books which have been composed by certain Westerners, yet he who desires thoroughly to comprehend their sprit must trace to the fountain-head. In the ordinary intercourse of life, he who is desirous of gaining the esteem and affection of those with whom he converses, will be careful not to offend against their religious precepts and notions of right and wrong, with which precepts and notions he can become acquainted by consulting their won records.

Furthermore, it behoves those ministers and missionaries of the Christian faith whose zeal leads them the labour in the propagation of their own doctrines and in attempts to refute the tenets and precepts of other religions, to be well acquainted with those things which they undertake to impugn.

The learned Roland (I) has shown that "Christian writers of no small eminence in point of learning and reputation have egregiously misrepresented the doctrine of Muslim faith, and bestowed much useless labour, in confuting opinions which the followers of the Arabian Prophet never maintained; thus exposing themselves to the charge of ignorance and the contempt of their adversaries; and injuring the cause they had undertaken to defend, by making it appear to stand in need of false allegations for its support."

Indeed, it is misrepresentation and misinformation, from which Muslims chiefly suffer. They have had imputed to them that which has no existence whatever in their teachings and policy; baseless charges have been advanced against Islam; nay, the very beauties which Muslims account amongst their exclusive possessions have been denied them, and the very evils which came to eradicate and did succeed in so doing, are ascribed to it. It is certainly a great pity that, with all this outpouring of learning and literature, very little real effort has been made to clear away the clouds of misrepresentation and defective knowledge which still envelop the religion of the Arabian Prophet in Europe and America.

It is a happy sign, however, to find plans for a universal religion being discussed in certain advanced circles in both continents, and a desire to create a better understanding among the adherents of the various denominations of the world.

To achieve this desirable end, it is inconsistent with the advanced culture of enlightened European or America enquirers that information on Islam — a religion which at present is a powerful factors in humanising millions hitherto living in ignorance and barbarity — should come through any adulterated channels and from the writings and works of propangandists hostile to Islam.

Undoubtedly a true knowledge of the Prophet and of his principal teachings is full to interest to those who desire to increase their general stock of information. Indeed the doctrines of Islam tend in general to promote the welfare and prosperity of mankind, inasmuch as they cultivate charity and good will to all people.

The Prophet said "No man's faith shall be perfect unless he wishes for his brother whatsoever he wishes for himself."

That Islam was admittedly the torch-bearer of light and learning in the West when Europe was enshrouded in ignorance and darkness, and that the followers of the Holy Prophet were undoubtedly among the very few factors creating the conditions leading to present culture and advancement, are in themselves cogent to justify and appeal to the Westerner's sense of duty and justice in judging Islam and the Muslims.

An honest student of the tenets of Islam and the labours of

Muslims for the regeneration and edification of mankind, especially of Europe, cannot fail to find much for which Islam should be thanked.

I quote Major Arthur Glyn Leonard in this connection :

"Never to this day has Europe acknowledged in an honest and wholehearted manner the great and everlasting debt she owes to Islamic culture and civilisation. Only in a lukewarm and perfunctory way has she recognised that when, during the dark ages, her people were sunk in feudalism and ignorance, Muslim civilisation under the Arabs reached a high standard of social and scientific splendour that kept the flickering members of European society from utter decadence.

"Do not we, who now consider ourselves on the topmost pinnacle ever reached by culture and civilisation, recognise that, had it not been for the high culture, the civilisation and intellectual, as well as the social splendours of the Arabs and soundness of their school system, Europe would to this day have remained sunk in the darkness of ignorance? Have we forgotten that the Muslim maxim was that, the real learning of a man is of more public importance than any particular religious opinions he may certain, that Muslim liberality was in striking contrast with the then intolerant state of Europe? Does the magnificent valour of the Arabs, inspired as it was by a theism as lofty as it was pure, not appeal to us? Does not the moderation and comparative toleration shown by them to the conquered, notwithstanding the fierce and burning ardour to regenerate mankind that impelled them onward to conquest, also appeal to us? Does it not all the more appeal to us when we contrast this the bitterness of the attitude of the Christian sects towards one another? Especially when we consider that in Christendom, as it was then constituted, extortion, tyranny and imperial centralisation, combining with ecclesiastical despotism and persecution, had practically extinguished patriotism, by substitution in its place schismatic and degenerate Church?"

Further the same writer continues to say :

"Is it possible that Europe is unmindful of, and has the ingratitude to ignore the splendid services of the scientists and philosophers of Arabic? Are the names of Assamh, Abu Othman, Alberuni, Albeithar, Abu Ali Ibn Sina (Avicenna) the great physician and philosopher, Ibn Rushd (Averroes) of Cordova, the chief commentator of Aristotle, Ibn Bajja (Anempace) besides a host of others but dead letters? Is the great work that they have done and the fame they have left behind them in their books to be consigned to the limbo of oblivion, by an ungrateful but antipathetic Europe?

"It cannot be that already we have lost sight of the amazing intellectual activity of the Muslim world during the earlier part of the 'Abbaside' period more especially. It cannot be that we have quite forgotten the irrecoverable loss that was inflicted on Arabian literature, and on the world at large, by the wanton destruction of thousands of boozs that was promoted by Christian bigotry and fanaticism? It cannot be surely said of Christian Europe that for centuries now she has done her best to hide obligations to the Arabs; yet most assuredly, obligations such as these, are far too sacred to lie much longer hidden." (I)

For further enlightenment as to the far reaching beneficial effects of Islam I quote Bosworth Smith, M.A., Asst. master in Harrow School and late fellow of Trinity College, Oxford :

"Nor does Islam lack other claims on our attention. Its ultimate acceptance by the Arabs, the new direction given to it by the later revelations to Mohammed, its rapid conquests, the literature and civilisation it brought in its train, the way in which it crumpled up the Roman Empire on one side and thc Persian on the other, how it drove Christianity before it on the West and north and fire worship on the East and South; how it crushed the false prophets that always follow in the wake of a true one, as the jackals do the trail of a line, how it spread over two continents, and how it settled in a third and at one time all but overwhelmed the whole... all this is matter of history, at which I can only glance.

"And what is the position now?

"It numbers at this day more than one hundred millions, probably one hundred and fifty millions(I) of believers as sincere, as devout, as true to their creed, as are the believers in any creed whatever. It still has its gript on three continents, extending from Morocco to the Malay Peninsula, from Zenzibar to the Kirghis horde....

"...Africa, which had yielded so early to Christianity, nay, which had given birth to Latin Christianity itself, the Africa of Cyprian and Tertullian, of Antony and Augustine, yielded still more readily to Mohammed; and from the Straits of Gibraltar to the Isthmus of Suez may still be heard the Cry which with them is no vain repetition of "Allah Akbar", God is Great, there is no God but God and Mohammed is His Prophet.

"And if it be said, as it often is, that Islam has gained nothing since the first flame of religious enthusiasm fanned, as it often was, by the lust of conquest, had died out, I answer that this is far from the truth.

"In the extreme East, Islam has since then won and maintained for centuries a moral supremacy in the important Chinese province of Yunnan, and has thus actually succeeded in thrusting a wedge between the two great Budhist empires of Burmah and of China...

"Throughout the Chinese Empire there are scattered Mussulman communities who have higher hopes than Bhudhism or Confucianism, and a purer morality than Taoism can supply. The Panthays themselves, it is believed, still number a million and a half, and the unity of God and the mission of God's Prophet are attested day by day by a continuous line of worshippers from the Atlantic to the Pacific Ocean.

"Nay, even beyond, in the East Indian Archipelago, beyond the straits of Malacca if I may venture just now so to call them, in Java and Sumatra, in Borneo and Celebes, ISLAM has raised many of the natives above their former selves and long been the dominant faith...

"It cannot of course, be supposed that race so low in the scale of humanity as are of the Indian islanders, Islam would be able to do what it did originally for the Arabs or for the Turkish hordes; but it has done something even for them. It was propagated by missionaries who *cared very much for the souls they could win, and nothing for the plunder they could carry off.* They conciliated the natives, learned their language, intermarried with them and in larger islands their success was rapid, and, so far as nature would allow, complete.

"The Philippines and the Molaccas, which were conquered by Spain and Portugal respectively, did not become Muslims for they had to surrender at once liberty and their religion. It is no wonder that the religion, known to the natives chiefly through the unblushing rapacity of the Dutch, has not extended itself beyond the reach of their swords. Here, as elsewhere in the East, the most fatal hindrance to the spread of Christianity has been the lives of Christians (2)....

"In Africa again Islam is spreading itself by giant strides almost year by year. Everyone knows that within half a century of the Prophet's death, the richest states of Africa, and those most accessible to Christianity and to European Civilisation, were torn away from both, by the armies of the faithful, with hardly a struggle or a regret; but few, except those who have studied the subject, are aware that even since then Islam has been gradually spreading over the northern half of the continent.

"Starting from the north west corner, it first marched southwards from Morocco, and by the time of the Norman Conquest had reached the neighborhood of Timbuctoo, and had got firm hold of the Mandingoes, thence it spread southwards again to the Foulahs, and then eastward by the thirteenth century to Lake Chad, where finally the Arab missionaries from the West joined hands with those from the East in the very heart of Africa..

"We hear of whole tribes laying aside their devil-worship or immemorial Fetish and springing at a bound, as it were, from the very lowest to one of the highest forms of religious belief. Christian travellers with every wish to think otherwise, have remarked that the negro who accepts Islam, acquires at once a sense of the dignity of human nature not commonly found even among those who have been brought to accept Christianity.

"It is also pertinent to observe here, that such progress as any large part of the negro race has hitherto made, is in exact proportion to the time that has elapsed, or the degree of fervour, with which they originally embraced, or have since clung to Islam. The Mandingoes and the Foulahs are salient instances of this; their unquestionable superiority to other negro tribes is as unquestionably owing to the early hold that Islam got upon them, and to the civilisation and culture that it has always encouraged. The Government Blue Books on our West African settlements, and the reports of missionary societies themselves, are quite at one on this head. The Governor of our West African Colonies, Mr. Pope Hennesay, remarks that the liberated African are always handed over to Christian missionaries for instruction, and that their children are baptised and brought up at the public expense in Christian schools, and are, therefore, in a sense, ready made converts, yet the total number of profession Christians, 35,000 out of a population of 513,000, very few even of these, as the Governor says, and as we can unfortunately well believe from our experience in countries that are not African, being practical Christian — fall far short of the original number of liberated African and their descendents. On the other hand the Rev. James Johnson, a native clergyman, and a man of remarkable energy and intelligence, as well as of very Catholic spirit, deplores the fact that of the total number of Muslims to be found in Sierra Leone and its neighbourhood three fourths were not born Muslims, but have become so by conversion, whether from a nominal Christianity or from Paganism.

"We are assured on all hands that the Muslim population has an almost passionate desire for education, and those in the nieghbourhood of our colonies would throng our schools, first if the practical education given was worth having, and secondly, if the teachers would refrain from needlessly attacking their cherished and often harmless customs. Wherever, Muslims are numerous, they establish schools themselves, and there are not a few who travel extraordinary distances to secure the best possible education. Mr. Pope Hennessy mentions the case of one young Muslim Negro who is in the habit of purchasing costly books from Trubner in London and who went to Foulah, two hundred and fifty miles away, to obtain an education better that he could find in Sierra Leone itself. Nor is it an uncommon thing for newly converted Muslims to maze their way right across the desert from Bornu or from Lake Chad, or down the Nile from Darfour or Wadi, a journey of over one thousand miles that they may carry on their studies in *El-Azhar*, the great collegiate Mosque at Cairo, and they may thence bring back the results of their training to their native country, and from so many centres of Muslim teaching and example.

"Nor as to the effects of Islam when first embraced by a negro tribe can there be any reasonable doubt. Polytheism disappears almost instantaneously, sorcery with its attendant evils, gradually dies away; human sacrifice becomes a thing of the past. The general moral elevation is most marked; the natives begin for the first time in their history to dress and that neatly. Squalid filth is replaced by a scrupulous cleanliness; inhospitality becomes a comparatively rare exception. Though polygamy is allowed by the Koran, it is not common in practice; and, beyond the limits laid down by the Prophet, incontinence is rare; chastity is looked upon as one of the highest and becomes in fact one of the commoner virtues. It is idleness henceforward that degrades, instead of the reverse. Offences are henceforward measured by a written code instead of the arbitrary caprice of a chieftain — a step as everyone will admit, of vast importance in the progress of a tribe. The Mosque gives an idea at all event higher than any the negro has yet had. A third for literature is created, and that for works of science and philosophy, as well as for commentaries on the Koran. There are whole tribes, as the Jalofs on the river Gambia and the Haussas, whose many qualities we have had occasions to test in Ashantee, which have become to a man Mulims, and have raised themselve infinitely in the process; and the very name salt-water-Muslims given to those tribes along the coast, who, from admixture with European settlers, have relaxed the severity of the prophet's laws, is a striking proof of the extent, to which the stricter form of the faith prevails in the far interior.

"It is melancholy to contrast with wide spread beneficial influences of Islam, the little that has been done for Africa till very lately by the Christian nations that have settled in it, and the still narrower limits, within which it has been confined. Till a few years ago the good effects produced beyond the immediate territories occupied by them were absolutely nothing. . .

"The message that European traders have carried for centuries to Africa has been one of rapacity, of cruelty and of bad faith. It is a remarks of Dr. Livingstone's (I) that the only art that the nations of Africa have acquired from their 500 years' acquaintance with the Portuguese, has been the art of distilling sprits from a gun-barrel; and that the only permanent belief they owe to them, is the belief that man may sell his brother man; for this, he says emphatically, is not a native benefit to Africa; but if we except the small number of converts made within the limits of their settlements, it has been the only benefit conferred by Europeans.

"Truly if the question must be put, whether it is Muslim or Christian nations that have as yet done most for Africa, the answer must be that it is not the Christian."

I think I can occupy no more space in this introduction by making further quotations to discuss the relation of Islam to modern civilisation and the position which it holds among the recognised religions of the world. It is a matter of pure history that Islam has been beneficial to humanity in general and that it had, and still has, an everlasting influence on the development of human character.

The Muslim School embraces all branches of human knowledge and research — theology, medicine, history, astronomy, grammar, economics, physics, racial philosophy and racial psychology and ethics. It is an important educator on all systems of purely human origin, and its creed adores, worships and acknowledges the Creator or the Universe, in the most sublime, lofliest and expression, never to be found in the liturgy of other religions. The Islamic conception of God is that He is *'Allah'* and there is no deity beside Him; He alone is to be worshipped. He begets not and He is not begotten. He was before time began its race. He is 'Allah' Who hath raised different prophets of men throughout the ages. His greatness is immeasurable. Allah is He That abideth from eternity to eternity. This is but a fractional part of the Muslim Creed — a creed which strictly, forbids the worship of images and the artistic representation of anything that resembles the human form. Yet in Christian literature, periodicals and other publications Muslims have been alluded to, and spoken of, as pagans, idolaters, polygamists, sunworshippers and what not. Our sacred edifice has been characterised as the Mosque of swords, our heaven as a heaven of sensual bliss, and that after death we sink into space, soul-less, and have no account to give. In the romance of "Turpin" quoted by Renan, Mohammed, the fanatical destroyer of all idolatry, is turned himself into an idol of gold, and under the name of Mawmet, is reported to be the object of worship at Cadiz. In the song of Ronald, the National Epic of France, Mohammed appears with the chief of the Pagan Gods on the one side of him and the chief of the Devils on the other. Human sacrifices are supposed to have been offered to him; in the imagination and assertions of Christian writers of the tenth and eleventh centuries he appeared under the various names of Bafum, or Maphomet, or Mawmet. Malaterra, in his history of Sicily describes that island as being, when under Saracenic rule, a land wholly given up to idolatry. It is not a little curious that the English and French language still bear witness to the popular misapprehension; the French by the word "Mahomeric", the English by the word "Mummery", still used for absurd or superstitions rites. "Mammetry", a contraction of Mahometry was used in early English for any false religion, especially for worship of idols, insomuch that "Mammet" or "Mawmet" came to mean an idol. In Shakespeare the name is extended to mean a doll : Juliet, for instance, is called by her father "A whinning mammet".

In the twelfth century "the god Mawmet" passes into the heresiarch Mahomet, and as such, of course he occupies a conspicuous place in the 'Inferno'.

Dante places him in his ninth circle among the sowers of religious discord; his companions being Fra Dolima, a communist of the forteenth century, and Berterand de Born, a fighting Troubadour.

The Romances of Baphomet, so common in the fourteenth and fifteenth centuries, attribute any and every crime to him, just as the Athanasians did to Arius. He is a debauchee, a camel stealer, a cardinal, who having failed to obtain the object of every cardinal's ambition, invents a new religion to revenge himself on his brethern.

With the leaders of the Reformation, Mohammed "the greatest of all Reformers" meets with little sympathy, and their hatred of him, as perhaps was natural, seems to be proportionate with their knowledge. Luther doubts whether he is not worse than Leo; Melanchton believes him to be either Gog or Maggog, and probably both.

In the imagination of the Biblical commentators the Arabian Prophet divides with the Pope the credit, or discredit, of being the subject of social prophecy in the books of Daniel and the Revelation. "He is Antichrist, the Man of Sin, the Little Horn" and I known at what the eighteenth century, trees of him as otherwise than a rank impostor and false prophet.

England and France were the first to take a different view and to have begun that critical study of Arabian history or literature which in the hands of Gibbon and or Muir, of Caussin de Perceval and of St. Hilaire, of Weil and of Springer has provided some material for a comparatively fair and unbiassed judgment within reach of everyone. But most other writers of the 18th century such as Dean Prideaux and the Abbe Maracci, Boulainvilliers and Voltaire have approached the subject only to prove a thesis. With them the Prophet was to be either a hero or an impostor. "From them is learnt much that has been said about Mohammed, but comparatively little of Mohammed himself."

Gagnier has then proceeded to write a history of the Prophet claimed to have been based on the work of Abul Feda. Gagnier's history was still not free wrong inferences and efroneous allusions.

Then followed the translations of the "Koran" by Sale and Savary into English and French respectively. Gibbon has then written his "three masterpieces of biography": Athanasius, eulian and "Mohammed." Gibbon's treatment of Islam is considered to be generally fair and philosophic, "in spite of occasional uncalled—for sarcasms and characteristic innuendoes." It seems that Gibbon's so-called unfair treatment of Christianity prevented the Christian world from doing justice to his generally fair treatment of Islam; and consequently most Englishmen who do not condemn the Arabian Prophet unheard, derive what favourable nations of him they have , not from Gibbon, but from Carlyle."

It was really a great surprise and an epoch in English intellectual and religious life, as Bosworth Smith has rightly observed, when it was found that Carlyle chose for his "Hero as Prophet" "not Moses or Elijah or Isaiah, but the so-called *Impostor Mohammed."*

Now it is time to conclude this my introduction. The reader will see and judge for himself the extent to which European writers of various reputations and in various ages have, in their different treatments of the Prophet Mohammed and of Islam, been either misleading or themselves misled.

In conclusion I wish to express my heart-felt-obligation to my numerous friends both in Egypt and abroad for their kind assistance and encouragement which enabled me to bring this work to the completion. I wish it were possible for me to name them all, but certain considerations prevent my doing so.

My gratitude is due to His Eminence Sheikh Mohammed Mustapha El Maraghi, Grand Rector of Al Azhar University, through whose personal suggestion my book on Islam has been accredited by that great Muslim Institution for publication as a supplement to Al Azhar Official Monthly Organ.

Special mention must, however, be made of Professor Mohammed Khaled Hassanein of Al Azhar University, for their help.

In my human endeavours I humbly implore the Almighty God, God of all mankind, to grant that my labour may serve as a basis, if not for an ultimate agreement between Christendom and Islam, at all events for mutual understanding and forbearance, for sympathy and respect.

REFERENCES

1. Roland, De Relig. Mohammedica, L. II.
2. Bosworth Smith, Mohammed and Mohammedanism.
3. Major Arthur Golyn Leonard, Islam, "Her moral and spiritual value."
4. Crawford's Indian Archipelago, II, 275 and 315.
5. Livingstone's "Expedition to the Zambesi", p. 240.
6. Renan "Etudes d'historie religiouse", p. 223.

2

Islam—The Religion of Submission: An Introduction

MUSHIR UL-HAQ

(Abstract: Presents an over-view of the history of Islam, faith and socio-political issues, all under the main frame of reference: Surrender to the Will of Allah-al Islam).

In the name of Allah, the Merciful, the Compassionate,
Praise be to Allah who all the world made,
The Merciful, the Compassionate,
The King of the Day of Fate,
Thee do we worship, and of Thee do we seek aid.
Guide us in the path that is straight,
The path of those to whom Thy love is great.
Not of those on whom is hate,
Nor of those who deviate.

This is *Al-Fatihah*, the Opening, the first chapter, or *Surah* as it is called in Arabic, of the Qur'an. Muslims recite it several times in day and night. The mere recitation, with understanding, will certainly remind a man that before Allah, the Islamic equivalent for God, he is naught. He cannot walk even on straight path without his guidance. Nor, without his mercy, can he check himself from going astray. Hc has constantly to be on guard against incurring divine wrath.

Since man cannot attain God without His help, God, in order to make Himself attainable, has from time to time been sending his guidance to him in different ways. The last time when he decided to make Himself known to the people. He chose the medium of 'letter' that is the Qur'an, the Recital.

The year was 610 : the city was Mecca in Arabia. It was one of the last ten nights of the month of *Ramadan*, the tenth month of the Islamic calendar, when God sent down the first revelation upon the Prophet Muhammad.

Muhammad was born in the year 570 A.D. At an early age he lost his parents and was brought up by one of his uncles. In his youth he earned his livelihood by working as commission agent to wealthy traders of mecca carrying their merchandise to other neighbouring cities. On one such occasion he was employed by Khadijah, a rich widow in Mecca, to take charge of her caravan. He discharged his mission very successfully. Impressed by his honesty and fair dealings she, even though many years senior of him, sought his land in marriage.

Relieved of the necessity of earning his living. Muhammad now had time to give himself to reflection. In a cave of a nearby mountain called Hira, he spent hours and days thinking of life and its meaning. There he began to have strange experiences of a mystical character. He saw vision, and heard voices. It was in some such moment that there came to him the tiding that he was a prophet, and he received his first revelation.

There are references in the Qur'an as to how it was revealed for the first time. The details, however, are found in the books of *Hadith*, the collections of the Prophet's sayings and doings. It is stated that one night when, sitting in his usual hide-out, he was absorbed in his thoughts that he visualized someone standing before him, identified later as the archangel Gabriel, who asked him to recite in the name of his Lord. Aware of his limitations the Prophet was at first hesitant, but as the angel persisted in his demand, words came out of his mouth:

Recite in the name of the Lord who created,
Created man out of mere clot of congealed blood:
Recite! and thy Lord is most bountiful,——
He who taught the use of the pen,—
Taught man that which he knew not.

This was a novel and strange experience which shook him completely. Shattered and trembling he returned home, and confided in his wife: "could it be that this was a call from God?" She was convinced that it certainly was. She was the first to believe in him as the true Prophet of God. Confidently he later told some of his close associates of his experience, and they too believe in him.

Thenceforth the Prophet remained receiving revelation throughout his life. Sometimes it consisted of only one or two verses, and sometimes a whole *surah* of full length like the twelfth one consisting of one hundred and eleven verses.

When the Prophet told his townsmen that he was receiving revelation from God they made fun of him. After listening to the Qur'an, some called him a poet while others equated him with soothsayers and regarded him out of his mind. But the Qur'an exonerated him from such charges and declared: "We have not instructed the Prophet and poetry" "O people, your companion is not one possessed."

People were also sore about the fact that it was Muhammad, a relatively poor and uninfluential man of the town, who was chosen for prophethood. Their criticism and objection are found in the Qur'an. They used to say; "Why is not the Qur'an sent down to some leading man in either of the two chief cities?" Or, "Say those without knowledge; why speaketh not God to one of us? or why cometh not unto us a sign?' Also, "they say: we shall not believe until we receive one exactly like those received by God's apostles."

In spite of their objections and criticism, however, people started listening to the Qur'an and accepting it as the true revelation from God. The language and style of the Qur'an were so attractive that most people found its message irresistible. The number of believers increased with such a speed that those who opposed it were just startled. Finally they tried to stop people from listening to the Qur'an by hooting them away. But that was all in vain, for in the final it is the truth which prevails.

Gradually in 23 years was completed the revelation in the form of the Qur'an which contains in it 114 *surahs* of varying length, 6,236 verses, 77,934 words and 3,23,621 letters. Unlike the first revelation, there is no unanimity among the Muslim scholars on the chronologically last verse revealed to the Prophet. The majority, however, is of the opinion that the last two verses of *surah* 9 were revealed only nine days before the death of the Prophet. Thereafter, he received none. However, what lies between the first and the last revelation in a book which has undoubtedly left a lasting mark on the religious, social and political history of mankind. Hardly can any scripture be compared with the Qur'an in its immediate impact upon the lives of the people who were its initial recipients. They, and after them the generation that followed them, have always found the Qur'an supplying satisfactory answers to all of their queries. It is quite possible that Muslims occasionally might have misconstrued the answer, or might have departed from the spirit of its message, but the fact remains that to the believers the Qur'an always represents the ultimate manifestation of God's grace to man, the ultimate wisdom, and the ultimate beauty of expression: in short, the true word of God.

The word of God emphasises the oneness of God and His concern with the welfare of man. Besides, it speaks of the creation of the world and specially of man, good and evil spirits, man's responsibility for his actions, the coming of the Day of Judgement, the final account, reward and punishment. In addition, we find in the Qur'an rules and regulations regarding worship and the life of the community, including quite special laws concerning family life such as marriage, divorce, inheritance. Several sets of commands are found scattered in the Qur'an. If arranged properly, they can be taken, like the Decalogue of the Moses, as definite Qur'anic commandments. The most systematic bunch of these found in one place, is in *surah* 17, verses 23-40. They are:

1. Put not any other god with Allah;
2. Be Kind and respectful to parents, especially in their old age;
3. Give what is due to kinsmen, the poor and travellers;
4. Be not wasteful;
5. Slay not your children for fear of poverty;
6. Go not near fornication;
7. Slay not the soul which Allah has forbidden you, except for just cause;
8. Draw not near to the wealth of the orphan;
9. Fulfil your contracts;
10. Give just measure and weight;
11. Follow not that of which you have no knowledge;
12. Walk not proudly on earth.

The Qur'an has been revealed in chaste language and best of style. It was the only literary style, at that time, acceptable to the Arabs. Those who opposed the Prophet raised a number of objections regarding his claim to prophethood, but they never failed to find any fault with language or the style of the Qur'an. The most that they could say was that Muhammad was tutored by some foreign teacher. But the Qur'an challenged them to explain as to how a non-Arab could be the author of such pure and chaste Arabic. In this whole dialogue the reference to a non-Arab is very significant. It means that the contemporary Arabs knew that no Arab could compose a piece like that of the Qur'an. Confronted with the quality of the language and style they had to confess that the source of the Qur'an was superhuman, even though for many reasons they could not say it openly. The simplest way out, therefore, was to tell the people that Muhammad had a supernaturally eloquent teacher from somewhere outside Arabia.

The contemporary Arabs never complained of "confusion"

or "crudeness" in the Qur'an. It is a later phenomenon, especially that of the non-Arabs. It is a fact, however, that while a believer reciting the Qur'an in its original language sees beauty most non-believing readers often claim to discern therein crudity. Passages which to a Muslim are expressive of sublime wisdom often sound flat and uninspiring to many non-Muslims. The coherence of the Qur'anic world-view and its relevance to the human conditions escape them altogether. It sound to them what is frequently described as an "incoherent rambling". Thus, critics of the Qur'an point out to its allegedly incoherent reference to God—often in one and the same phrase—as He, God, We, or I, with the corresponding changes of the pronouns from His to Ours to My, or from Him to Us or Me. They seem to be unaware of the fact that these variations are not accidental, and not even what one might describe as 'poetic licence'. They are *deliberate*: a linguistic device meant to stress the idea that God is not a 'person' and cannot, therefore, be really circumscribed by the pronouns applicable to finite beings.

About the present textual arrangement of the Qur'an the books of tradition say the Gabriel taught the Prophet the right place of each verse. The Prophet used to tell his companions where a particular verse was to go. Similarly once a *surah* was completed the Prophet was informed of its exact location in the Qur'an. In this connetion we should remember that the Qur'anic verses are of two kinds: legal and non-legal. In so far as the legal verses are concerned, the Qur'an is direct and precise. It is only the non-legal verses wherein the message has been repeated. And it was necessary. The Qur'an is meant to put may on its right path; therefore, monosyllabic orders were not enough. For the same reason the Qur'an could not be arranged according to subject matter. For, then all the verses, say, dealing with the oneness of God, the Prophethood, the virtuous living, and so on, were to be put together. Imagine what a dull and boring reading it then could have been.

So long as the Prophet Muhammad, after receiving the revelation, carried on his mission in secret, all went well. Bitter opposition arose only when he publicly claimed that he was a prophet of God, and all were to follow him. As a prophet he was not a mere bearer of God's revelation: he was required to convey it to others. A prophet's mission as a matter of fact does not end but begins with the recitation of the revelation. This has been clearly stated in the Qur'an:

> "He it is who hath sent among the unlettered ones a messenger of their own, to recite unto them His revelation and to make them grow, and to teach them the scriptures and wisdom, though heretofore, they were indeed in error manifest."

It then appears that Prophet Muhammad had before him three important tasks. First he had to transmit the revelation to his fellowmen and explain to them its meaning and its implication. The second was to urge them to give up their evil practices, and live a life of piety, love and devotion. The third was to lay the foundation of a new society. For all these basic prophetic tasks he had to come forward courageously. He fearlessly, therefore, attacked the Meccans' belief in idols housed in the House of God, the *Ka'bah*. This they could not tolerate, and the Prophet and his followers were to bear the consequences. The persecution became so severe that the Prophet with his companions had finally to move out of the city in A.D. 622 and settle down in Yathrib, later called al-Madinah (The City), about 200 miles north of Mecca.

Even in Madinah life for the Prophet and his companions was not peaceful in the beginning. The local non-believers, Jews and others, finding themselves incapable of stopping the rapid expansion of Islam, conspired with the people of Mecca, who themselves did not like to see a strong centre of their opponents established so close to the trade route by which their caravans passed. Soon skirmishes began between the two groups. Finally, the Meccans surrendered, and in a ten years' time the Prophet became the master of the whole of Arabia.

When the Prophet died in 632, he left the whole of Arabia under the sway of Islam with Madinah as its capital. Immediately after his death some neighbouring tribes revolted against the authority of Madinah. Abu Bakr, the first Caliph, who remained on the scene for a little more than two years, took strong action and curbed the revolt. After his death in 634 'Umar, the second Caliph, took the charge. In his days Islam reached beyond the borders of Arabia. Syria and Jerusalem were conquered, and by 637 A.D. he had brought under Islamic control almost the whole region that had once constituted and Babylonian and Assyrian Empires. In 640 Egypt was conquered and in 642 the whole of Persia fell before him. By the end of his caliphate in 644 Islam reigned from Egypt on the west to the borders of India on the east. During the remainder of the century Muslim armies swept across the whole of north Africa, and in the year 711, entered Europe through Spain. Northward they pushed their way steadily until they occupied almost half of France.

For about three decades after the death of the Prophet. Madinah continued to be the centre of the Muslim world. In 661, however, Damascus became the seat of the Caliphate. It was later transferred to Baghdad in Iraq in the eighth century. In the eleventh century the Turks took up the cause of Islam, and in the fifteenth century they overran all of Asia Minor and entered Europe through Constantinople. Steadily they advanced through Central Europe and reached up to Vienna in Austria. About 1000 A.D. in the east having already reached Afghanistan and Baluchistan, Islam had entered the northern plains of India. The South of India was already exposed of Islam through Arab traders. Within a comparatively short time a great Muslim empire was established in India was its capital at Delhi which was ultimately wiped out by the British in 1857.

In the Far East Islam reached China in the 9th century where even today its followers number several millions. The Malaysia and Indonesia became gradually almost wholly Muslim. Evidence shows that by the 16th century Islam was already well established in Philippine Islands. From the narrow rim around the north end of Africa, bordering on the Mediterranean, Islam had pushed southward across the Sahara taking tribes after tribes of Africa into its fold.

This is the story of the expansion of Islam. This rapid expansion of Islam has created a misunderstanding in the minds of people about the use of sword in the spread of Islam. We must, however, remember that Islam does not approve of compulsion in matters of religion. The Qur'an clearly says: "let there be no compulsion in religion." Still there exists a general disposition on the part of many writers to charge Muslims with the use of sword as a converting agency. The fact is that people usually do not distinguish between political conquest of a religious community and wars to compel acceptance of religion as a faith. However, there are historian and scholars who are convinced beyond any doubt that much of the spread of Islam has been by peaceful preaching.

The Muslims believe that Prophet Muhammad was not the first man to whom God spoke; there had been many before him bestowed with this honour. The uniqueness of the Quranic revelation to Prophet Muhammad, according to Islamic belief, lies in the fact that this was complete and final: afterwards God did not speak, and will not speak to any human being. This final divine speech, however, does not negate the previous revelations; nor does it claim to be something new, something novel. This is the same which has been revealed before—but the followers of its recipients corrupted it. The question of corruption in divine scriptures is an important issue in Islamic theology. According to Muslim understanding of the Qur'an, God has been sending prophets to each nook and corner of the world. So long as the people remained faithful to the revelation and did not corrupt the scriptures, new messengers or prophets did not come. It was only when the scriptures were vitiated that the prophet came. According to the Qur'an, all revelations which preceded it, were distorted and altered by their followers. The Qur'an came to remind them that they should purify their own scriptures from all corruption and accretions. Once this was done, the Qur'an says, they would see for themselves that their religion and Islam were identical.

The Qur'an cannot and will not be altered: God has Himself promised this. History also bears witness to the fact that so far not a single letter of the Qur'an has been changed. Hence no more prophet after Muhammad.

To become a Muslim one has to accept the tenets of Islam in totality. Anyone who surrenders himself to the will of God is a Muslim. This complete and unconditional submission is not, however, easy. One has to undergo severe ordeals. The state of real submission before God has been well described by a Muslim saint of India, Shaikh Fariduddin Shakarganj. Once he was asked about the *zakat*, which, according to the Islamic law, every Muslim who fulfils the given condition has to pay for distribution among the poor at the rate of two and a half per cent of his annual savings. Shaikh Farid considered the rate merely the following of the letter of law. To him it was better to keep two and a half per cent with oneself and give the rest in the way of God. The most praiseworthy, however, were those who gave all. Besides the submission before God, it is stressed that one also has to accept Muhammad as the last prophet of God. In other words, a Muslim has to confess and believe that there is but one God, and Muhammad is his prophet. Many, besides Muslims, may be found sharing belief in the first part of this formula but it is the latter half of it which distinguishes a Muslim from the people of other faiths.

The stress on the prophethood of Muhammad did not allow Islam to remain merely a body of individual religious beliefs. Religious individualism in fact was replaced in Islam by religious collectivism haloed by the personality of the Prophet. Everything which developed in Islamic society had to have the sanction from the prophetic tradition. This produced two novel conceptions: the *sunnah* (tradition) and the *bid'ah* (innovation). The former means all these acts for which a precedent from the life of the Prophet can be quoted, whereas all the rest come under the latter category, and hence are disapproved. Since the life lived by the Prophet was considered to be an ideal life for those who wanted to attain to God, the adherence to the sunnah of the Prophet became essential for the achievements of this goal. This pushed the Islamic community into the sphere of law.

It has been shown earlier that without divine guidance man cannot find the right path. *Hidayat* (guidance), therefore, is one of the most important terms in the Islamic vocabulary. A Muslim is enjoined upon to always look for guidance. Considered in this sense the law of Islam is but an effort to make divine guidance as explicit and detailed as possible. In its broadest sense the law in Islam is called the *shari'ah*.

Thus, the *shari'ah* becomes the eternal divine will for man, and Islam becomes a commitment to follow the *shari'ah*.

"The first and most important thing about the *shari'ah*," it is said, "is the fact that it is a divine law. In the history of mankind many different sanctions for legality have emerged, some having derived the authority of law from the traditions of old, others from the decrees of rulers, other from the consent of the governed, etc. Islamic law accepts none of these but claims its origin and authority, from the very word of God Himself. According to the Islamic understanding man a mere creature, with his unaided faculties is incapable of distinguishing between right and wrong or the determining how he should live. God had decreed a way of life for men, and this decree is the sole and determinative norm. All obligations as well as all rights arise because God in his wisdom had decreed them; their character is juridical. There is no question of human rights or of other `natural' bases of moral judgement. What is right because God has directed it and not the other way round. If he had so chosen, there would have been nothing to prevent God in His freedom from making what he decreed as right to be wrong, for there is no moral order apart from His eternal decree. A law which thus represents the eternal will of the Creater of the Universe is infallible, and man's attitude towards it should be one of humble submission." Thus, law in Islam or the *shari'ah* regulates a number of things which is modern understanding fall outside the scope of law. A cursory glance at any major work in Islamic law will convince us that there is hardly any aspect of life for which no direct or indirect guidance is found in the *shari'ah*. For example, *Hidayah* of Al-Marghinani, an *opus magnum* of Islamic law, has in it fifty seven chapters on various aspects of human life. The first five deal with purification and cleanliness, rules and regulations for basic religious duties like prayer, fasting, alms giving and pilgrimage etc. Then come the questions concerning marriage, divorce, slaves offences and punishments, war and peace, state taxes, the public treasury, apostasy, rebellion, business partnership trust, commercial transactions, administration of justice, evidence, deposits, gifts, wages, misappropriation, pre-emption, assessment of rents and dues from agricultural land and orchards, mortgage, capital crimes and compensation to victims of such crimes and other losses, sanctuary and asylum, will, and so on.

The subject matter of the Islamic law can, therefore, be divided into (1) obligations to God (*'ibadat*), such as the profession of faith, performance of prayers and other religious duties, and (2) obligations to other fellow beings (*ma'amalat*) or all those acts which affect our individual and social life. Among the obligations to God belief in the oneness of God and the prophethood of Muhammad, as stated above, is one of the foremost and basic acts. Along with this there are four basic duties to God which are known as pillars (*arkan*) of Islam. They are *salat, sawam, zakat and hajj*. *Salat* is the most important of all other obligations to God. It is, as the Prophet stated, the point of distinction between belief and disbelief. It is offered five times a day, at dawn, midday, afternoon, immediately after sunset and in the early part of the night, preferably in congregation in a mosque, otherwise individually at home. The midday prayer on Fridays is offered in congregation only in important mosques of the town.

Sawm is the whole day fasting during the entire month of *Ramadan*, the ninth month of the Islamic calendar. Fasting is abstaining oneself from eating, drinking, smoking and sexual pleasure. What distinguishes this fast from the fast of other religions is that in Islam one has to fast only during the day from the dawn to the sunset.

Zakat is an obligatory charity at the rate of two and a half per cent of yearly savings. One is not to wait for an official collector to come and receive the amount. He must voluntarily pat it if he desires to follow the dictates of God. The rates differ in the case of agricultural and commercial produce.

Hajj is a pilgrimage to the 'House of God' the *ka'bah*, in Mecca. Every Muslim is required to visit it on a prescribed day of the year at least once in his lifetime, if he has the necessary means for performing the journey.

Law—especially if it carries with it divine reward and punishment—is hardly followed with love, sincerity and devotion, for it infuses a certain degree of fear. This happened in the case of Islamic law also. It certainly developed well as a science—many schools of Islamic jurisprudence were established in course of time—but like any other legal system it remained remote from the hearts of the people. And thus the rigidity and formalism of Islamic legal system found its reaction in the development of mystic thought. The Muslim mystics did not agree with the jurists' assumption that 'physical cleanliness' would ultimately result in 'spiritual cleanliness'. To the mystics the real purpose of Islam was to bring man nearer to God, and this, they stressed, could not be achieved without first purifying the soul. In fact, both these legalistic and mystical attitudes had in view the same goal of attaining to God but they were differing from each other in their approach. Legalism laid stress on the correctness of the outward actions of man, whereas mysticism was more concerned with the purity of heart. The following couplet beautifully illustrates the mystic attitude towards legal formalism:

> You cannot see God in *Kanz* or *Hadiyah*,
> Look into the mirror of your heart,
> For there is no book better than this.

Mysticism, in the Islamic context, is called *tasawwuf*; a mystics is a *sufi*. The etymology of the word *tasawwuf* is not yet known for certain. However, it is usually traced to the rough woolen robes (*suf* in Arabic) that were the identifying badges of the early mystics. There is not doubt that the first stage of development of Islamic mysticism was market by ascetic practices. Very soon, however, emerged an active quest fro experiences of intimate relationship with God, which are the climax of real mysticism. Eventually an elaborate system of mystical thought and practices came into existence.

Love of God and love for man are the two pillars on which stands the edifice of Islamic mysticism. To the *sufis* faith in God is not complete without love for his creature. Shaikh Nizammuddin Auliya, a famous sufi of India, once remarked: "Devotion to God is of two kinds : *lazimi* (intransitive) and *mauta'addi* (transitive). The benefits accrued in the former are confined to the devotees alone. It can be achieved through prayers, fasting, recitation of the Qur'an and so on. The transitive devotion, however, brings advantages and comfort not only to the devotees but to others also. It is performed by helping people, spending money on the poor, and by all other means through which a man strives to help his fellows. The reward of transitive devotion, says Nizamuddin Auliya, is endless. Since the stress in Islamic mysticism was on 'salvation through service' it very soon assumed the form of a movement for the spiritual culture of Islamic society. Gibb's remark in this connection that "the movement of popular religion in Islam is closely connected with the history of Islamic mysticism" is quite indicative. Mysticism has attracted more people to it than any other movement in Islam. Since the mystics, contrary to the men of law, believed in patience, they, instead of passing judgment against the 'sick' soul, embraced it and waited for the cure. This, however much against their wishes, created a kind of laxity among many of their followers. Hence, it is correct to say that "within the ranks of the mystics there were wide gradations, ranging from men of great intellectual attainments and character to whom mysticism offered a rich spiritual experience, strengthening their grasp of the truths of their religion down to those who found in mysticism an emotional and moral satisfaction and cared little whether their practices and postulates were in harmony or not with Islami doctrine."

The spread of Islam beyond the confines of Arabia and the advancement of theological and philosophical knowledge gave rise to serious difference in the interpretation of the divine revelation and the prophetic teachings. This was bound to divide the community into sects which are many. Among them, however, two are noteworthy and these are the Sunnites (Sunni) and the Shiites (Shi'ah). They differ from each other basically on two points: succession to the prophet Muhammad and the religious authority in Islam after the prophet. The Sunnis follow the line of succession from among the companions of the Prophet, beginning with Abu Bakr. Also the basis of authority in Islam after the Prophet, according to the Sunnis, is the Qur'an and the tradition of the prophet as understood and confirmed by the consensus of the community, or its leaned people, the ulema. The Shi'ahs hold that the succession was restricted to the family of the Prophet through his daughter, Fatimah. They, therefore, place Ali, the son-in-law of the Prophet, and the fourth Caliph of Islam in the historical sequence, as his first rightful heir. Religious authority for them finds its basis, as against the Sunnis, in the person of an inspired Imam, a member of the Prophet's family, who is infallible in all doctrinal and practical declarations. They believe that cognition of the Imam and submission to his authority is incumbent on all Muslims.

According to the Sunnis, as we have seen, the Muslim community after the Prophet was not bound to accept an individual as a final religious authority. Even the Caliphs remained essentially the political heads of the community.

Caliph is the anglicized version of the Arabic word *khalifah* meaning the 'successor.' This title was first given to Abu Bakr who was, after the death of the Prophet, entrusted by his fellow companions with the responsibility of conducting the affairs of the Muslim community. Later, all those who were called to the highest political and administrative office of the state were called *khalifah.* The early Muslims had made no distinction between the 'religious' and the 'temporal'. Since there was no clear-cut demarcation between these two regions, the Caliph who was essentially a political head was often mistaken for an authority in religious matters also. But as a matter of principle, he was only the political head of the community and not the spiritual heir to the Prophet. It was clearly understood and agreed upon that the Qur'an and the prophetic traditions were more than enough to guide the community. Nonetheless 'legalism' and 'letterism' produced a class of religiously learned people, the ulema, who in course of time unofficially became the 'official' spokesmen of Islam.

The two groups of Islamic community, the 'ulema and the sufis, often did not see eye to eye with each other. The 'ulema criticized the mystical approach of attaining to God as something alien to the prophetic tradition. The mystics, in their turn, condemned the ulema as being merely the followers of the 'letter'. Much of their bickerings, however, were the outcome of the rigid letterism of one group and the apparent laxity of the other with regard to religious practices. This internal conflict gave birth to many reform movements in the history of Islam.

To an outsider these internal conflicts of the Muslim community may appear as a sign of disintegration. However, there is a pervasive undercurrent of unity which asserts itself at critical junctures and draws the members of diverse groups into a single community. This has so far saved the community from internal erosion as well as external pressure.

Today the Muslim world faces a peculiar problem. In the past, usually the 'ulema in their collective or individual capacity, stood up to check the community from going astray. All their efforts were directed to what may be called revivalism. Not the situation is different. The 'ulema, is most cases, have been replaced by the state. In almost every Muslim country it is the state which is trying to bring about reforms by advocation the 'modernization' of the shari'ah to suit the changed circumstances of to-day. One the other hand, the 'ulema contend that the shari'ah is immutable. Hence, modernization is out of question. This conflict between the ulema and the state is one of the chief characteristic of modern Islam and, if it continues, it may vitally affect the future course of its history.

Revised and edited; originally published in Islam and the Modern Age, vol. IX: no. 3.

3

Exposition of the Religion of Islam

E.A. POLIAKOVA

(Abstract: Presents a comparative view of the Christian and Islamic concepts, ideas and details of faith and belief. In addition, it also has a Christian specialist writing on Islam, and quotes Muslims sources dealing with Christianity).

The word Islam which literally signifies 'resignation' (to God's will), is a comprehensive name commonly applied to the religion of the followers of the Prophet Mohammad. It embodies the various sections of the Muslim Law which God has established for the guidance of the people, both for the worship of their Lord, and for the duties of life.

These sections are five number, namely : Beliefs; Practical Devotion; Transactions; Moralities and Punishments.

Section I— Beliefs

Belief embraces the six articles of the Islamic faith, namely:

(a) God; (b) His angels; (c) His books; (d) His prophets; (e) The day of Resurrection; (f) Predestination.

Section II — Devotions

Devotions are sub-divided into five articles of practice: (a) Recital of the Creed; (b) Prayer; (c) Paying legal alms; (d) Fasting the month of Ramadan; (e) Pilgrimage to Mecca once in a lifetime, if means allows it.

Devotion also embrace legal warfare for the defence of the

religion of Islam.

Section III — Transactions

Transactions include such duties as are required between man and man, and may be divided into three sub-divisions, namely:—Contests; Nuptials; and Securities. Almost all the various sections of civil jurisprudence relating to barter, sale, agency, larceny, marriage, divorce, dower, partnership, claims etc., are embraced under those three heads.

Section IV — Moralities

Moralities embrace the consideration of all those moral excellences which are enjoined in the Koran and in the teachings of the Prophet, such as, Sincerity; Confidence in God; Humility; Resignation; Keeping worldly ambitions within bounds; Giving good counsel and advice; Contentment; Liberality; Love to God and man; Patience; Ethical instructions and rules of conduct relating to (1) salutations, (2) asking permission to enter a house, (3) shaking hands, and embracing, (4) rising up, (5)sitting, sleeping and walking, (6) sneezing and yawning, (7) laughing, (8) names, (9) poetry and eloquence, (10) backbiting and abuse, (11) promises, (12) joking, (13) boasting and party spirit.

Section V —Punishments

Punishments include (1) penalties exacted for manslaughter or serious bodily injuries, (2) punishment for theft by the loss of a hand, (3) punishment for fornication and adultery : stoning for a married person, and one hundred lashes for an unmarried person, (4) punishment for slander by eighty lashes, (5) punishment for apostasy by death, (6) punishment for inebriation by eitghy lashes.

My object in writing this vulume, however, is quite limited. It is to deal only with the first section of the religion of Islam, namely Beliefs—which embrace all matters of faith.

Devotions which include all matters of practice, as well as the articles embodied in the rest of the sections shall be the subjects of volumes II to fellow.

The creed of Islam demands faith in the following :

(1) God; (2) The Angles of God; (3) The Books of God; (4) The Apostles of God; (5) The day of Judgment or Resurrection; (6) Predestination.

I will now deal with each of these articles separately:

I. Belief in God

Belief in God is best represented by the following formula which every sunni, or orthodox Moslem must profess sincerely:

God is one and has no partner; Singular, without any like Him; Uniform, having no contrary; Separate, having no equal; Ancient, having no first; Everlasting, having no end; Ever-existing, without termination; Perpetual and constant, with neither interruption nor termination; Ever qualified with the attributes of supreme greatness; nor is He bound to be determined by lapse of ages or times. But He is the Alpha and Omega (the First and the Last), and the Evident (1), and the Hidden (2).

What God is not

God is not a formed body; nor a measurable substance; neither does He resemble bodies, either in their being measurable or divisible. Neither is He substance, nor do substances exist in Him; neither is He an accidental form, nor do accidentals exist in Him.

He is not like anything that exists, neither does anything resemble Him. He is not determined by dimensions, nor contained within bounds; nor is He surrounded by sides; nor is He comprised within the heavens or earth. He sits upon the throne, after the manner which He Himself has described, and in that same sense which He Himself meant: It is a sitting, far removed from any notion of contact, or resting upon, or local situation; but both the throne, and whatsoever supports it, are sustained by the goodness of His power, and are conquered by His will. He is above His throne and above all things, but so above, as at the same time not to be a whit nearer to the throne and the heaven, or farther from the earth.

God is exalted by infinite degrees above the throne, no less than He is exalted above the earth, and at the time, He is near to everything that has being; may, he is nearer to men than their jugular veins, and is witness to everything: though His nearness is not like the nearness of bodies; neither is His essence like the essence of bodies. He does not exist in anything, nor does anything exist in Him; but He is too exalted, to be contained in any place, and too holy, to be determined by time; for He existed before He created time and place; and He is now as He always existed. He is also distinct from the creatures by His attributes neither is there anything besides Himself in His essence, nor is His essence in any other besides Him.

He is too holy to be subject to change, or any local motion; neither do any accidents dwell in Him, nor any contingencies befall Him; but He abides through all generations with His glorious attributes, free from all dissolution. As to the attribute of perfection, He wants no addition of perfection. As to being, He is known to exist by the apprehension of the understanding, and seen as He is by the eyes, through a favour which will be vouchsafed out of his mercy and grace, to the holy in the eternal mansion, completing their joy by vision of His glorious presence.

God's Life and Power

God is living, powerful, mighty, omnipotent, not liable to any defect or impotence, neither slumbering nor sleeping, nor being subject to decay or death. To Him belongs the Kingdom, the power and the might. His is the dominion and the excellence and the creation and the command. The heavens are folded in His hands, and all creatures are held within His grasp. He is the sole creator of beings and producer of things, and He is the communicator of existence, and from Him everything has its beginning. He created men and their works, and destined their maintenance, and determined their lives. Nothing that is possible, can escape His grasp, nor can the vicissitudes of things elude His power. The effects of His might are innumerable, and the objects of His knowledge infinite.

God's Knowledge

God knows all things that can be known, and comprehends whatsoever comes to pass, from the extremities of the earth to the highest heavens: even the weight of an atom cannot escape His knowledge, either in earth or heaven. He knows all things hidden or manifest. He knows the number of leaves of the trees, of the grains of wheat and of sand. Events past and future are known to Him. He knows what enters into the heart of man, and what he utters with his mouth. He alone, except those to whom He has revealed them, knows the invisible things. He is free from forgetfulness, negligence and error. His knowledge is internal, it is not posterior to His essence.

God's Will

God wills those things to be that exist, and disposes of all accidents. Nothing passes in the earth or in the heavens, neither little nor much, nor small great, nor good nor evil, nor profitable, nor faith nor infidelity, nor knowledge nor ignorance, nor prosperity nor adversity, nor increase nor decrease, nor obedience nor rebellion, but by His determinate counsel and decree, and His definite sentence and will. Nor does the wink of him that sees, nor the subtlety of him that thinks, exceed the bounds of His will; but it is He who gave all things their existence or being. He is the Creator and Restorer and the sole operator of what He pleases; there is no one to reverse His decree, or delay what He has determined, nor is there any refuge for man from rebellion against Him, but only His help and mercy; nor has man any power to perform any duty towards Him, but through His love and will. Though men, genii, angels and devils should conspire together, either to put one single atom in motion, or it to cease its motion, without His will and approbation, they would not be able to do so. His will subsists in His essence, with the rest of His attributes, by which He willed from eternity the existence of those things that He decreed, which were produced in their proper seasons, according to His eternal will, without any Before or After, and with agreement both With His knowledge and will, and not by methodising of thoughts, nor waiting for a proper time, for which reason no one thing is in Him a hindrance from another.

God's Hearing and Sight

God — praised be His name — is Hearing and Seeing, and Hears and Sees. No audible sound however still, escapes His Hearing; nor is anything visible so small as to escape His sight; for distance is no hindrance to His hearing, nor darkness to His sight. He sees without pupil or eye-lid, and hears without any passage or ear, even as He knows without a brain, and performs His actions without the assistance of any corporeal limb, and creates without any instruction, for His attributes are not like those of men, any more than His Essence is like theirs.

Good's Word

God commands, forbids, promises, threatens by an eternal words, subsisting in His essence. Neither is it like the word of the creatures, nor does it consist in a voice, arising from the commotion of the air and the collision of bodies; nor in letters which are separated by the joining together of the lips, or the motion of the tongue. The Koran, the Law, the Gospel and the Psalms are Books sent down by His Apostles. The Koran, indeed, is read with tongues, written in books and kept in hearts: yet, as subsisting in the essence of God, it does not become liable to separation and division, when it is transferred into the hearts and the papers. Thus Moses also heard the Word of God, without voice of letter, even as the saints behold the essence of God, without substance. And since as these are His attributes, He lives and knows and hears and sees and speaks, by life knowledge and will and hearing and sight and word, not by His simple essence.

God's Works

God— praised be His name— exists after such a manner, that nothing besides Him has any being, but what is produced by His operation, and flows His justice, after the best, most excellent, most perfect and most just model. He is, moreover, Wise in His works, and Just in His decrees. But His justice is not to be compared with the justice of men. For a man may be held to act unjustly by invading the possessions of another; but to God, inasmuch as there is nothing which may belong to any other besides Himself, no wrong is imputable, for He cannot be considered as meddling with things not appertaining to Him. All things, Himself only excepted, genii, men, devils, angels, heaven, earth, animals, plants, substance, and their attributes, all are His creation. He created them by His power out of nothingness, and brought them into existence, when as yet they were nothing at all, but He alone existing from eternity, neither was there any other with him. Now, He created all things from the beginning, for the manifestation of His Power and His Will, and for the confirmation of His word which was true from all eternity; not that He stood in need of them, nor wanted them; but He manifestly declared His glory in creating and producing and commanding, without being under any obligation, nor out of necessity. *Loving, Kindness, favour, and grace and beneficence,* belong to Him; whereas it is in His power to pour forth upon men a variety of torments, and to afflict them with various kinds of sorrows and disease; and should He do this, His justice would not be arraigned, nor would He be chargeable with injustice. Yet He rewards those who worship Him for their obedience, on account of His promise and beneficence, not for their merit or of necessity, since there is nothing which He is under an obligation to perform; nor can any injustice be supposed in Him, nor can He be under any obligation to any person whatsoever. That His creatures, however, should be bound to serve him, arises from His having declared by the tongues of the Prophets, that it was due to Him by them. The worship of God is not simply the dictates of the understanding, but He sent messengers to carry to men His commands and promises and admonitions: the veracity of these messengers He proved by manifest, whereby men are obliged to give credit to them in those things which they relate.

Mr. George Sale rightly comments on the Mohammadan notion of God as follows:

"The both Mohammed and those among his followers who are reckoned orthodox, had and continue to have, just and true notions of God and His attributes, appear plains from the Koran itself and all the Mohammedan divines, so that it would be *Loss of time, to refuse those who suppose the God* of Mohammed to be different from the true God and only a fictions deity or idol of his own creation."

I will now give interpretation of some quotations from the Koran, bearing on the essence of God; this subject forming such an important feature of the teachings of the religion of Islam:

The Unity of God: "Say : He is God, the Singular, God the Support He begettheth not, nor is He begotten, nor is anything equal unto Him."

"Truly your God is but one. Lord of the Heavens and of the Earth, and of all that is between them and Lord of the East and of the West. God. There is no deity but He, Most excellent are His attributes."

Proofs of His existence "The (God) bringeth forth the living out of the dead, and He oringeth the dead out of the living, and He quickeneth the earth after it hath been dead; and in like manner shallye be brought forth (from your graves) of His sign (one is), that He hath created you of dust; and behold, ye((are become) men, spread over the face of the earth. And of His signs (another is), that He hath created for you, out of yourselves, wives, that ye may cohabit with them; and hath put love and compassion between you: verily herein are signs unto people who consider. And of His signs (are also), the creation of the heavens and the earth, and the variety of your languages, and of your complexions; verily herein are signs unto men of understanding. And of His signs (are), your sleeping by night and by day, and your seeking (to provide for yourselves) of His abundance; verily herein (are signs unto people who hearken. Of His sign (other are) that He showeth you the lightning, to strike terror, and to give hope (of rain), and that He sendeth down water from heaven, and quickeneth thereby the earth, after if hath been dead: verily herein are sign unto people who understand. And of His signs (this also is one, namely) that the heavens and the earth stand firm at His command: here-after, when He shall call ye out of the earth at one summons, behold, ye shall come forth..."

"When adversity befalleth men, they call upon their Lord, turning unto Him; afterwards, when He hath caused them to taste of His mercy, behold, a part of them associate (other deities) with their Lord; showing themselves, a part of them associate (other deities) with Lord; showing themselves ungrateful for the favours which We have bestowed on them"..(Koran).

"When We cause men to taste mercy, they rejoice therein;; but if evil befalleth them, for that which their hands have before committed, be hold, they despair. (It is) God Who Hath created you, and hath provided food for you; hereafter will He cause to die; and after that, will He raise you again to life" (Koran).

"(It is) God Who created you in weakness, and after weakness hath given (you) strength; and after strength, he will (again) reduce (you) to weakness, and grey hairs: He created that which He pleaseth; and He (is) the Wise, the Powerful" (Koran).

God's Omnipresence Asserted

"There is no private discourse among three persons, but He is the fourth of them; nor (among) five, but He is the sixth of them; neither (among) a smaller number than this, nor a larger, but He is with them, wheresoever they be: and He will declare unto them that which they have done, on the day of resurrection; for God knoweth all things" (Koran).

God's Omnipotence

"God, There is no deity but He, the Living, the Self-subsisting: Neither slumber seizeth Him nor sleep; He, whatsoever is in the heavens, and whatsoever is no the earth. Who is He that can intercede with Him, but by His permission? He knoweth what hath been before them and what shall be after; yet nought of His knowledge shall they grasp, save what He willeth. His seat reaches over the heavens and the earth, and the upholding of both is no burden unto Him; and He is High and the Great" (Koran).

Creator of all Things

"He cause the dawn to appear, and hath ordained the night for rest, and the sun and the moon for computing time. The ordinance of the Mighty, the Wise" (Koran).

"And it is He Who hath ordained the stars for you, that ye may be guided thereby in the darkness of the land and of the sea. Clear have We made Our signs to men of knowledge" (Koran).

"And it is He Who produced you from one man, and hath) provided for you) and abode and resting place. Clear have We made our signs to men of knowledge" (Koran).

"And it is He Who sendeth rain from Heaven, and We bring forth by it buds of all the plants, and from them bring We forth the green foliage, and the close growing grain, and palm trees with sheaths of clustering dates, and gardens of grapes, and the olive and the pomegranate, like and unlike. Look ye on their fruits, when they ripen and bear fruit. Truly herein are signs unto people who believe... This is God your Lord. There is no deity but He, the creator of all things, therefore worship Him alone; and He watched over all thing..." (Koran).

"We created the heavens and the earth and all that is between them in six days, and no weariness touched Us" (Koran).

Perfect in His Works

"Blessed be He in Whose hand is the Kingdom and over all things is He potent.

"Who hath created death and life, to prove who of you will be most righteous in deed, and He is the Mighty, the Forgiving" (Koran).

"Who hath created seven heavens one above another. No defect canst thou see in the creation of the God of mercy; repeat the gaze: seeest thou a single flaw? (Koran).

Then twice more repeat the gaze: the gaze shall return to thee dulled and weary."

The Light of Heaven and Earth

"God is the Light of the Heavens and of the Earth. His light is like a niche in which there is a lamp — the lamp encased in glass — the glass, as it were a glistening star. From a blessed tree it is lighted: the olive tree neither Eastern nor Western, whose oil shines out as it were, even thought fire touched it not. It is light upon light. God guideth whom He willeth to His light, and God setteth forth parables to men, for God knoweth all things" (Koran).

Provides for All

"Whose chooseth this quickly passing life, quickly will We bestow thereon that which We please — even on him We choose; afterwards We will appoint hell for him, in which he shall burn— disgraced, outcast.

"But they Who choose the life to come and strive after it, as it should be striven for, being also believers — as for these, their striving shall be grateful (to God).

"To all — both to these and those — will We prolong the gifts of (Us We) your Lord; for not to any shall the gifts of the Lord be denied.

"See how We have caused some of them to excel others; but the next life shall grater in its grades, and greater in excellence.

"Set not up another Lord with God, less thou sit thee down disgraced, helpless (Koran).

The Lord ordained that ye worship none but Him..." (Koran).

His Words are Countless

"Say : Should the sea become ink, to write the words of my Lord, the sea would surely fail, ere the words of my Lord would fail, though we brought (other seas) like it in aid.. (Koran).

"If all the trees that are upon earth were to become pens, and if God should after swell the sea into seven seas (of ink) His words would not be exhausted; for God is Mighty and Wise" (Koran).

Has no Offspring

"And they say, 'God hath a son' : No; Praise be to Him. But — He is whatever is in the Heavens and the Earth. All obey Him. (Koran).

"Sole make of the Heavens and of the Earth. And when He decreeth a thing, He only saith to it, `Be' and it is ..(Koran).

"Yet have they assigned the jins to God as His associates, though He created them; and in their ignorance they have falsely ascribed to Him sons and daughters. Glory to be Him, and high let Him be exalted above that they attribute to Him (Koran).

"Sole maker of the Heavens and the Earth; how, when He hath no consort, should He have a son? He hath created every thing, and He knoweth every thing.

"This is God your Lord. There is no deity but He, the creator of all things; therefore worship Him alone; and He watches over all things. They say; 'The God of Mercy hath gotten offspring'. Now have ye done a monstrous thing. Almost might the very Heavens be rent thereat, and the Earth cleave asunder, and the mountains fall down in fragments, that they ascribe a son to the God of Mercy, when it beseemeth not the God of Mercy to beget a son.."

Created All Beings to Adore Him

"I have not created Jins and men, but that they should worship Me" (Koran).

How He Speaketh with Man

"It is not for man that God should speak with him, but by vision, or from behind a veil: Or, He sendeth a messenger to reveal, by His permission, what He will: for He is exalted (and) Wise.

"Thus have We sent the Spirit (Gabriel) to thee with a revelation, by our command; Thou knewest not, ere this, what the 'Book' was, or what the (true) faith was. But We have ordained it for a light: by it will We guide whom We please of our servants. And thou (O. Mohammad), shalt guide their feet into the right way" (Koran).

God is creator of good and Evil Deeds, and Yet Good is from him, but Evil from Man in Consequence of his Ignorance or Disobedience:

"By the sun and his noonday brightness; Be the moon when she followeth him; By the day when it revealeth his glory; By the night when it enshroudeth him; By the earth and Him Who spread it forth; By a soul and Him Who perfected it revealed to it the way of wickedness and the way of piety (to choose between them) — Blessed now is he who hath kept it pure, and undone is he who hath corrupted it." "If good fortune betide them, they say, 'this is from God' and if evil betide them, they say 'this is from thee (the Prophet). Say: All is from God: Whatever good betideth thee, is from God, and whatever betideth thee, of evil, is from thyself; and We have sent thee to mankind as an apostle: God is thy sufficient witness" (Koran).

Omniscient and Omnipotent

"And with Him are the keys of the secret things; none knoweth them, but He: He knoweth whatever is on the land and in the sea; and no leaf falleth but He knoweth it, neither is there a grain in the darkness of the earth, nor a thing green or sere, but it is noted in a distinct writing."

All-Seeing but Unseen

"The eyes do not reach Him, but He reaches the eyes: and he is the Subtle, the All-informed."

"It is He Who in six days created the Heavens and the Earth, then ascended His throne. He knoweth that which entereth the earth, and that which goeth forth from it, and what cometh down from Heaven, and what mounteth up to it; and wherever ye are, He is with you, and God beholdeth all your actions.

His is the Kingdom of the Heavens and the Earth: and to God shall all things return. He causeth the night to pass into the day, and He causeth the day to pass into the night; and He knoweth the very secrets of the bosom".

The Existence of God

Of all the doctrine and beliefs that have objected to in this age of materialism, the greatest is the belief in the existence of God. The first demand which an atheist makes is : "If you show God to me, I will believe in Him. How can I believe in Him without seeing Him?" Western influences have gone a long way towards effacing from the hearts of many men, the imprint of the Divine Being, and hundreds of college students and others, have begun to deny existence of God. There are thousands of persons who, though refraining from an open declaration of their views through fear of the community, have really no faith in Him; therefore, I submit the following suggestions on the subject, that haply some fortunate soul may be benefited thereby.

May knows, different things by means of different senses. Some things we know by means of seeing, some by tasting. A colour is known by seeing, not by smelling, touching or tasting. If anybody should say, that he will acknowledge a colour, only if he is made to hear the sound of it, would not such a proposition be considered unreasonable? Similarly, fragrance is known by means of smelling. Now, if anyone should say that he will consider a rose to be fragrant, only if he is made to taste its fragrance, would such a person be regarded as wise? On the other hand, if anybody seeks to know, by smelling, things which can be known by tasting, such as sourness and sweetness, bitterness and saltiness, he will never be able to do so. Therefore, it is not right, that we should accept those things only which we can behold with our eyes, and disbelieve those things which are not recognisable by the eye. How absurd is, then, the demand that God must be shown to us before we believe in Him.

Moreover, there are certain things in man himself, the existence of whcih he recognises, without having seen them. We do not know all things merely by seeing, but they are known by means of five different senses. Now, there are many things which are not knowable, even by these gateways of knowledge, there being other ways of knowing them. For instance, reason, memory and intelligence are things which are not denied by anybody; yet nobody has ever seen, heard, tasted, smelt or touched them. How did we, then, come to know that there were such things as reason, or memory, or intelligence? Again, has anybody ever seen, smelt, touched or tasted energy? Even the simplest man can see that we have no known these things by means of the five senses, but that there are other evidences that have us to the knowledge of their existence. We see that then a man is confronted with a difficulty, he thinks for a while, and then devices a plan, by which he is able to solve his difficulty. When we see difficulties being removed in this way, we conclude that there is something in man which is of service to him on such occasions, and we call it reason. Thus, we do not become aware of the existence of reason directly though the five senses, but we obtain a knowledge of it means of its wonderful manifestations. Similarly when we see able to carry heavy loads, and some, able to carry heavier weights than others, we infer that there is a capacity in man, which enables him to bear these burdens, and which some persons possess in a greater degree than others. This capacity we call strength. We have not seen strength, but we have seen the deeds that are done by strength, and from these we have concluded its existence.

Thus, we find that the more subtle a thing is, the more hidden it is from the human eye, and it is by actions, and not by the five senses, that we perceive the existence of such things.

But God is the subtlest of all. How unjust is it, then, to say that we cannot believe in the existence of God, unless He is shown to us. Has anybody ever electricity? But can we, then, deny the transmission of messages and signals to long distances, lighting and, the working of machinery by means of electricity? The discovery of ether has brought about a revolution in the world of physical science, but has any scientist been able to find it by means of his five senses? But if we deny its existence, we find ourselves to explain, how the rays of the sun reach the earth. How unjust is, then, the demand that in order to be believed in, God must be visible to the eye, while there are so many things which are believed in, though they are not visible to the eye, or perceptible by any other of the five senses. God is visible, but only to the eyes that are capable of seeing Him. But if any anybody is desirous of seeing Him, He is before the whole world through His powers, and in spite of His being hidden, He is the most apparent of all. This fact has been briefly, but very exquisitely mentioned in the Holy Koran in the following words :

"The eyes not do not reach Him, but He reached the eyes : and He is the Subtle, the All informed."

In this verse, God draws the attention of man to the fact, that his eyes are not capable of seeing Him, for He is subtle, and subtle things cannot be perceived by the eyes. What, then, is the way of knowing God? The koran answers this question by saying : "And He reacheth the eyes:" namely though the eyes of man are not capable of seeing Him, yet he reveals Himself to man by a display of His powers, and by a manifestation of His attributes. Manifold are the ways in which He reveals Himself to man. He display His unlimited power sometimes by terrorstriking signs, sometimes by signs of mercy, and at others, by accepting prayer. If God were to be believed in, only if He were perceptible by the eye, then we should have to deny the existence of about four-fifths of the things of the world, or the existence of all things, if we accept as true the view of certain philosophers who allege, *that nobody can the substance of anything in the world, and that it is only the form that we see.*

We know very little of God, and yet we know that God exist; that there is a Great Mysterious Power, at behind the Universe.

In ancient times, Nature, or the forces of Nature, were deemed to be freakish, capricious powers, personified, to popular intelligence, as demons, and the like. Now we know that there is nothing freakish or capricious about Nature, that Nature works in accordance with a fixed law — the law of the Universe, the law laid and establish hed by the Great Mysterious Power at work behind the Universe.

All we know of that Great Mysterious Power is compounded of all we know of the various laws — discovered from time to time — which govern the Universe.

There are three main laws in the Universe — the Law of Creation, the Law, of Substance and the Law of Evolution; so if we seek, as it were, to personify the Great Mysterious Power, and clothes Him with attributes that we mortal men can comprehend, we shall endeavour to visualise him as Creator, Sustainer and Evolver.

The Arabic language has one word which comprises all three ideas — *Rabb-ul-Alameen;* the word *Rabb* signifying Creator, Sustainer, and one who has endowed every object with the capacity of ultimate development, — thereby anticipating the doctrine of Evolution, many centuries before Darwin gave his theories to the world.

At every evolutionary stage of matter, however transient it be, we find a course prescribed, and an organisation pre-ordained. . . . Nature everywhere obeying the Law.

As the Holy Koran says: "And to Allah does obeisance whatever is in heaven and earth — willingly or unwillingly."

Over and over again, the Holy Koran lays down with great clarity, that a Reign of Law exists, dominating the whole material world; and every day, fresh discoveries of science do but prove inspired accuracy of the Sacred Book. For after all, this is the sum-total of all scientific discovery, — that all growth and all development of every element in Nature, is under the Rule of the Law.

Is, therefore, this Reign of Law, — this mechanism, as it were, of rule and regulation, — intentional? Or is it accidental?

Call it mechanism if you will; but can you dissociate mechanism, from mind?

The machine itself cannot think; but what of the mind that made it? Mechanism cannot construct itself.

In all human mechanism, we believe in the priority of laws and principles, on which certain mechanism is working. We acknowledge the pre-existence of the mind that devised the machine, and set it working.

Why do we hesitate, when we come to the great mechanism of Nature? I suppose, we are afraid lest, if we once make such an admission, we shall have to accept Law, as separate from Matter, — to admit that Mind has priority over Substance.

About seventy years ago, the Atomic theory was the popular craze. The Atom was our great God, our first cause and origin; but later, we found this god itself a slave to Low. It was found to be, not an origin, but a product of some electronic specialisation, which in its turn receive its birth, not as an accident, but under a Law — the Law of Condensation — from the collocation of ethereal specks. But this ether, as it is called, is, in its turn, a law-ridden entity.

Ernst Haeckel and others, refusing to admit the priority of Mind to Matter, sought a way out by regarding matter and energy as one and the same thing, with "law-abidingness" as a permanent characteristics, and calling it Law-Substance. Law-Substance, therefore, is a first cause, self-created, and the creator of other things, — self-existing, and the maintainer of subsequent growth, omnipresent, and all-pervading, indestructible and infinite; add to these the attributes of all-knowing all-powerful, designer and regularizer, though you style yourself atheist or free-thinker, you believe in the God of Islam. As the Holy Koran says: "And to Him doth obey what is in the heavens and the earth. And a sign to them is the night; we draw forth form it the day, then lo, they are in the dark; and the sun runs on to a term appointed for it; that is the ordinance of the Mighty and the knowing. And as for the moon, We have ordained for it stages, till it becomes again as an old dry palm-branch. Neither is it allowable to the sun, that he should overtake the moon, nor can the night outstrip the day. All float on in a sphere" (Koran XXXIV:37-40. Thus is the whole Solar System under Divine Ordinance.

What was the Law — the LAw of Gravity, — "evolved from accidence", what made the earth stand on its orbit, with its axis inclined?

What a contradiction in terms — Law and accident. To what lengths will we not go 'to avoid belief in the Divine Ordinance.

Is the camera an accident? The lens, the sensitive paper. The light regulating contrivance, and so forth, all suggest design and mind; and yet the camera is but the crudest copy of an which is, presumably, a thing evolved at random. And what about the feeling that the image reflected produces? The lens of the camera reflects the image, but it does not see, it does not feel; whereas the eye sends a thrill into the very soul, when we see anything beautiful.

Can we give or receive a telephone message without an "exchange"? Some *design* to connect the giver and the receiver is indispensable.

The brain of an army — known in modern parlance as General Head Quarters — is preeminently the product of design. Is the brain of man just a haphazard contrivance, meaningless in the inception?

We assign a distinct design to every one of the hundred and one pipes fixed, in the machinery of an ordinary steam engine. Are the million and one nerves that work so miraculously in our bodies, purposeless and without intent?

Yet, I could even worship this Fetish of Accident, if all these defined movements of our planet had failed to produce desirable results, making for our benefit. And this being so, I am compelled to believe in some Will, under whose control Nature works, not blindly. The alternation of day and night — which causes changes in the weather, affecting the atmosphere, changing the course of the winds, bringing the rainy seasons and the dry weather, in a desired order; the withering of Nature, and its resuscitation; these, and the life of man himself, depending on the peculiar bend of the earth sphere towards its orbit, are these all at random?

You will note find a single thing in the realm of Nature which is unconnected with your own existence. As the Book says: "Those who remember Allah... And reflect on the creation of the heavens and the earth, (say): Our Lord — Who looks to our sustenance and maintenance,— Thous has not created all this in vain. Glory be to Thee." (Koran III:190).

The unintelligible phenomena of yesterday are, today, instinct with a great and real purpose; and so it will be with the milliards of things which still baffle us. This being the case, I have every right to suppose that every object in Nature of my using it for my benefits — if only I know how, — and is subservient to me under the ordinance of some mind, which I call Allah; for, did you ever think of a contrivance, or scheme out a design, in the working out of which you did not find the necessary aids already existing in Nature?

But you will say, things in themselves are not subject to design; it is only man's intelligent use of them that makes them useful.

We all know that light, and the colour known as green, strengthen the sight; and green is the prevailing colour in Nature after light. But, it is said, the green colour was not made intentionally to strengthen sight; rather the eye became accustomed to it, and so derived benefit from it.

But consider the case of the mole. The mole has eyes, but being generally away from the light, it is blind. It cannot make its surroundings subservient to its sight. Whence, it may be seen, to what an extent the eye is indebted to light and green colour.

In support of his theory, that Nature is to with purpose intrinsically, but that its purpose is, as it were, of man's contriving. Ernst Haeckel adduces the illustration of powder.

Powder was for ages lying useless and unused; — by finding use for it we have invested it with a purpose. But that is tantamount to asserting that inquiries have invested powder with its properties, or in other words that the purpose of the explosive was already in it, but in a dormant state; and that it is due to us, that it has become active. All of which tends rather to prove design, than otherwise. But there are other ways of looking as it.

If a mind works upon material, giving it shape to seve a certain purpose, it is impossible for another person, to use that material in a way other than in which it was designed by its maker. If you deny the design of its maker, you are looking for trouble and wasting your effort.

Here are pieces of iron and wood before me: I use them in making a machine, and any person desirous of using that machine, must do so in the way intended by me, and in that way only.

Can you use the things that God has made, otherwise than in the way intended by Him?

Your body is a wonderful machine, — endowed with numerous faculties, to which are added Free-will, and the power of discretion. But can you use your nose for seeing? Or can you eat through your ear?

This machine of your body has been fashioned by an Intelligence and a Mind, and if you act contrary to its designs, your actions will not be acceptable in the realm of Nature. For thus says the Holy

Koran: "Is it, then, other than Allah's way that they seeks to follow; and to Him submits whoever is in the heaven or on the earth, willingly or unwillingly. . . And whoever desires a way other than submission (Islam) it shall not be accepted from him; and in the end, he shall be the loser" (Koran III. 82-84).

Again, if a particular form of matter involves, in its being, certain principles, the knowledge and application of which, alone make the realisation of that purpose possible, then it is certain that a mind has pre-ordained it. If the small form of matter had existed independenly of such principles, and if there had been no need of their knowledge, nor had any advantage accrued to us in our application of such knowledge, then one might, perhaps, deny the purpose behind it.

The Holy Koran tells us, the everything in Nature is for our benefit, and further apprises us of the principles which will enable us throughly to make use of them: "The Beneficient God taught the Koran. He created man, taught him the mode of expression. The sun and the moon follow a *reckoning, and the herbs do obey (Him).* And the heaven: He raised it on high; and He made the *measure;* that you may not be *inordinate in respect of the measure;* and keep up the *balance* with equity, and do not *make the measure* deficient. And the earth He has set it and the grain wit (its) husk and fragrance. Which then of the bounties of the Lord will you reject"? (LV. 1-13).

Note the words in italics. The whole universe has been regulated with mathematical precision; and that we may derive the best advantage from it, we must respect the *measure,* — find out these *reckonings* and measures, and not make them *deficient.*

Every created thing, from the stars of heavens to the smallest herbs that grow on the earth, observe rules laid down with mathematical reckoning, and observes measures, prescribed for its creation and development.

In short everything that is created in this universe, is based on mathematical principles; and all our scientific researches owe their existence to this science of measure and reckoning.

I could agree with Ernst Haekel, if man, in this search for purpose in Nature, could disregard these mathematical principle. In reality we did not create purpose for Nature; we simply discovered those measures and rules which had been laid down for the working out of the purpose.

Can we, then, deny, behind the working of Nature, the existence of some Great Mind... the Regularizer, the Reckoner and the Measurer? Let us, in the words of the Holy Koran, "glorify the Name of Our Lord Most High, Who creates, them balances; Who measures, then guides."

Does evolution of matter really consist in the development of its potentialities? Is not the human organism proved, by biological research, to be the final and best evolution of matter?

The consciousness which is evolved out of animated matter, in the animal kingdom, in the form of impulses, evolves into natural passion in man. But this is not the final growth. In its turn, it must evolve ethics and high philosophy. Where, then, is the constructive ability, inherent in matter, which should now work all the more vigorously, to sublimate my consciousness into high moral and philosophic growth? Do I possess a nature which automatically distinguishes between Right and Wrong? Or must I cultivate such a nature, through guidance? Do I, by nature, nauseate at wrong philosophy? Do I, by instinct, spurn things injurious to my intellect? Do I discern between wholesome and unwholesome food, without guidance? Man, who represents the highest possible form of evolved matter, is hopelessly destitute of that constructive ability for the evolution of this intellect, which discriminates so unerringly in the physical building of organism. The very fact that, as far as the unconscious growth of matter goes, this constructive ability works so splendidly, but disappears on the rise of consciousness, proves conclusively, that it was not an inherent faculty in matter, but an external guidance, — guidance form the Source that has been called

Rabb— Who is the God of Islam.

If, then, the scientific world agree, that Law predominates in matter, force and energy and if it also believes in Monism, it follows that it must believe in one design and in one mind. There may be a hundred and one laws at work in Nature, but they go all at converge on one purpose. In short, Law is, and must be obeyed, if the world is to on all. Law is the "Obeyed" Entity and in this connection, the reader may be interested to learn, that the word Allah, Who is the object of worship with Moslems, literally, means "The Obeyed".

"God says", according to the Prophet "do not abuse the Universe, because *I am the Universe.*" — a great truth and undeniable reality! It means, that all the manifestations of Nature are the manifestations of the God-head, and that all the forces and laws of Nature are the features and characteristics of that Great Being.

To be in touch with Nature, is the secret of all success, of all felicity in life; and if in Islam, the dictum has been pronounced, in a somewhat different language, "to imbue ourselves with Divine Attributes", it means the same thing. For the attributes of God, as mentioned in the Holy Koran, do perfectly and completely index the working of Nature; and if, to believe in God, is to accept Him, as the Source of all Law, and to worship Him means simply to obey His Law, how can we disbelieve in the God of Islam?.

2. Belief in the Angels of God

The angels are created of light, and endowed with life, speech and reason. They are free from desire and the disturbance of anger: they disobey not God in what He has commanded them, but do all that they are commanded. Their food is, to celebrate God's glory; their drink, to proclaim His holiness; their conversation, to commemorate God; their pleasure, to worship Him. The angels are created in different forms and with different powers.

The number or angels is very great; it can be known to no one except to God. Four of the angels are archangels, namely, Jibril

(Gabriel), the angel of revelations; Mikhail (Michael), the angel of rain; Israfil, the angel who will announce the advent of Resurrection; Azrail, the angel of death.

Every man is attended by two recording angels, called the "Kiram-ul-Katibeen", or the illustrious writers, one of whom records his good actions, and the other his evil actions. There are also two other kinds of angels, called 'Monkar' and 'Nakeer', who examine the dead in the grave.

There are also two celebrated angels, 'Radwan' who is in charge of Paradise, and 'Malik' who is in charge of Hell.

The angels intercede for men, while celebrated the praise of God; they implore forgiveness for the dwellers of earth. They also act as guardians for men. Each man has a succession of angels before and behind him, who watch over him by God's behest.

3. Belief in the Scriptures of God

The fundamental position, on which the superstructure of the Mohammadan Religion is erected, is that, from the beginning to the end of the world, there has been, and for ever will be, but one true orthodox religion. This true religion consists as to matter of faith, in the acknowledge of the only true God, and in the belief in, and obedience to such messengers or prophets of God, as He has been pleased to send from time to time, with credentials, to reveal His will to mankind; and as to matter of practice, the religion of God consists in the observance of the immutable and eternal laws of right and wrong, together with such other precepts and ceremonies, as God ordained as fit, for the time being, according to the different dispensations in different ages. These precepts and ceremonies were in themselves non-essential, but they became strictly obligatory by God's positive command; and were, therefore, temporary and subject to alternation, according to His will and wisdom. Hence, the name 'Islam', signifying absolute surrender to the will of God' is used commonly to denote the Mohammadan Religion. This name, however, (Islam) also applies to God's religion, since the beginning of the World, inasmuch as all true religion is nothing, but absolute submission to God's will.

As to scriptures, the Moslems, are taught, that God, in divers ages of the world, gave revelations of His will Books, to several prophets. The number of these sacred Books is said to be 104: ten Books were given to Adam, fifty to Seth, thirty to Idris (Enoch), ten to Abraham; and the other four, being the Pentateuch, the Psalms, the Gospel and the Koran, were successively delivered to Moses, David, Jesus and Mohammad. No further revelation to man-kind is to be expected. The Prophet Mohammad is, as taught by the Koran, the seal of God's messengers and prophets.

All of those divine Books, except the four last, are believed to be now entirely lost. As to the Pentateuch, the Psalms and the Gospel, the Moslems give no credit to the present copies of these Books, which they believe to have undergone many alterations corruptions, though there might possible be some part of the true word of God therein. Any passages in the present copies which in sense are not in harmony with the teachings of the Koran, as far as matters of faith are concerned, are held by Moslems to be no true revelation. Hence, such statements in the present copies of the Old and New Testaments, as attribute to God a son, or to the Divinity a plurality or a corporal form, are dogmatically and emphatically condemned as schismatics.

On the other hand, if any precept, tenet, law or regulation, relating to mode of worship, or rules of right and wrong, found in the Koran, is in harmony with similar precepts, as taught by the Testaments, it is because such tenets are immutable and eternal, and relate to that part of God's one, true orthodox religion which is subject to no change or alteration, inasmuch as such laws were saved from corruption.

Apparently it is due to the misunderstanding of this fundamental superstructure of the Mohammadan Religion (to wit: that from the beginning to the end of the world, there has been, and still for ever will be, but one true religion), that some of the prejudiced class of Western historians and commentators have been apt to wrongly describe such systems, rites or rules of the Religion of Islam, of which the like exist in the Jewish Scriptures, as 'borrowed' from these books. Such cities, if absolutely innocent, conscientious and well-informed, must needs admit, that these common precepts are but confirmed by the Koran as immutable in themselves.

It must be again re-iterated until the basis of the Religion of Islam is well understood, that this religion does not profess to be a new religion, formulated by the Prophet Mohammad, but a continuation of the true religious principles, established by God through His revelations to Adam, North, Abraham, Moses and to other inspired Messengers of God. The revelation of God's prophets, prior to the advent of Mohammadanism, are held to have been partly corrupted by the hand of man, through the various renderings and divers of same. All portions of the World of God that were by chance, or otherwise, saved from corruption,.. such as relate to that part of God's religion which is eternal and immutable,.. have been preserved and confirmed by the Koran, together with other corrected beliefs and dogma of faith, and such additional rules of practical devotion, as God judged fit for the new and eternal dispensation. Hence, it is out of place and entirely misleading, that any critic should suggest, that Mohammadanism is 'indebted', either to the Jewish or any other dispensation, for any elements in its system.

In brief, it is enjoined upon every Moslem, to believe in God's previous Books of revelations, from Adam to Jesus, in so far as the contents of any extant book of them are not contradicted by the Koran.

At the advent of Islam, the World of God, as revealed in the Old and New Testament, was wrapped up in various superstitions, and was spoiled by an admixture of ungodly beliefs and imaginations. The Jews were openly charged, in the early chapters of the Koran, with having corrupted their Scripture, with stiffing passages. They obstinately and impiously denied the advent of Jesus. They believed that Christ was yet to come. They spoke ill, and most wrongly and indecently, of the acknowledge Jesus Christ and of his revered mother, the Virgin Mary. They attributed to God the adoption of a son in the person of Ezra.

With regard to Christianity, its real and pure doctrine were exceedingly and abominable corrupted. A sect substituted the Virgin Mary for God, or worshipped her as such. These were called the Mariamites.

Christians also believed in the divinity of Jesus. They worshipped him as God, called him the son God, and even God Himself.

Dr. Hughes, commenting on the state of degradation, into which the Christian Church had fallen, at the advent of Islam, writes as follows:

"The bitter dissensions of the Greeks, Nestorians, Eutechians and Monophysites, are matters of history, and must have held up the religion of Jesus to the ridicule of the heathen world. The controversies, regarding the nature and person of our Divine Lord, had begotten a sect of Tritheists...

"The worship of the Virgin Mary had also given rise to a religious controversy the Antidues, Mariamites and the Collyridians; the former holding that the Virgin Marry was not immaculate and the latter, raising her to a position of a Goddess. Under these circumstances, it is not surprising to find that the Arabian reformed turned aways from Christianity."

The Gospel of St. Barnabas commonly considered by Christian theologians as "apocryphal", — is most in harmony, as to matters of faith, with the Koran Jesus Christ is spoken of in that Gospel as the servant of God; the word of God and a Spirit from God. His miraculous birth, being born without a father was even supernatural than the creation of Adam who was created by God's power with neither father nor mother.

The crucifixion of Jesus by the Jews is entirely refuted, according to St.Barnabas and the Koran.

In that Gospel, it is asserted, that Judas, the traitor, was he who was crucified, in the place of the Lord Jesus. "Of this Gospel", writes Mr. Sale, "the Moriscoes in Africa have a translation in Spanish, and there is in the library of Prince Eugene of Savoy, a manuscript of some antiquity, containing an Italian translation of the same Gospel made, it is supposed, for the use of renegades.."

In St. Barnabas' Gospel, the Prophet Mohammad is foretold by name, as the Periclyte, that is, the famous or illustrious, that being the signification of the name of Mohammad in Arabic; thereby justifying the passage in the Koran(chap.61) where Jesus is formally asserted to have foretold his coming, under his other name of Ahmad, which is derived from the same root as Mohammad and of the same import.

George Sale states that he inspected a Spanish translation of the Italian copy to St. Barnabas' Gospel, of which he gives the following account:

"There is a preface prefixed to it, wherein the discoverer of the original MS., who was a Christian monk called Fra Marino, tells us that, having accidentally met with a writing of Irenacus (among others), wherein he speaks against St. Paul, alleging for his authority the gospel of St. Barnabas' he became exceedingly desirous to find this gospel; and that God, of His mercy, having made him very intimate with Pope Sixtus V (1521-90) one day, as they were together in that Pope's library, His Holiness fell asleep and he, to employ himself, reached down a book to read, the first he laid hand on proved to be the very gospel he wanted; overjoyed at the discovery, he scrupled not to hide his prize in his sleeve, and on the Pope's awaking, took leave of him carrying with him that celestial treasure, by reading of which he became a convert to Mohammadanism.

"This Gospel of Barnabas contains a complete history of Jesus Christ, from His birth to His ascension, and most of the circumstances of the four real gospel are to be found therein, but many of them turned, and some artfully enough, to favour the

Mohammedan system... The passages produced from the Italian MS. by M. de la Monnoye, are to be seen in this Spanish version word for word."

The Koran

The practical side of both the Jewish and Christian dispensations, as concerning social matters and civil law, is most deficient; and that deficiency is made good by the Koran, it being the last divine Word of God.

Let us now make a swift survey of the Koran, as far as our limited space in this work allows; for to describe it in detail would require unlimited time and space. For various reasons, all being much to the advantage of the non-Moslem reader, — I shall content myself with a number of quotations of what was written on the Koran by the pen of non-Moslem critics, whose writings on the subject can be passed by a Moslem, as giving a sufficiently true picture of the Holy Koran. However, it must be remembered that, as a miraculously Divine Book, the Koran, when translated into a foreign language, necessarily loses a great deal of its supernatural elegance and purity of Style.

Mr. Sale addresses the reader of his English versions of the Koran in the following words:

".. though the reader must not imagine the translation to come up to the original, notwithstanding my endeavours to do it justice".

In another places, the same writer comments on the Koran as follows:

"The Koran is universally allowed to be written with the utmost elegance and purity of language, in the dialect of the tribe of the Koreish, the most noble and polite of all the Arabians; but with some mixture though very rarely, of other dialects. It is confessedly the standard of the Arabian tongue and, as the more orthodox believe and are taught by the book itself, inimitable by any human pen, and therefore insisted on as a permanent miracle, greater than that of raising the dead, and alone sufficient to convince the world of its origin.

"And to this miracle Mohammad himself chiefly appealed for the confirmation of his mission, publicly challenging the most eloquent men in Arabia which was at the same time stocked with thousands whose sole study and ambition it was, to excel in elegance of style and composition, to produced even a single chapter that might be compared with it I will mention but one instance out of several, to show that this book was really admired for the beauty of its composition by those who must be allowed to have been competent judges. A poem of Labib Ebn Rabia, in Mohammeds' time, being affixed to the gate of the temple of Mecca, an honour allowed to none but the most esteemed performances, none of the other poets durst offer anything of their own in competition with it. But the second chapter of the Koran, being affixed near it soon after, Labib himself (then an idolater) on reading the first verse only, was struck with admiration, and immediately professed the religion taught therein, declaring that such words could proceed from an inspired person only. This Labib was afterwards of great service to Mohammed, in writing answer to the satires and invectives that were made on him and his religion ."

Von Goethe, the renowned German author, speaking of the Koran in his West-Oestlicher Divan, State:

"However often we turn to it, (the Koran), at first disgusting us each time afresh, it soon attracts, astounds and, in the end, enforces our reverence... Its style, in accordance with its contents and aim, is stern, grand, terrible, — ever and anon truly sublime — Thus, this book will go on exercising, through all ages, a most potent influence."

Dr. Steingass, the learned compiler of an English-Arabic and Arabic English Dictionary (W.H.Allen and Co.) has recorded his opinion on the Koran in Dr. Hughes' Dictionary of Islam. After alluding to the above words of Goethe Dr. Steingass writes: "These words seem to me so much the more weighty and worthy of attention, as they are uttered by one who, whatever his merits or demerits in other respects may be deemed to be, indisputably belongs to the greatest masters of language of all times, and stands foremost as a leader of modern thought and the intellectual culture of modern times." (Here Dr. Steingass quotes the words of Goeth and then says) "A work, then which calls forth so powerful and seemingly incompatible emotions, even in the distant reader, — distant as to time, and still more so, as to mental development — a work which not only conquers repugnance with he may begin its perusal, but changes this adverse feeling into astonishment and admiration. Such, a work must be a wonderful production of the human mind indeed, and a problem of the highest interest to every thoughtful observer of the destinies of mankind. Much has been said, in the preceding pages, to acknowledge, to appreciate, and to explain the literary excellences of the Koran, and a more or less distinct admission, that Buffon's much-quoted saying:

"Le style est l'homme", is here more justified than ever, underlies all these verdict. We may well say, the Koran is one of the grandest books ever written, because it faithful reflects the character and life of one of the greatest men the ever breathed. "Sincerity, writes Carlyle, 'sincerity, in all senses, seems to me the merit of the Koran'. This same sincerity, this ardour and earnestness in the search for truth, this neverflagging perseverance in trying to impress it, when partly found, again and again upon his unwilling hearers, *appear to me as the real and undeniable 'seal of prophecy' in Mohammad.."*

But the approaches to truth are many, and he who devoted all his powers and energies, with untiring patience and self-denial, to the task of leading a whole nation by one of these approaches, from a coarse and effete idolatry, to the worship of the living God, has certainly a strong claims to our warmest sympathies, as a faithful servants and noble champion of truth.

It is, however, not my intention to dwell here any longer upon this side of the question. Praise has been bestowed in this work on the Koran and is author, without stint or grudge, and the unanimity of so many distinguished voice, in this respect, will no doubt impress the general reader in favour of the sacred book of the Mohammadans which until now he may have known only by name.

Dealing with the opinion, expressed on the Koran by some European authors who dwelt upon the pretended inferiority of the later positions of the Koran in comparison with the earlier chapters, Dr. Steingass ably remarks as follows:

"Not being an Arabic scholar himself (Goethe), he knew the Koran only through the translations existing at the time which follow throughout the order of the received text... Those critics, on the other hand, who view the Koran with regard to the chronological order of its constituents, follow the descending scale in their estimate. But if we consider the variety and heterogeneousness of the topics, on which the Koran touches, uniformity of style and diction can scarcely be excepted; on the contrary, it would appear to be strangely out of place. Let us not forget that in the book, as Mohammad's newest biographer, Ludolf Krehl (Das Leben des Mohammed, Leipzig 1884) expresses it, 'there is given a complete code of creed and morals, as well as of the law based thereupon. There are also the foundations laid for every institution of an extensive commonwealth, for instruction, for the administration of justice, for military organisation, for finance, for a most careful legislation for the poor: all built up on the belief in the one God Who holds man's destiny in His hand. Where so many important objects are concerned, the standard of excellence, by which we have to gauge the composition of the Koran as a whole, must needs vary with the matter treated upon in each particular case. Sublime, and chaste, where the supreme truth of God's unity is to be proclaimed; appealing in high-pitched, strains to the imagination of a poetically-gifted people, where the eternal consequences of mans' submission to God's holy will, or of rebellion against it, are pictured; touching in its simple, almost crude earnestness, when it seeks again and again encouragement or consolation for God's messenger, and a solemn warning for those, to whom he has been sent, in the histories of the prophets of old: the language of the Koran adapts itself to the exigencies of everyday life, when this everyday life, in its private and public bearings, is to be brought in to harmony with the fundamental principles of the new dispensation.

"Here, therefore, its merits, as a literary production should, perhaps, not be measured by some preconceived maxims of subjective and aesthetic taste, but by the effects which it produced in Mohammad's contemporaries and fellow-countrymen. If it spoke so powerfully and convincingly to the hearts of his hearts, as to weld hitherto centrifugal and antagonistic elements into one compact and well organised body, animated by ideas, far beyond these which had until now rules the Arabian mind, then its eloquence was perfect, simply because it created a civilised nation out of savage tribes, and shot a fresh woof into the old wrap of history.

"When a long period of conquests scattered the Arabs to the farthest East and to the farthest West, their spoken language might deviate from its pristine purity, slurring over unaccented syllables and dropping terminations. But the fine idiom of their forefathers, as deposited in the Koran, remained the language of their prayer and their pious meditation, and thus lived on with them, as a bond of unity, an object of national love and admiration, and a source of literary development, for all times."

The Koran, therefore, is the last Scripture from God which has superseded by its new dispensation all preceding Scriptures, containing all comprehensible instructions and laws, all matters concerning the relation between the Creator and His creature, and between man and man. It is a miraculous book which is a poem, far beyond the power of poets to imitate, a code of laws bearing on every institution of an extensive commonwealth, on instruction, on the administration of justice, on military organisation, on finance, on a most careful legislation for the poor; and a complete code of beliefs and morals; all built up on the perfected belief in the one God Who holds man's destiny in His Hand. It embodies a correct summary of the true religion which former prophets from the time Adam had taught to their respective countries, and a solemn warning to all mankind, to whom the "Seal of Prophets" had been sent to reclaim and to reform. It exposes and refutes the pretensions and incorrect interpretations of rabbins and priests who had misled their people. These latter were often called upon, in the Koran, to come to a reasoning with the followers of the new faith and, then, to judge for themselves, as to whether Mohammadanism was to be rejected by pure reason cleared of every grain of partiality. But the high voice from Heavens was not hearkened to and differences of a religious nature still continue between Moslems and non-Moslems.

The Koran is a Divine Book which from the day of its revelation through the message of the Arabian Prophet and Apostle of God, up to this moment, has undergone no alteration whatever. It is the Scared Book that continues to reign over the hearts of its hearers, to convince them, through their own conscience and spiritual nature of its Divine origin. No human pen, however powerful, can venture to imitate it. The miraculous nature of the Koran has, long ago, been solemnly confirmed by those who were the most competent judges. The Arabians could boast of no other literature than witty poems of eloquence in their own language, — though as they paid due honour to any distinguished poem by their famous poets— were struck with infinite admiration, when they heard the Prophet of God rehearsing certain portions of God's new Gospel to them. Their own celebrated Rabiaa, whose poem was attached to the Sacred Pantheon of the Kaaba, could, without much trouble or hesitation, judge that the Koran of Mohammad was rightly a Divine Book, and that the *illiterate orphan was the true messenger of God.* From the perusal of the concise, but accurate history of the Prophet, in part II of this essay, it is clear enough, how the obstinate minded Arabs of the Desert received the Book with adoration and perfect reverence. Again, the contents of the Koran most readily answer all questions that may be raised on religious or civil matters. I will quote here some interpreted passages from that Holy Book, as specimens of the rest, and leave them to recommend themselves:

1. Calling the Jews and Christian to Come to Agreement with the Moslems

"Say, O ye who have received the Scripture (Jews and Christians) come to a just determination between us and you; that we worship not any except God, and associate no creature with Him; and that the one of us takes no other for Lord, beside God. But if they turn back, say; bear witness that we are true believers."

2. Ordering the Prophet to Praise God

"Say, O God, possessor of the Kingdom, thou givest dominion to whom Thou wilt, and Thou takest away Kingdom from whom Thou wilt: Thou exaltest whom Thou wilt, and thou Humblest whom Thou wilt, in Thy hand is Good, and Thou art the Almighty: Thou causest the night to succeed the day, and Thou causest the day to succeed the night: Thou bringest forth the living out of the dead, and Thou bringest forth the dead out for the living and thou art the provider of substinance to whom Thou wilt, without measure."

3. Good and Evil Deeds

"Say, whether ye conceal that which is in your hearts, or whether ye show it, God knoweth it: He knoweth is in heaven and whatever is on earth: and He is the Almighty. On the Day of Judgment, every soul shall find present and he happy with the good which it wrought while the evil which it wrought, will cause it such a disgrace, that it shall wish that there was a vast distance between itself and that evil."

4. Belief of the Faithful

"The Apostle (Mohammad) believeth in that which hath been sent down unto him from his Lord, as do the faithful (also). Everyone (of them) believeth in God and His Angels, and His Scriptures, and his Apostle: We make no distinction between any of His Apostle. And they say "We have listened, and so we obey. Thy mercy, O Lord, for unto Thee (O Lord) must we return'. God will not burden any soul beyond its power. It shall enjoy the good which it hath gained, and shall bear the evil which it hath wrought. O Lord, punish us not, if we forget or fall into sin; O Lord, lay not on us a burden, like that which Thou hast laid on those who have been before us, neither makes us, O Lord, to bear what we have no strength to bear, but be favourable unto us, and spare us, and be merciful unto us. Thou art our patron, help us therefore against the unbelieving people."

With regard to the New Testament, Moslems hold the belief that, although God revealed the Gospel to His Messenger Jesus Christ, the So-called gospels ascribed to the four saints do not represent the true world of God as revealed to the Teacher of Nazareth. With Moslems these books *are mere historical works, dealing with the history of Jesus*, and they contradict each other in certain statements. Three of the authors of the four gospel, did not see Jesus at all.. St. Mark did not see Jesus, until the year he was taken up to heaven. After the ascension of Jesus, (1) St.Mark wrote in the city of Alexandria, his gospel, in which he gave an account of the birth and life of the Master of Christianity, mentioning several events which are not to be traced in the other three gospel. (2) St. Luke also did not see Jesus, but he was converted to Christianity by St. Paul, the latter being an Israelite who himself had not seen Jesus, but was converted by St. Ananias. (3) St. Matthew also did not see Jesus, but was converted to the Christian faith by St. Peter, sometime after the ascension of Jesus; he took his gospel from St. Peter in the city of Rome. St. Matthew's gospel contradicts several statements of the other three Gospel.

St.John was the nephew of Jesus. It was at the wedding of John, Jesus converted water into wine. Witnessing this miracle, John immediately became a Christian proselyte, left his wife and followed Jesus. He was the author of the fourth gospel, called after him, written in the Greek language, in the city of Ephesus.

These are the four gospel of the Christian New Testament, although Moslems do not believe them to contain the uncorrupted word of God. They are nothing more than biographical works which are liable to defects and errors. There was but one Gospel, namely, the "Evangel" which God vouchsafed to give to Jesus, for him to preach to the Israilities. The Book containing the True Word of God must needs be free from all discrepancies; yet it is written in St. Mark's gospel, that in the book of the Prophet Isaiah it was said by God: 'I have sent Angel before Thy face', namely, before the face of Jesus; whereas the words *are not* in the book of Isaiah, but in that of Malachi (see St. Mark). Again it is related in St. Matthew's gospel (Matt. xii.40) that Jesus said 'My body will remain in the belly of the earth three days and three nights after my death, just as Jones was in the whale's belly', and it is evident this was not true, for St. Matthew himself agrees with the three other writers of the gospel, that Jesus died at the sixth hour on Friday, and was buried at the first hour of the night and rose from the dead early on Sunday morning, so that he remained in the belly of the earth two nights only.

Islam and the Four Gospels

As already pointed out, Moslems do not admit the authenticity of the Gospels, or the creed contained therein, or the leading events in the life of the Holy Prophet Jesus, as depicted by these same Gospels. In this attitude Moslems are supported by the scholarly researches of devout Christian even.

It seems, however, that the laity in Christendom are generally as ignorant, with regard to these vital question, as non-Christians, to whom Christian literature is inaccessible in the main. A brief account of these question is, therefore likely to be of interest and use.

According to the doctrine of Islam, the four Gospels are not revealed by God. Nor was it the Holy Ghost that moved the writers of the said Gospel to write them. But it was the example of other writers, that inspired them with the desire of compiling brief biographies of Jesus.

1. St. Luke's Gospel

St. Luke's own words to this effect are :

"For as much *as many have take in hand* to set forth, in

order, a declaration of those things which are most surely believed among us.

"Even as they delivered them unto us, who from the beginning were eyewitness, and ministers of the word;

"It *seemed good to me also*, having had perfect understanding of all things, from the very first, to write unto thee in order, most excellent Theophilus.

"That thou mightest know the certainty of those things, wherein thou hast been instructed" St. Luke

St. Luke has very plainly set forth the grounds of his inspiration, namely : (1) the example of other writers of Jesus' life; (2) his consciousness of possessing "perfect understanding of all things from the first"; and (3) to import reliable information to Theophilus. Thus, St. Luke does not call his Gospel a divine revelation, but he claims for it (a) diligence in collecting all available material, (b) fullness, (c)careful investigation, (d) orderly arrangement and (e) accuracy.

The Rev. Grieve, M.A.,D.D., Principal of the Congregational Hall, Edinburgh, and a joint Editor of Peake's famous Commentary, explains Luke's preface in the following words : "The writer, *influenced by the attempts* of others, to record the primitive tradition of Christianity, as it was handed down by the first generation of disciples, essays the same task, and having taken pains to collect, examine, sift and arrange the contents of the *written oral tradition,* presents the result to Theophilus, a Roman official of some standing — a literary patron of the Evangelists — who needed fuller acquaintance with the historic basis of the oral teaching about Christianity which he had received."

God reveals books for the guidance of a nation or nations, as the case may be, but St. Luke dedicates his books to the *"Most excellent Theophilus."*

The Encyclopaedia Biblica throws further light on this dedication: "The dedication of Luke shows, that we have passed into a new literary province. The Muratorian fragment calls attention to the fact, that the author writes in *his own name, a novelty* among Evangelists. He also dedicates his work to someone who, if not an imaginary 'God beloved', would appear to be a patron, a man of rank. The apostles — the 'eyewitnesses and ministers of the world' — appear to have delivered their testimony by oral tradition, and to have passed away. To supply their places, (I-i) 'many' had attempted to draw up a formal narrative concerning the matters fully established in the Church. These writer had clearly not been eyewitnesses, nor were they, in Luke's judgment so successful as to make unnecessary any further attempts. Apparently they had failed in the three points, in which he hopes to excel: (1) they had not traced everything up to the source, and this (2), as far as it went, not 'accurately' and (3) they had not written 'in order.'"

The same book further discusses the point whether or not the work of St. Luke's justifies the claims of that Apostle: "We are led to the conclusion that, though Luke attempted to write 'accurately', and in `order', *yet he could not always succeed.* When deciding between an earlier and a later date, between this and that place and occasion, between metaphor and literalism, between what Jesus himself said and what he said through his disciples, he (Luke) had to be guided by evidence which sometimes led him aright, *but not always.*"

We further read in the same work: "Luke's absolute omission of genuine and valuable traditions — especially in connection with Christ's appearance to woman after the Resurrection, and with Christ's promise to go to 'Galilee' —. . . seriously diminishes the value of his work. It is probably the best adapted for making converts. But if hold bare facts are in question, *it is probably the least authoritative of the Four.*"

Luke's failure has evidently been ascribed to his attempts being human, and his sources mortal, which could 'not always' guide him aright. If his work had been revealed, he could not have been accused of having omitted some most important incidents, or of his book being "the least authoritative".

The quotations cited above clearly buttress the Islamic belief, that the Christian gospels are but human attempts to draw up accounts of the life of Jesus, and as such are neither complete nor satisfactory. Revelation alone can make a recipient immune from error; for it suspends, for the time being, all other mental activity of the person, upon the Word of God descends. His Word and Will were revealed to holy prophets, like Abraham, Moses, Jesus and Mohammad. But the followers Jesus were animated, or inspired, to compile what was already known to them. They had but to collect, sift and arrange the material which was in the possession of the people. As such the works of the Apostles are necessarily characterised by normal shortcomings. Even the devout Christian scholar admits it, and is ready to bear testimony to the fact, that the record of the gospel is not altogether complete and reliable. We cannot do better than quote some of the most scholarly and popularly admitted opinions which carry weight and conviction in this connection.

The Rev. Dummelow, M.A., expresses his opinion as follows:

"Speaking broadly, the Christians mean by their inspiration an impulse from God, causing 'certain persons to write, and directing them how to write, for the edification of others. Though it is closely connected with *revelation,* it is not identical with it. By *revelation,* God makes known to a soul truths which were unknown to it before *But it is not at all necessary,* that an inspired writer should receiver any new truths by way of revelation. Thus St. Mark was inspired to write his Gospel, but be was inspired *to write down truths* which were already familiar to him and to others through the instruction given by St. Peter."

2. The Gospel of St. Matthew and that of St. Mark

The foregoing also applies to both St. Matthew's and St. Mark's Gospel. "St. Mark is the oldest of the Synoptists, and has been used by St. Matthew and St. Luke, who have incorporated the bulk of his gospel into their own with comparatively few alterations."

It is thus plain, that Christian scholars of sacred literature do not claim divine origin for Christian Gospel. They, on the other hand, admit that the said books were compiled by mere men who were by no means experts. They were consequently liable to mistakes, I quote the Rev. Dummelow once more on this point: "We must not regard the Bible as *an absolutely perfect book, in which God is Himself the author using human hands and brains only as a man may use a typewriter...* Their inspiration did not involve a suspension of their natural faculties, nor abolish the differences of training and character; it did not even make them perfectly free from earthy passion. Therefore, we find that their knowledge sometimes is no higher than their contemporaries, and their indignation against oppression and wrongdoing sometimes breaks out into desire of revenge. It surprises us in the Bible, because of our theory of Verbal Inspiration."

The same Commentary further throws light upon the insufficiency and incompleteness of these sacred records, and thus precludes any chance of claiming their divine origin. "To-day we realise, that the life of Jesus can never by written. The material is wanting. Neither in quality, nor in extent, do the Gospel satisfy the requirements of a modern biography. At best, they offer us certain memorabilia of the public ministry of Jesus, hardly adequate to construct the story of the year or year, during which he evangelised his people, and barely sufficing to mirror the chief feature of his message. Where the modern mind is most curious, the Gospel seem to be least communicative. Men would fain trace the development of innermost convictions which condition his activity as prophet. But the facts that the Gospel tell us little or nothing of the early life of jesus, and that almost every story consists of a simple record of outward act and utterance, with few hints as to inward feeling or historical setting, seem at first sight to defeat the hopes of analysing motive, and tracing growth."

3. The Four Gospels

Dealing with the sources of the four Gospels of the Christian faith, the Encyclopaedia Biblica comments as follows:

"These documents are of varying value from a historical point of view. Critical opinion is much decided as to the fourth, that which bears the name of John, the judgment of many critics being, that it is the *least Transt-worthy as a source, whether for words or for the acts of Jesus*. By comparison, the first three, from their resemblances called synoptical are regarded by many as possessing a considerable measure of historical worth, but even these, from a critical point of view, are not of equal value, nor to do the contents of any of them possess a uniform degree of historical probability. They present to the critic a curious, interesting, and perplexing problem, still far from final solution. By their resemblances and differences, agreements and disagreements, they raise many questions as to origin, relative dates, and literary connections, which have called forth a multitude of conflicting hypotheses and a most extensive critical literature."

In the opinion of the best English scholar of the New Testament, the Gospel are not to be looked upon as revealed books, the sole source of which should have been God and not man. But they are to be regarded, on the other hand, as inadequate attempts, made by pious but not talented followers of Christ, at the description of his life. It is a great pity, that the world never availed itself of the collection of those life inspiring words that were uttered by the Holy Prophet of Nazareth. However, piety and veneration, for a long time, assured the credulity of the early Christians, that the Gospel revealed the Word of God, and in consequence were infallible. There was a time, when every article of it was firmly and reverently believed to have directly proceeded from God. In short, what had been written by man, passed for the word of God. This is clear to those clergy who have undergone university training. But the pity of it is, that they have not the moral courage to enlighten their congregation on the subject. It would only seem, that pious anxiety dictates, that a character of infallibility should still be given to what has been written by human hands, and that crude attempts at the biography of the Holy Prophet of Nazareth, should continue to be believed to have been revealed by God Himself.

Anyhow, what scholarship and research have now brought to light, was revealed over thirteen centuries ago in the Koran:

"Do they not know, that God knows, what they keep secret, and what they make known; and there are among them ignorant, who know not the Book, but only idle stories, and they do but conjecture; woe, then, to those who write the book with their own hands, and then say. This is from God, so that they may obtain therewith a small gain; therefore, woe to them, for what their hands have written, and woe to them, for what they have earned." Dr. Murray's illustrated `Bible Dictionary' which is a valuable commentary, enlightens us thus:

Gospels:— "The first point which attracts our notice in reading the Gospels is, that the first three Gospels are distinct from the fourth. The first three Gospels confine themselves almost exclusively to the events which took place in Galilee, until Christ's last journey to Jerusalem. If we had three Gospels alone, we could not definitely say, that our Lord went to Jerusalem during his ministry, until he went there to die. The difference in character is no less, than the difference in scene. Further, *the synoptists do not* be eyewitnesses of our Lord's work ; the first three Gospels are usually called the synoptic Gospels... It is obvious, that not only all the three synoptic Gospels differ from John, but they differ *widely* from each other. The account of the birth and infancy of Christ in Matthew *differs widely* from that in Luke. The incidents of the temptation of our Lord are recorded in a different order in Matthew and Luke, and the temptation is recorded without these incidents in Mark. All three Gospels give a slightly different account of the inscription on the cross, and the words spoken by the centurion at the death of Jesus, very in Luke from the words in Matthew and Mark. Also the language differs and differs in a very singular manner."

From the above quotations it is very clear, that the material for Mark's Gospels was supplied by St. Peter's preaching, and that Mark was freely drawn upon by Matthew and Luke; which establishes the fact, that the synoptic Gospel are no revelations at all, but are purely and simply human compilations. It remains to deal with St.

John's Gospel.

The Twentieth Century New Testament makes the following observation on John :

"The writer apparently proposed to himself to illustrate the spirit of the 'Gospel of Love' by such incidents in the life of Jesus, as best suited his purpose. There is no attempt at a regular connected narrative; and the writer allows himself such freedom, in commenting upon the teaching of Jesus, that it is not always easy to tell where that teaching ends and the writer's comments being. It is to the great struggle between Light and Darkness, Death and Life, — words much in use and much debated in the current philosophy of Ephesus, — that the writer devotes his attention, rather than to the external incidents of a story which has already been told, and which is plainly viewed by him from a greater distance of time, than is the case with the compilers of the three other Gospels."

Another eminent authority, namely Dr. Weymouth, in his Introduction to John, observes:

"It must be owned that, although the fourth Gospels makes on assertion which contradicts the character of Teacher and Reformer attributed to Him by the synoptists, it presents to us a personage so enwrapped in mystery and dignity, as altogether to transcend ordinary human nature. This transcendent personality is, indeed, the avowed centre of the whole record, and his portrayal is its avowed purpose".

Now, these quotation, point very clearly to the fact, that there is a general agreement, as to John having played the role of an interpreter or a commentator of the three other Gospels. There is not an allusion or a reference, made to John having received a revelation from Heaven, or having been inspired to furnished the world with an explanation of the doctrine of Christ. We learn on the other hand, that, while the authors of the three other Gospels compiled the incidents of the life of Jesus, John gave a mystical meaning to them. He himself does not lay claim to revelation, or to consequent perfection. He has, on the contrary, confessed the imperfection of his attempts, to depict the incidents of the life Jesus. Likewise, he admits that he is but a recorder of incidents of signs. 'There were also a great number of signs which Jesus performed in the presence of the disciples, which are not recorded in this book; but these have been recorded, in order that you may believe, that he is the Christ, the son of God, and that, through believing, you may have Life through his name."

This text, which reveals the object of the fourth Gospels, announces that this is a partial record of some of those signs which Jesus performed before his disciples. To record events or signs which are known to many, or all, of the disciples and others, does not require the aid of revelation which supplies information which is not already in the possession of human beings.

Some Important Discrepancies

Jesus said to them (who took offence at him and who were not prepared to recognise his claims simply because he was a carpenter's son and had other humble ties): "A *prophet* is not without, but in his own country, and among his own kin, and in his own house" (Mark). This statement was curtailed by Matthew, and still more by John. Luke ignored it altogether.

"But of the day and that hour knoweth no man, not, not the angels which are in heaven, neither the Son, but the Father" (Mark xiii, 32). This text embodies a confession by Jesus, eloquent of his limited knowledge and avowed ignorance; while Luke and John, however make no mention of that humiliating reference.

The Rev. Dummelow's Commentary makes the following remarks on "Neither the Son": This is the true reading not only here (in mark) but in Matthew xxiv, 36, where it has been *altered* in many MSS., probably as being a difficulty to faith." Peake's Commentary offers the following note on it :

"Mark xiii. 32 — This is one of 'Schmiedel's pillar-passages'. A passage admitting a limit to Christ; knowledge must be trustworthy history, according to Schmiedel. Certainly later commentators found the verse difficult."

"My God, my God, why hast Thou forsaken me? (Mark xv. 34) These words have been copied by Matthew only. They picture the inborn weakness of Jesus. This expression of his human nature was unworthy of record, in the opinion of Luke and John.

Interpolations

Of many interpolations, mention will be made here of a few only:

(A) *John* vii 53 and viii. i-ii, that is, the last verse of the seventh chapter, with its continuation in the first eleven verse of the eighth chapter, which relate the story of an adultress, is an interpolation. This is admitted universally. The Rev. Dummelow's Commentary has the following observations on it : "The woman taken in adultery — All modern critics agree, that this section (vii.53. i-ii) is no original part of the fourth Gospels. It is not in the author's style; it breaks the sequence of our Lord's discourses and *is omitted by most of the ancient authorities."*

Peake's Commentary comments on the story at the end of John vii. 53-vii-i-ii, *Jesus, and the woman accused of sin* : "The well-known story of the woman taken in adultery has no claim to be regarded as part of the original text of this. . . It is supported by no early Patiristic evidence. The evidence proves it to be *an interpolation of a 'western' character"*.

Dr. Weymouth's 'New Testament in modern English' mark the section as an interpolation. 'The Twentieth Century New Testament' has excised it, and placed it in such a place as indicates clearly, that it has no connection with John 'The Complete Bible in Modern English' writes in a footnote: "The narrative of the sinful woman (chap. vii 53 to viii-i-ii) is rejected by the most competent authorities as a *spurious interpolation.*

(B) *John xxi:* In the opinion of the Rev. Dummelow, the last two verse at least, 24 and 25 — *are really doubtful*, and they "may have been added by the Ephesian elders, who first put the Gospel in circulation, after the death of the Apostle, and who wished to testify to its genuineness and trustworthiness".

(C) *Mark xvi:* 9-20 *is another interpolation.* Dummelow's Commentary observes that "Internal evidence points definitely to the conclusion, that *the last twelve verse are not by St. Mark."* It further supplies the following information on the subject: "When at the close of the apostolic age, and attempt was made (probably in Rome) to collect the authentic memorials of the Apostles and their companions, a copy of the neglected second Gospel was not easily found. *The one that was actually discovered, and was used to multiply copies, had lost its last leaf, and so a fitting termination (the present appendix) was added by another hand.*"

The unanimous verdict given in the New Testaments Of Dr. Weymouth, Dr. Moffat, Ferrar Fention, and in the Twetieth Century New Testament, is that *Mark VXI-9-20, is an addition.*

(D) *Luke xxiv.* 51 is another interpolation, as is conceded on all hands. It elicits the following comment from the Rev. Dummelow: "A few ancient authorities omit these words. *If they are omitted, it is possible to regard this event, not* as the ascension, but as a miraculous disappearance of Jesus at the end of the interview begun in verse 36".

Peake's Commentary makes remarks; "The words 'and was carried up into heaven' are omitted in some of the best MSS, and have probably crept in form Acts. i-9f."

The Twentieth Century New testament and Dr. Moffat's "New Testament" Mark it as an interpolation.

Ascension

Our co-religionist, Maulvi Sadr-ud-Did, B.A., from whose interesting essay, "Are the Gospels inspired". I have chiefly reproduced the above chapter, makes the following conclusion to his work:

"If according to Christ and Mohammed (peace be upon them and all the other prophets), the essence of religion lies in our perfect love of God, which can only be manifested in our willing obedience to His Divine will, we must be assured, as rational being, of the genuineness and credibility of God's message, as much as of the soundness of the truth, that it reveals. It is this natural craving, that had led to what is known as the higher criticism of the Bible. A similar test has been applied to the Holy Koran as well, to which reference has been made previously. The result of the higher criticism of the four Gospels has partially been presented in this treatise, with the object of making the laity and non-Christians in general acquainted with it. In doing so, I have purposely refrained from quoting the opinions expressed in the learned commentaries of the Non-conformists, and in the books issued on the subject by the *Rational Press*. I have, on the contrary, restricted the treatment to the views expounded by the *Clergy of the Church of England* in the main, and to the views of those who are rather conservative. I have also deliberately overlooked the question, whether, we can ascribe with certainly the authorship of the Gospels to the Evangelists, whose names they bear now. All the commentaries are agreed upon the fact, that the original copies of the Gospels, were without indication as to the authors' names. It was guessed, later, who were the most probable writers of them. The Probable conjecture has not yet reached certainty. The authenticity of the names, to which, the Gospels are attributed, is open to doubt, as can be seen by referring to any commentary."

What, we have learnt with respect to the origin of the Christian Gospels, and the creed preached therein, can be recapitulated in a few words. *Mark was the first Gospel, and not Matthew* as is generally indicated by the present arrangement of the four books. Mark, who was a convert and interpreter of St. Peter, penned at the instance of 'his hearners,' what St. Peter had adopted and preached to his Roman audiences. Mark has been incorporated into Matthew and Luke. But Matthew has represented the words the works of Jesus as fulfilling the prophecies of the Old Testament. No less than sixty-five references have been made to Old Testament texts, to establish that the advent of the Messiah was in strict accordance with the Jewish ideals. This conception and purpose pervade the whole of Matthew, and distinguish it from the other three. *Luke represents St. Paul's views, which are in conflict with St. Peter's.* Thus we have in Luke an altogether different point of view. *It opposes Matthew and Mark most boldly,* and places its litteral and Catholic description of Christianity in striking contrast to Matthew and Mark, who confine God's blessings and ministrations to the elect alone. John strikes an entirely different note. If offers, to interpret Christianity for us. We may respect his opinion, as an individual one, and as different from the other three; but we cannot be assured, that his vague and mythical representation of Christianity is identical with the definite and plain teaching of the holy Prophet Jesus. In a word, the Gospels are as divergent, in expressing the Christian doctrines, as their versions are discrepant, in the reproduction of the works and works of Jesus. They have not been safeguarded against mistakes and interpolations. On the contrary, they are replete with extraneous matter. Sometimes glosses and editorial notes have been absorbed in the body of the book, and sometimes *irrelevant additions* have been made. Matthew and Luke have either toned down or omitted what they deemed objectionable in Mark. They do not teach that, because the depending anxiety of Jesus, in alliance with a fear of treacherous betrayal on the part of some of his disciples, led to his sudden and skilfully planned disappearance, we should believe that he soared upwards to heaven. Their accounts of the incident of the crucifixion do not show that God saved Jesus from the cursed death on the cross. The plain and useful teachings of Jesus, as pronounced in the Gospels, however, make the belief in the atoning and propitating power of the crucifixion unnecessary. His disciples also betray total ignorance of such a dogma as the vicarious atonement. Jesus himself believed in one God, worshipped Him, and prayed to Him, and laid all possible stress on good living and cherishing love for one's neighbours.

This brings the treatment to a close, with my sincerest hopes that it will be of some interest and benefit to God's people.

The Koran

As to the Koran, it consists exclusively of the revelation or commands which the Prophet professed, to have received from time to time, as a message direct from God; and which, under divine direction, the Prophet delivered to those about him.

Every syllable of the Koran is of divine origin, eternal and 'uncreated' as the Deity Himself. It is one of the Mohammadan arguments against the Jewish and Christian Scripture, that they are not exclusively oracles professing to proceed from God.

The Prophet himself neither read nor wrote. His being an illiterate man, enhances the marvel of his revelation. 'Learning' says the Rev. Margoliouth, 'He had none, or next to none'.

At the moment of inspiration or shortly after, each passage was recited by the Prophet in the presence of friends or followers, and was generally committed to writing by someone amongst them, at the time or afterwards, upon palm-leaves, leather, stones, or such other rude material as conveniently came to hand. These divine messages continued throughout the twenty-three years of his prophetic life, so that the last portion was not received till year near the time of his death.

The Koran, being the divine revelation and the corner-stone of Islam, the recital of a passage from it formed as essential part of daily prayer, public and private; and its perusal and repetition were considered to be a great privilege. The preservation of the various chapters during the life-time of the Prophet, was not altogether dependent on their being committed to writing. The Koran was committed to memory by so many adherents of Islam, and the extent, to which it could be recited, was one of the chief sources of distinction, in the early stages of Islam.

Amongst a crowd of warrior martyrs, he who had been the most versed in the Koran, was honoured with the first burial. The person who in any company could most faithfully repeat the Koran, was ipso facto entitled to conduct the public prayers, and in certain cases to pecuniary rewards.

The retentive faculty of the early Arabs favoured the task; and it was applied, with all the ardour of an awakened spirit, to the Koran, Several of the Prophet's followers could, during his life-time, repeat with scrupulous accuracy, the whole as then in use. Four or five such persons are named; and several others also who could very nearly repeat the whole, before the Prophet's death.

"However retentive the Arab memory, remarks Sir William Munir, we should still have regarded with distrust a transcript made entirely from that source. But there is good reason for believing, that many fragmentary copies, embracing amongst them the whole Koran, or nearly the whole, were during his life-time made by the Prophet's followers.

"Such was the condition of the text during Mohammad's life-time, and such it remained for about a year after his death, imprinted upon the hearts of his people, and fragmentary transcript increasing daily."

Further the same writer states: "The contents and arrangement of the Koran speak forcibly for its authenticity. All the fragments have with artless simplicity, been joined together."

"Even the frailties of the Prophet, as noticed by the Deity, have with evident faithfulness been entered in the Koran."

"In fine, we possess every internal guarantee of confidence (namely in the authenticity of the Koran, as it exists in the present copy)."

". . . There is otherwise every security, internal and external, that we possess the text which Mohammad himself gave forth and used."

"So carefully, indeed, has it been preserved that there are no variation of importance — we might almost say no variations at all — to be found in the innumerable copies scattered throughout the vast bounds of the Empire of Islam."

"Yet, but One Koran has been current amongst them; and the consentaneous use by all of the same Scripture, in every age to the present day, is an irrefragable proof, that we have now before us the very text prepared by command of the unfortunate Caliph (Othman who was murdered sometime after compilation of the Koran)."

There is probably in the world no other work, which has remained twelve centuries (1861), with so pure a text. This is only because the various revelations in the Koran, regarding its divine nature, and its remaining for ever free from corruption or contradiction, are rightly confirmed. Here are a few verses bearing on this point :

"We have surely down the Koran; and we will certainly preserve the same from corruption."

"This Koran could not have been composed by any, except God; but it is a confirmation of that which was revealed before it, and explanation of the Scriptures; there is no doubt thereof; sent down from the Lord of all creatures. Will they say, (Mohammad) hath forged it?

Answer, Bring therefore a chapter like unto it; and call whom ye may (to your assistance), besides God, if ye speak truth."

"Say, Verily if men and genii were purposely assembled, that they might produce (a book) like this Koran, they could not produce one like unto it, although they assisted each other. And we have variously propounded unto men in this Koran, every kind of figurative argument; but the greater part of men refuse to receive it, merely out of infidelity."

The Rev. Rodwell states :

"It must be acknowledged too, that the Koran deserves the highest praise for its conception of the divine nature, in reference to the attributes of power, knowledge and universal Providence and Unity — that its belief and trust in the One God of Heaven and Earth, is deep and fervent."

"It is due to the Koran, that the occupants, in the sixth century, of an arid peninsula, whose poverty was only equalled by their ignorance, have been become not only the fervent and sincere votaries of a new creed, but, like Amru and many more, its warlike propagators."

"The simple shepherds and wandering bedouins of Arabia, are transformed, as if by a magician's wand, into the founders of empires, the builders of cities, the collectors of more libraries, than they at first destroyed, while cities like Fostat, Baghdad, Cordova and Delhi, attest the power, at which Christian Europe trembled. And thus, while the Koran, which underlies this vast energy and contains the principles which are its springs of action, reflects to a great extent the mixed character of its author, its merit as a code of laws, and as a system of religious teaching, must always be estimated by the changes which it introduced into the customs and beliefs of those who willingly or by compulsion, embraced it. In the suppression of their idolatries, in the substitution of the worship of Allah for that of the powers of nature and genii with Him, in the abolition of child murder, in the extinction of manifold superstitious usages, in the reduction of the number of wives to a fixed standard, it was to the Arabian an unquestionable blessing, and a revelation of Truth; and while every Christian must deplore the overthrow of so many flourishing Eastern churches by the arms of the victorious Moslems, it must not be forgotten that *Europe*, in the middle ages, *owed much* of her knowledge of dialectic *philosophy* of *medicine and architecture to Arabian writers*, and the Moslems formed the connecting link between the West and the East for the importation of numerous articles of luxury and use...

"For if he (mohammad) was indeed the illterate person the Moslems represent him to have been, then it will be hard to escape their inference, that *the Koran is*, as they assert it to be, *a standing miracle.*"

The Kornic Conception of Man

The Hole Koran represents man as a free and responsible being, gifted with the faculty of distinguishing between right and wrong. Then according to the Koran, man is capable of obeying the law of God. He needs nobody to atone for his sins, but himself; for the Lord is merciful and will forgive him his sins. The Holy Book of Islam mentions no original sin which we inherit at our birth. It does not represent man as coming into the world with a load of sin on his back. On the contrary, it represents him as an unconscious Moslems at the moment of creation.

The Prophet of Islam says: "Every child is born with a Moslem heart", and it is the external influences that makes it what it becomes after wards in life. If bad influences happen to be at work, the child generally surrenders to such influences, unless God Himself undertakes to nurture the little soul. When the child grows into manhood, he may use the God-gifted faculty of discrimination and may become what he chooses in life. Indeed, God gives him many a chance in life, that he may recover himself from sin and iniquity. He may make or mar his fortune, even in the spiritual sense. If in him, faith asserts its power, if true repentance places him in the right attitude towards God, if the spirit of God impels him to do virtuous deeds, if he feels the hand of God working in the smallest concerns of his life, and, above all, if he accepts death with a smilling countenance, and loses himself to save himself, why this is sufficient atonement in the sight of the Lord, whose pre-eminent attribute is Mercy.

To understand the Koranic conception of man, a reference to the following verse is necessary: "Of goodliest fabric We created man, then brought him down to be the lowest of the low; save who believe and do things that are right, for theirs shall be a reward that faileth not". These verse indicate that man, at the moment of his creation, is perfectly sinless. It is afterwards, that sin tries to assert it self and bring him down to the level of the brutes. But he has also the divine in him, — the power to offer, if he so wills, a stubborn resistance; and by the help of this power, he may "grow up to a saint". Although his own force is feeble, there is the Spirit of God, which will cooperate with him in this work of self-regeneration, only if he shows genuine desire to turn to God, to believe, and to do things that are right. The Holy Koran is very clear on this point. It does not ask us to believe in the doctrine of original sin; and so atonement, in a Christian sense, has no place in the Islamic Scripture. What God wants of us, is this, that we for our part, should make the utmost endeavour to secure His pleasure and grace, white He for His part, undertakes to direct us into His way. "And who so maketh his utmost endeavour towards Us, We will surely direct him into Our ways", says the Koran. This utmost endeavour on our part, to reach God, involves the idea of personal atonement and sacrifice which the Moslem is required to offer. We find the same thought clearly expressed elsewhere in the Word of God: "They who set their face with resignation God-ward, and do what is right, — their reward is with their Lord; no fear shall come on them, neither shall they be grieved". Turning his face towards God, gradually proceeding towards Him, till he realises himself in Him — herein lies the salvation of man, according to the Koran. The Moslem is taught the high truth, that "the good drives away the evil in man", and so he requires not anyone, to take the burden of his sin and to undergo punishment as his substitute. He develops his faculties, and tries his very best, to make use of them in doing good deeds and working out the will of his Maker; and hopes that his little will be accepted as much by the Most Merciful Lord.

Everywhere, in the Holy Koran, man is represented as the crowed and glory of creation. He is the central figure of this beautiful universe. In Adam, he is God's viceregent on earth. Out of love, God hath created man. And He hath created for him the heavens and the earth, and sendeth down water from he heaven, and so on bringeth forth the fruits for his food. And him He hath subjected the ships, so that by His command they pass through the sea; and to him He hath subjected the sun and the moon in their constant courses; and to him He hath subjected the day and the night; of everything which he may ask Him, giveth He to him; and if man would reckon up the favours of God, man can never count them.

"And the cattle, for you He created them; from them ye have warm garments, and they are useful in many ways; and of them ye eat; and they obery you well when ye fetch them home and when ye drive them forth to pasture: and they carry your burdens to lands which ye could not else reach, but with travail of soul: truly, your Lord is full of goodness, and merciful: And He hath given you horses, mules and asses, that ye may ride them, and for your pleasure: And things, of which ye have no knowledge, hath He created. It is God who shows the right way, since some other ways are misleading. Some (Of you) turn aside from it; but had He pleased, He would have guided you all aright."

According to the Koran, God hath endowed us with the power of self-government which is an almost incredible trust. By this power, God not only trust our destinies to ourselves, but He actually trusts, or seems to trust, the whole final outcome of His creative work to our treatment of it. This earth, at least, is put into our hands, to make what we will of it and of ourselves, its inhabitants. It is stored with all possible helps to us, in natural forces and materials; we are given intelligenc, to find them out and to use them for the enrichment and beautifying of our lives; we are given the understanding of a Rule of Right in our conduct towards each other, that will keep us in perfect harmony and happiness together, for the common good; we are given a complete code of regulations, to guide us as to what is right and what is wrong; we are drawn towards well-doing, in accord with the Rule of Right, by a feeling created in us, which will not let us forget it or violet it without wilful intent; but (and here lies the grandeur of the part man performs in creation) we are trusted with the freedom, to do with all this what we will. The outcome, good or evil, is what we and our fellows of the human race, past and future, are helping, or have helped, or will help, to make it. The glory of triumph or the shame of failure in the creation of mankind is to belong to the race itself.

The Realities of Human Nature

The Koran also dwells on the weaknesses, to which the flesh is heir, and constantly reminds man of his inconstancy, injustice and ingratitude. "Man is created weak". "Surely man is unjust and ungrateful". "Man is hasty". "Man is covetous". "Verily, mad is created extremely impatient". "Verily, man is ungrateful unto his Lord." It must, however, not be inferred from verses like these, that man stands condemned before his Creator, as deserving only death and perdition. These verses rather breathe a noble sympathy for the weakness of man and the infirmities of the Flesh. They contain in them promises of God's grace and forgiveness. In reminding man of the infirmities of his nature, God desires, that man should realise his weakness and powerlessness, bow down his head before the Lord, turn to Him for strength and assistance, and pray constantly, that He may guide Him into the right, straight path. Indeed, the Moslem is enjoined to throw himself in this attitude towards his Maker, and to offer such prayers repeatedly day and night. He is taught to say: "Praise be to God, Lord of the worlds; the Compassionate, the Merciful, King of the day of Reckoning. These only do we worship, and to Thee do we cry for help. Guide Thou us in the right path, the path of those, unto whom Thou hast been gracious: — and not of those, who are convicted nor of those who go astry".

As will be seen, this human prayers is full of sympathy towards the weakness of man. In it the Lord reaches His servants, to beg of Him spiritual blessings. In it He indirectly asks them not to sink in despair, and indirectly promises, to guide them into the path of holiness and to give them strength, to bear the yoke of His law. What an uplifting hope is breathed into our hearts, when He tells us, that He was gracious in the past, unto those who sought Him, and even so to-day He is ready, to be gracious unto us, if we only turn to Him and look up to His Grace, as our true Saviour.

But, as Shakespeare said : "The course of true love never did run smooth" with equal truth it may be said of divine love, that its course never runs smooth. Trial and tribulations are bound to come. Many a trial the seeker after God has to undergo, before he can expect to receive the grace of God. "Think ye", says the Lord, "To enter Paradise, when no such things have come upon you, as on those who flourished before you? Ills and troubles tried them; and so tossed were they by trials, that the Apostle and they who shared his faith, said, 'when will the help of god come? — Surely the help of God is nigh!". Even the Patriarch Abraham, was tried by God, when He commanded him to leave his home and country, and to offer his beloved son as a sacrifice.

No doubt, it is rather a difficult task, to secure the blessings of God, and to perform the divine laws. But, let not man stagger under the difficulty of the task that lies before him. Let him take courage, and, with a firm trust in God and a cheerful hearts, undertake the performance; and above all fear the Lord; for it is God's premise, that "He will make His command easy to him who feareth Him". The God of Islam, it should always be remembered, is not a niggardly, exacting God, but "He is gracious unto His servants". Elsewhere, we read a surpassingly comforting verse, which comes as a message of hope to each and all of us. "God desireth, to be gracious unto you.. God desireth, to make your burden light: for man hath been created weak". Again we read; "God wisheth you ease and never wisheth you discomfort". A world of mercy and forgiveness is surely concealed behind, and breathed out by these verses. God is offering His grace; we have only to throw ourselves in the right attitude of Faith, and ourselves up to God, and His Hand will lead us to His blessing. We have but to consess our weakness and ask from our Lord power and strength, and His spirit will descend upon us.

There is another remarkable passage in the Holy Koran which presents to us a just, but at the same time a merciful God, and then gives a most beautiful prayer, so comforting to the helpless man who, toiling up the spiritual heights, sits down totally unnerved, looking up to God for strength and support: "God will not burden any soul beyond its power", so run the words of God, "It shall enjoy the good which it hath acquired, and shall bear the evil, for the acquirement of which it laboured. Our Lord, punish us not if we forget, or fall into sin; Our Lord, lay not on us a burden, like that which Thou hast laid on those who have been before us;

neither make us, O Lord, to bear what we have not the strength to bear; but blot out our sins, and forgive us, and have pity on us thou art our Patron; help us, therefore, against those who do not believe".

The Koran and the Doctrine of Personal Holiness

Islam has taken due cognisance of the frailties of human nature, and this constitutes its chief excellence as a system of religion. Thus the laws of Islam exhibit an elasticity which is a proof of their beneficence and usefulness. Though Islam no doubt points to a lofty idealism it is at the same time, thoroughly practical. The merit of Islam, as a religion, consists, in a happy harmonious blending of the ideal and the practical. It favours no form of asceticism, and never asks any man, to do what he has not the power to do. There is, however, one thing, on which it lays the greatest emphasis. It is personal holiness, and purity of heart. It is the grand purpose, for which the Prophet was sent down, as it appears from the prayer of Abraham: "Our Lord, raise up among them an apostle who may rehearse Thy signs unto them, and teach them the Book, and the Wisdom, and purify them". The reader will observe, that the verse gradually ascends to a climax. Purification of men being put last, as the most important part of the functions of the Prophet of Islam. "He who is purified, hath obtained felicity", says the Koran elsewhere. Again, after mentioning the blessings of heavenly life, the Holy Book adds: "And this shall be the reward of him who shall be pure". That a very important place is given to purity of mind and personal holiness, will be seen from another verse, where sinners are threatened with the punishment, that God shall neither speak unto them nor shall He purify them: "Moreover, they who conceal any part of the scripture which God hath sent down unto them — God shall not speak unto them, on the day of resurrection, neither shall He purify them,and they shall suffer a grievous punishment." It is clear, then that communion with the Deity and personal holiness are the keynote of Islam.

But even here, man is not held responsible for the evil thoughts that inspite of himself, pass through his mind, like flashes of lightning. To render man responsible for such passing fancies, over which he has little control, would be sheer injustice. Commission of a wrong act, without previous intention and deliberation, does not make one a sinner, far less a passing thought that rises like a bubble only to die and disappear the next moment. Adam ate of the forbidden fruit and thereby committed a mistake, as all men are liable to commit mistakes; but he was never guilty of committing sin, and the Holy Koran clear him of the false accusation, just as it has cleared other prophets, like Moses and Jesus, of similar charge. For it say : "We heretofore gave a command to Adam, and *he forget it*; and We found *no intention* in him (to disobey) our command."

This, indeed, an important principle, and it has important bearings on the doctrine of sin, as presented by the Holy Koran. For, elsewhere we read: "God will not punish you for an inconsiderate word in your oaths; but He will punish you for that which your hearts have assented unto it". This verse clearly lays downs, that a wrong act, or an evil thought, is a sin, if it is deliberate. Shorn of intention and deliberation, a wrong act or an impure thought is a mere accident which, however deplorable, cannot prove the doer a guilty sinner in the sight of God.

But, if the element of intention is present, even the faintest thought is enough, to render a man guilty before his Maker, not to speak of a deed which is manifestly wrong. God forbids both kinds of sin — open and secret — equally in the same verse: "Draw not near unto sin; neither open nor secret". "Leave both — the outside of iniquity and the inside thereof". Again: "Say, verily, my Lord hath forbidden sins, whether open or secret, and iniquity and unjust violence."

These verse sufficiently establish the doctrine of personal holiness in Islam; but to crush the objection of the critics absolutely, we give one more verse which shows, that not only the eyes and the ears, but also the heart, will be required, to give evidence on the Day of Judgment, if any sin has been committed through them. And the verse is this: "And follow not that, whereof thou hast no knowledge; for the hearing and the sight and the *heart* — each of these shall be examined."

Personal holiness, it must be remembered, depends largely on a thorough belief in the Omniscience and Omnipresence of God. And nothing is more striking to the reader of the Holy Koran, than the force with which it impresses upon us these two attributes of the Deity. The belief, that the Supreme Being sees our actions and knows even the innermost secrets of our hearts, is a most powerful check upon the tendency to commit sin. So long as a man realises, that he works and moves under the great Task-master's eyes, he keeps himself from vice: but whenever this consciousness in him grows dim, and he thinks he is not watched by God, he exposes himself to constant danger.

4. Belief in the Apostles of God

The fourth article of the Mohammedan creed is faith in all the Apostle of God. A Moslem must believes, that the Merciful Creator sent in divers ages certain messengers or apostle, to reclaim mankind from infidelity and superstition, and to teach them the religion and laws of God, and to give them good tidings and admonitions. The number of these apostles is given as 313. Twenty-five of them must be remembered,since their names are distinctly given in the Koran; but it it not necessary to learn them by heart. The following are the names, according to chronological order:-

Adam, Noah, Houd (Heber), Saleh (Methuselah), Lot, Abraham, Ishmail, Isaac, Joseph Jacob, Shu'aib (Jethro), Haroun (Aaron), Moses, David, Solomon, Ayoub (Job), Zulkifi (Isaiah), Younis (Jonah), Ilias, Alyas'aa (Elisha), Zacharias, Yehia (John the Baptist), Jesus and Mohammad.

If a Moslem is asked about anyone of these men, he must confess his belief, that he was an apostle of God.

Moslems must also believe, that the apostles of God were truthful faithful and intelligent, and that they delivered in full God's message to their respective people. A moslem must further believe, that all apostle of God were, by their prophetic characteristics, free from (1) telling lies, (2) committing unlawful deeds, (3) stupidity, laziness or cowardice, (4) and from concealing any part of the message they were ordered to deliver.

The apostles of God were subject to the same human wants as the rest of mankind, such as eating, drinking, sleeping, marrying, etc.. They were also liable to ordinary but not disgusting maladies etc.

Since the nature, as well as the story, of Jesus Christ were matters of dispute between Christians and Mohammadans, I must give a summary of the Moslems' belief in this respect, according to the teaching of the Koran and the interpretations of the Prophet.

Moslems hold, that Jesus Christ was the blessed Apostle of God who was sent to reclaim the people of Israel. He was a spirit from God, His messenger, His servant and prophet, illustrious in this world and in the next. He was miraculously born of the Virgin Mary. The Jews having spoken ill of Mary, and charged her with unchasity, Jesus Christ, speaking in the cradle, vindicated his mother' honour. Jesus performed miracles by God's power; giving life to a clay figure of a bird, healing the blind, curing the leper, quickening the dead, and causing a table of food to be brought down from Heaven. He was sent by God, to confirm the law of Moses, and to preach the Gospel to the people of Israel. He proclaimed his mission by many manifest signs, being confirmed by the Holy Spirit. He foretold the advent of another apostle to succeed him, named Periclete or Ahmad. The Jews intended to crucify Jesus, but God saved him from the plot, took him up to Heaven, and stamped his likeness on a treacherous Jew who was apprehended and crucified in his stead. It is the constant doctrine of the Moslems, that it was not Jesus who underwent crucifixion, but someone else, resembling him in shape, namely, judas, who agreed with the Jews, to betray Jesus for some pieces of silver, and led those who were sent to take him. After the crucifixion of the wicked Judas, and the taking up of Jesus into Heaven, Christ, the Apostle of God, was sent down again to the earth, to comfort his mother and devoted disciples, and to tell them, how the Jews were deceived; and he was taken up a second time to Heaven.

"It is supported by several", writers Mr. G. Sale "that this story was an original invention of Mohammad's; but they are certainly mistaken; for several sectaries held the same opinion, long before his time. The Basilidians, in the very beginning of Christianity, denied, that Christ himself suffered, but that Simon the Cyrenean was crucified in his place. The Cerinthians, before them, and the Carpocratians next, (to name no more of those who affirmed Jesus to have been a mere man) did believe the same thing; that it was not himself, but one of his followers very like him, that was crucified. Photius tells us, that he read a book entitled. The Journey of The Apostle', relating the acts of Peter, John Andrew, Thomas and Paul; and among other things contained therein, this was one, that Christ was not crucified, but another in his stead, and that therefore, he laughed at his crucifiers, or those who thought they had crucified him".

St. Barnabas relates this part of Jesus Christ's history with circumstances approximating to the Mohammadan view. In that Gospel it is related, that: "The moment the Jews were going to apprehend Jesus in the garden, he was lifted up to heaven, by the ministry of four angels; that he will not die, till the end of the world, and that it was Judas who was crucified in his stead; God having permitted that traitor, to appear so like his master, in the eyes of the Jews, that they took and delivered him to Pilate. That this resemblance was so great, that it deceived the Virgin Mary and the disciples themselves; but that Jesus Christ afterwards obtained leave of God, to go and comfort them. That Barnabas having then asked him, why the divine goodness had suffered the mother and disciples of so holy a prophet, to believe, even for one moment, that he had died in so ignominious a manner. Jesus returned the following answer. "O Barnabas, believe me, that every sin, however small, is punished by God with great torment, because God is offended by sin. My mother, therefore, and faithful disciples, having loved me with a mixture of earthy love, the Just God has been pleased, to punish this love with their present grief, that they might not be punished for it hereafter in the flames of hell. And as for me, though I have myself been blameless in the world. Yet other men having called me God and son of God; therefore God, that I might not be mocked by the devils on the Day of Judgment, has been pleased, that in this world I should be mocked by men with the death of Judas, making everybody believe, that I died upon the cross. And hence it is, that this mocking is to continue till the coming of Ahmad, the messenger of God; who, coming into the world, will undeceive everyone who shall believe in the law of God, from this error".

The Moslems are also taught, that after Jesus had left this earth, his disciples disputed among themselves concerning his nature, some calling him God and others the son of God. They believe, that he will come again into the world, will slay antichrist, and will reign as just king for many years, marry and have children and die.

The following are a variety of translated passages of the Koran bearing on the story of Jesus Christ, and the disputed nature and life of the Great Teacher of Christianity:

1. Promised to Mary

(a) "And when the angels said: O Mary, verily, God hath chosen thee and hath purified thee, and hath raised thee above all other woman of the world : O Mary, be, therefore, devout towards thy Lord, and prostrate thyself and bow down in worship with those devotes who bow down to Him".

(b) "And when the angels said : O Mary, verily, God sendeth thee good tidings; thou shalt bear a word from Him, whose name will be Jesus, the son of Mary, and who will be illustrious in this world and in the next, and one of those men who are honoured with approach to the presence of God; and he shall speak to men alike when in the cradle and when he is grown up; and he shall be one of the most righteous: she said, How, O My Lord, shall I have a son, since a man hath not touched me? The angel said: Thus God will create what He will; when He decreeth a thing. He only saith

'Be', and 'it is'. He (God) shall teach him the scripture and wisdom and the law and the Gospel; and He shall appoint him an apostle to the children of Israel, and he shall say to them: Verily, I come unto you with a sign from your Lord, for I will make before you out of clay, as it were, the figure of a bird; then I will breathe into it, and it shall become an animated bird, *by the will of God;* and I will heal the blind and the leper, *by the will of God,* and I will raise the dead, *by the will of God;* and I will tell you what ye eat and what ye store up in your houses. Verily, this will be a sign to you, if ye believe. And I will come to confirm the law which was revealed before me, and to allow unto you as lawful, part of what hath been forbidden you; therefore, fear God and obey me. Verily, God is my Lord and your Lord; therefore serve Him. This is the right way. But Jesus perceiving their unbelief, said: who of you will assist towards the way to God?The disciples said: We are your helper towards the way to God: we do believe in God, and do thou bear witness, we are true believers. O Lord, we believe in what Thou hast sent down, and have followed Thy apostle; write us down, then,with those who bear witness (of his) message.

2. Birth of Jesus

(a) "And make mention, in the scripture, of Mary; when she retired from her family eastward, and drew a veil upon her to conceal herself from them; and We sent our spirit (Gabriel) to her, and he appeared to her in the form of a perfect man. She said :'I fly for refuge thee to the Most Merciful. If thou fearest Him'. He said: 'I am the messenger of thy Lord, that I may bestow on thee a purified son'. She said 'How shall I have a son, when man hath never touched me, and I was never unchaste"? He said : "So shall it be. Thy Lord hath said, it is a simple thing with Him, and that He will make him a sign to mankind, and a mercy from Him: This is a thing already decreed'. Therefore she conceived him; and she retired aside with him (in her womb) to a distant place, and the throes came upon her near the trunk of a palm-tree. (She said 'Would to God, I had died before this, and had become as one lost in oblivion'. And he who was below her (namely the newly born babe) came to her, saying, 'Be not grieved. Thy Lord hath provided for thee a rivulet at thy feet; and do thou shake the trunk of the palm-tree towards thee: it will drop fresh ripe dates to eat. Therefore, eat and drink and cheer thyself; and shouldst thou see any human being, say, Verily, I have vowed a fast to the Most Merciful; wherefore I will by no means speaks to human being this day'. So she came with the babe to her people. And they said to her 'O Mary, thou has committed a grave thing. O sister of Aaron, thy father was not a bad man, nor was thy mother unchaste'. And she made a sign to him (the infant). They said: 'how shall we speak to him who is an infant in the cradel?' He said: 'Verily, I am the servant of God: He hath given me the book (the Gospel), and He hath appointed me a prophet. And He hath made me blessed, wheresoever I may be, and hath commanded me to pray to him and to give alms, as long as I live; and hath made me dutiful towards my mother; and He hath not made me cruel or wicked. The peace of God was on me the day I was born, and it will be on me the day I shall die and the day I shall be raised again to life'. This was Jesus, the son of Mary, the word of truth, concerning whom they dispute.

(b) "Verily, the case of Jesus with God is the same as that of Adam. He created him (Adam) out of the dust, and then said to him 'Be', and he was. This is the truth from the Lord; be not, therefore, one of those who dispute".

One of the Miracles of Jesus

Remember when disciples said. "O Jesus, son of Mary' is the Lord able to send down to us a table of provisions from heaven?" He said : 'Fear God, if ye be true believers'. They said: 'We desire to eat therefrom, and to have our hearts assured, and to know that thou hast indeed spoken truth to us, and to be witness thereof' Jesus, the son of Mary, said : 'O God, our Lord' send down a table to us from heaven, that the day of its descent become a recurring festival to us, to the first of us and to the last of us, and a sign from Thee; and do Thou provide food for us, for Thou art the best provider'. God said: 'Verily, I will cause it to descend unto you; but whosoever among you shall disbelieve hereafter, I will surely punish him with more severe a punishment than I will punish any other of my creatures.

The Mission of Jesus

"We formerly sent our apostle with evident sign and miracles, and We sent down with them the Scriptures and the balance, that men might observe justice."

"And We caused Jesus, the son of Mary, to succeed them, and We gave him the Gospel: and We put in the hearts of those who followed him, compassion and mercy: but as to the monastic life, they invented it themselves: We did not prescribe it to them; they did it out of design to please God, yet this they did not probably observe. And We gave to such of them as believed, their reward: but many of them were evil doers."

(b) "We also caused Jesus, the son of Mary, to follow the footsteps of the Prophets, to confirm the Law which was sent down before him; and We gave him the Gospel, containing guidance and light, and confirming the preceding word and a direction and admonition unto those who fear God: so that they who have received the Gospel might judge, according to what God hath revealed therein. And who so will not judge according to what God hath revealed, they are certainly transgressor".

(c) "Some of the apostle We have endowed more than others. Those, to whom God hath spoken, He hath raised to the loftiest position. And to Jesus, the son of Mary, We gave manifest, signs, and We strengthened him with the Holy Spirit. And if God had pleased, they who came after them, would not have wrangled, after the clear signs had reached them. But into disputes they fell: some of them believed, and some were infidels: yet, if God had pleased, they would not have wrangled: but God doth what He will."

(d) "And Jesus, the son of Mary, said: 'O children of Israel. Verily, I am God's apostle to you who came to confirm the law which was given before me, and to announce an apostle who shall come after me whose name shall be Ahmad. But when he (Ahmad) presented himself with clear signs of his mission, they said: 'This is manifest sorcery'. Jesus said to them: 'I come to attest the law which was revealed before me, and to allow you part of that which had been forbidden you; and I come to you with a sign from your Lord: therefore, fear God and obey me; Verily God is my Lord and your Lord; therefore, worship Him; this is the right way."

Jesus not Crucified

(a) "The Jews were cursed for their unbelief and for their having spoken a grievous against Mary and for their saying; 'Verily, we have slain Christ Jesus, the son of Mary, the apostle of God'; yet they slew him not, and crucified him not, but he was represented to them by one in his likeness, and verily they who disputed about him, were in doubt, concerning this matter: they had no sure knowledge thereof, but followed only an uncertain opinion. They (the Jews) did not really kill him; but God took him up to Himself and God is Mighty and Wise".

Jesus and the Divinity

(a) "He (Jesus) is no other than a servant of God whom We favoured, and set forth as an instance (of divine power) to the children of Israel; and if We pleased, verily, We could have even produced angels from yourselves, to succeed you on earth".

(b) "And when Jesus came with manifest signs, he said: 'Now I am come to you with wisdom, and to explain to you part of those things, about which you disagree: therefore fear God, andobey me. Verily, God is my Lord and your Lord; wherefore worship ye Him: this is the right path'. But the different parties fell into disputes among themselves, but woe to those who thus transgressed, because of the punishment of a grievous day."

(c) "The Jews say :'Ezra is the son of God'; and the Christians say, 'Christ is the son God'. This is their saying with their mouths, following the example of those who misbelieved before them. May God resist them! How are they infatuated! They take their priests and their monks for their Lord, besides God, and (take) Christ, the son of Mary, (for their Lord besides God) altogether they are commanded to worship one Deity only; There is no Diety but He (the true God); far be those from Him whom they associate (with God)'.

The Trinity Condemned

(a) "They are surely infidels who say, 'Verily, God is Christ the son of Mary; since Christ said, O ye children of Israel, worship God, my Lord and your Lord; whoever, shall associate aught with Him, God shall forbid him paradise, and his habitation shall be hell fire; and the ungodly shall have none to help them. They are certainly infidels who say, God is the third of three for is no Deity, but God alone. And if they do not desist from what they say, a painful torment shall surely be inflicted upon those who misbelieved among them. Will they not turn unto God, and ask His pardon? Since God is Gracious and Merciful. Christ, the son Mary, is no more than an apostle: Other apostles preceded him, and his mother was true believer; they both used to eat food (as all other human beings do). Behold, how we declare unto them the signs (of God's unity); and then behold, how they turn aside (from the right path). Say, (O Mohammad) unto them, will ye worship, besides God, that which can cause you neither harm nor profit? God heareth (everything) and seeth (every thing) Say. O ye who have received the Scriptures, exceed not the just bounds in your religion, by speaking beside the truth, neither follow the desires of people who have heretofore erred, and who have seduced many, and have gone astray from the right path".

(b) "O ye who have received the Scriptures, exceed not thejust bounds in your religion, neither say of God otherwise than the truth. Verily, Christ, the son of Mary, was the apostle, of God and His Word which He conveyed to Mary, and a Spirit coming from Him. Believe, therefore, in God and His apostle, and say not: 'there are three (Deities)' desist: it will be better for you. God is the only Deity. Far be it from Him, that He should have a son; unto Him belongeth whatever is in heaven and on earth; and is the Protector, Christ doth not proudly disdain to be a servant to God".(c) " It beseemeth not a man, that God should give the Scripture and the wisdom and the gift of prophecy to him, and that then he should say to the people 'Be ye worshippers of me as well as of God's, but rather, 'Be ye perfect in things pertaining to God, since ye know the Scriptures, and have studied deeply."

(d) "And when God shall say (namely unto Jesus on the Day of Judgment), O Jesus, son of Mary, hast thou said unto the people, 'Take me and my mother for two deities, beside God?' He shall answer 'Glory be to Thee, it is not for me, to say that which I ought not in truth; if I had said it, Thou wouldst surely have known it: Thou knowest what is in me, but I know not what is in Thee; for Thou art the knower of all secrets. I have not spoken to them otherwise, than Thou didst command me. I said to them : Worship God, my Lord and your Lord; and I was a winess against them as long as I stayed amongst them; but when Thou causest me die, Thou hast been the Watcher over them, as Thou art the Watcher over all things, If Thou punish them, they are surely Thy servants, and it Thou forgive them, Thou art the Almighty and the All-wise."

REFERENCES

1. Al-Koran, Tr. G.Sale.
2. Muir, Life of Mohammad.
3. Ency. Biblica, p. 1790, 1793.
4. Rev. Dumatow's Commentary, p. 71, 131.
5. Murray's Bible dictionary.
6. The 20th century New Testament.
7. Dr. Weymouth's Introduction to St. John's Gospel.
8. Maulvi Sadr-ud-Din, "Are the Gospels inspired."
9. Al-Koran, tr., Rodwell, introduction by Rev. Margoliouth.

Revised and edited; originally published as Book III. Expostion of the Religion of Islam.

4

Some Aspects of Religious Life

MIR VALIUDDIN

(Abstract: Deals with purification of the self, blissful life, alienation, and reflection).

> When yau let knowledge minister to the heart, it proves a friend to you,
> When you employ it to subserve your body, it plays the serpent" (Rumi).

To be spiritual, says Santayana, is "to live in presence of the ideal." The meaning of spirituality and its relation to religion are expressed by Durant Drake in these words: "This disposition of the heart and will, through which a man comes to care for the highest things and to live in gentleness and inward calm above the surface aspects and accidents of life, we call in its inner nature, Spirituality; when it is embodied in outward forms and institutions and spreads among whole communities, we call it religion".

If we argue that way, religion loses its mysterious or dogmatic and oracular character and becomes the intrinsic response of the soul in need. It is not something the "truth" of which we have to question and argue about and seek evidence for. It rests upon the recognition of a realm of higher values and a kind of instinctive sympathy with them and longing for them. We aspire for higher values of this realm; we do not confine ourselves to the pleasures and attractions of the nether world. We do not busy ourselves with absorbing merely the "hay and seeds" of life; and since religion always places the higher values before us, it does not allow our hearts to be busy always in enjoying the delights and pleasures of this beautiful world only! Religion keeps our attention engaged in these values and it is therefore the loveliest thing in a man's life.

Do you know what is the source of the this Ideal? In whose presence to live is to be spiritual? Can you comprehend the origin of the higher values, concentration on which is termed living a religious life? It is none but that which had been spoken of as the Good by Plato, and regarded by him as the absolute beloved of the whole universe!

The love for good is in the very nature of every individual from eternity; every mind is in quest of it and every eye looks forward to it. Does not every person wish himself well? What else is it which he is after? Good is the only cherished object before you when you exclaim:

> "I cannot keep my heart and eyes busy elsewhere,
> The object that my heart and eye seek is the vision of
> The glory only.

It is probable that every person had draped his beloved in a different garment, but in spite of all apparent variations, the same one light is manifest in the entire universe. Every may seems to be enamoured of this beloved! The difference is marked by the degree of knowledge or ignorance one brings to bear on it, but the object—the beloved—is only one. After comprehending this point you cannot deny it.

> "He who had seen the dark and glossy hair of Laila,
> Knows well why Majnu was enamoured of her."

The "Good" itself has been termed 'God' by Plato. According to his system of philosophy. Good and God are synonymous. All religions and sects have expressed the same truth in different languages. God, Yazdan, Allah, Ishwar, Haqq etc. are the different names of the same One Being alone. The same one truth has been regarded as the source of all higher values. All the rays of values radiate from this one Sun only, who guards and preserves them. Religion, in the words of the German thinker, Harold Hoffding, is the faith in God as the guardian and conservator of these values. Its love in human nature is a divine gift. Love of good and regard for values is another name for loving the Being of God alone. Regarding this Being as the source of all ideal values, and living one's life in His contemplation, is spirituality, faith, or religion. It is through this process, as if piercing through the shadow one emerges before the original, he no longer merely hears Reality from a distance; he comes face to face with it. A gnostic has beautifully expressed the idea thus:

> "When I hold the Beloved's tresses in my hands, musk
> in liquid form drips from my fingers.
> When the Beloved comes into my arms, rays then
> emanate from myself and illumine the world".

I shall now give a brief description of the revolution wrought in life by living in the presence of this ideal:

1. Purification of the Self

When this ideal absorbs all attention, the truth of the Persian hemistich is realised:

"When a person concentrates his attention on one object, he seems to be ubiquitous, and the man who is everywhere, is, as a matter of fact, nowhere." When such is the case, that is to say when one gains unity of attention, moral vices begin to disappear and virtues begin to make their appearance instead."

He does this take place? It requires some explanation. The real substance in man is 'thought'. This alone is his reality, and according to Rumi, all the rest found in him is "bones and fibres" and has no value.

The thought is affected by the thing on which it is concentrated. It fills the atmosphere of the mind with its effects. This atmosphere becomes, as it were, tinged with its colour. There is a famous saying to the effect that the liquid which drips from a vessel is what that vessel contains. The same thoughts are manifested in practice which are felled in the vessel of thought. In other words, thoughts and ideals take the form of practice in the world of effects. Thinking is a reality and action is its manifestation. Thought is the real substance and action is its shadow. After discovering this truth the gnostic of Rum had loudly exclaimed:

> "O, brother; you are nothing else save thought,
> All the rest in yourself is fibres and bones.
> If you have ideas of flowers in your mind, you are, then, as it were, a garden.
> And if you have thoughts of thorns and dross you are like a kiln."

When one's gaze is concentrated on good, on values, and mind is engrossed in them, or changing the simile we may say, when the rooster of thought begins to keep watch on the egg of heart, the latter itself begets "ecstacy, noise and laughter"! If attention is concentrated on the flower and adverse thought does not enter the mind, that is to say, when the thorn cannot find its way in the atmosphere of the mind, the heart then finds all the effects of the flower in itself. Man begins to experience the same bliss, colour, perfume and felicity which have been bestowed on the flower by nature. On the other hand, if your gaze is riveted on the thorn, and the field of thought is full of thorns, your heart needs must feel their prick. This fuel for fire gets ablaze in the heart—sorrow, pain, anxiety or fear, is another name for these very states. When these states of the heart appear in the guise of actions or deeds, different forms of evil, then, make their appearance in the external world. They begin from the mind and terminate in the world.

If the ideal, the centre of gaze, is God, if it is the Whole whose different aspects alone are noble qualities and perfect attributes, it is evident, then, that the states of heart are pleasant and good, and deeds and actions are nothing but the manifestations or revelations of these states alone! All of them are good and are called good.

If you desire a further explanation of this principle, selecting a few from the list of moral vices and virtues, I would say, that if you wish to remove the emotion of hatred from your character, you should carefully guard the conception of love; if you desire to dispel fear, rivet your attention on courage and valour. Similarly instead of selfishness or egoism keep in view self-sacrifice and sympathy. Concentrate your mental forces on forgiveness instead of anger, on health instead of sickness, on good manners instead of rudeness, and on patience instead of fretting and fuming. You will then gradually become the ideal which is the object of your thought. The eminent Jami calls our attention to this principle thus:

> "If the thought of a flower enters your mind, you would then be a flower as it were,
> And if the thought of a restless nightingale finds its way into your mind, you will then be a nightingale, as it were,
> You are a part and God is the Whole; if you reflect a while
> On the whole, then, you too are the whole as it were!"

William James expressed this view in pragmatic terms: "The drama of life is a mental drama, all the trouble is a mental one". It means that a trouble commences from the mind alone. If matters are smoothed here and the path is cleared, the difficulties of life do not arise at all.

Keeping this principle in view, it may be asserted, that if you are in quest of the key to happiness you will not find it in any bazaar; do not search it outside. You can obtain this key by changing your mind, by creating virtuous attributes within yourself and by giving special training to your thought. So the method of acquiring it is:

> "Adopt virtue and be happy; always be looking at virtue and
> have a good opinion of others,
> Because these four things alone are the key to happiness.

In other words, if you have lived a virtuous life, searched virtue everywhere, considered always the good aspect of everything, gave place to good thoughts in your mind, formed a good opinion of others and experienced joy and felicity in such deeds, you have then mastered the secret of a happy life—the only way to a joyous and felicitous life!

Living in the presence of the ideal means that instead of concentrating your attention on vices, you should concentrate it on virtues, exert all your will power in achieving it and stamp it on the mirror of your mind. This practice should commence from the early stages of life. The nature of children is usually simple and pure and their imitative powers are very acute. Their disposition should be dyed in the colour of virtues and the loveliness of 'the colour of Allah' should be stimulated therein. The practice of keeping in view virtues and overlooking vices is very necessary. This practice creates virtuous attributes and keeps in check moral voices. It is imperative to know the basic moral virtues and vices. To aid the memory, a poet has expressed them in the following verses:

> "The virtues and vices are altogether twenty in number.
>
> If you are one of godly persons you should remember them well.
>
> (The vices are) vanity, stinginess, conceit, love of riches, desire for eating and coitus love for reputation, fury, jealousy and hypocrisy.
>
> (The virtues are) patience, thanks-offering, piety, sincerity, fear of God, good thoughts, moderate fear and hope, repentance and resignation."
>
> In the above list of vices lying and back-biting have been omitted. The following quatrain covers all these vices:
>
> "If you desire that your heart should become as clear as crystal,
>
> You should clear your mind of ten vices:

Avarice, greed, stinginess, iniquity, back-biting Lying, envy, pride, hypocricy and spite."

These vices should be completely eradicated from the heart, and the way to do so is to make virtues the ideal and live in their presence. Darkness should be met with light and evil should be fought with good. It would be, as it were, depths of darkness one above another, if darkness is matched against darkness. When these vices are rooted out from the heart, their off-shoots, then, which are vices and wicked deeds, cannot play any mischief. This very outcome has been spoken of by the moralists as purity of heart and good manners.

2. For Everlasting

Do you know in what do purification of heart, cleansing of mind or 'Catharsis' result? Socrates, Plato, Aristotle and all the moralists of the world have regarded virtue and happiness as twins. Virtue, piety, good deeds, good nature are synonymous. Their necessary and universal effect is joy, pleasure, happiness and bliss! An example or two will make this important correlation between cause and effect clear.

Suppose you are by nature envious, that is, if any other person is favoured with blessings, you feel sad and despondent, you owe the man a grudge, and desire for his down-fall. The pleasures enjoyed by him are a sore mortification for you!

You wonder why this happens. You wish to dispel your sorrow and it does not leave you, because you are helpless in depriving the man of the blessings he enjoys. But you have complete authority over your own self. You should wield that authority. Do not lose heart and you can eradicate the vice of envy. If a friend of yours happens to enjoy some favours, you too should feel pleasure. Let this pleasure lucidly reflect in your heart. A little effort on your part will help you in achieving this. Only a little courage could effect this. A little reflection on love and satisfaction with what is given would suffice to accomplish it. After doing this you will see that the fire of jealousy which had been consuming your heart and nerves will be completely put out, and you will gain freedom from the tortures of Hell in this life.

In the same way think over the evils of anger! Suppose you are a victim of the emotion of maddening fury. A slight cause provokes you to anger. Your brain in filled with dark smoke. Now, in the external world every thing is not arranged according to one's taste. If every crooked thing infuriates you, and fills your mind with dark thoughts, makes your blood toxic, you will not be able to differentiate between good and evil. The pure ties of love and friendship may be snapped; and one blow of yours may smash the relations of kith and kin. Then, pray tell me, can anybody claim friendship with a lunatic like you? Can you ever be destined to anything else save torments and tortures? Can you have any share of joy and peace of mind? Who has deprived you of all these values? Decidedly, nothing from the external! All this is due to your mental disease i.e. fury. Unless you cure this malady no recipe of the Messiah even will help you to get rid of it and you will not recover! You need not even seek a Messiah! Give up anger, always be meek and forgiving, concentrate your powers of thinking on meekness and forgiveness and contemplate on them while sitting or walking. This will put out the flames of your wild fury and you will get rid of constant torment and torture, and you will be enlisted in the circle of

> "Those who control their anger and are forgiving towards fellow beings"
>
> You will be rewarded with peace of mind and ataraxia!

Similarly, reflect on all vices one by one. Their presence in your character is akin to a host of venomous insects infesting your garments and continually biting you. They do not even for a moment spare you! Or, changing the simile, we can say, that your clothes are smeared with the worst stinking filth imaginable, the stench of which is intolerable for you even for a moment. The only way to tide over this difficulty is to change this dress, or to have it washed clean. From the beginning your aspiration, desire or prayer ought to be:

> "O, God Almighty, wash my sins with the water of hailstones and ice and free my heart from sins, just as dirt is cleansed from a white cloth. Create a gulf between myself and my sin, as is found between the West and the East".
>
> "O, Almighty God! make my mind pious and stainless.
> Thou alone art the best purifier and Thou alone art its
> Lord and Master"!

At the outset, living in the presence of the ideal is nothing but this, that the attributes of virtues should take the place of the attributes of vices. As soon as prayer, desire, aspiration, contemplation and austerity effect this change, the fountain of life-giving bliss wells out from the recesses of the heart, and one is blessed with everlasting joy.

> "The flower plants that sprout from the earth in garden perish eventually
> But the flowers growing out from the heart know no decay". (Rumi)

3. Takhlia-i-Sir

By living in the presence of the ideal, a change takes place in the heart, which I have tried to describe by the phrase, 'takhlia-i-Sir'. By keeping ourselves busy in purifying our hearts, we grasp the point intuitionaly and become convinced that such is the practice approved by God, and such is the settled or prevailing course of the perfect wisdom by the All-Wise, that the more a man is involved in bodily limitations, the more he is confined by external causes, and has his attention diverted towards material things. The more he suffers tribulations, mental worries, cares and forgetfulness of the remembrance of God. Further, to the extent he is engrossed in catering for his bodily needs or in nourishing his body, and in showing off his vanity, to that extent the condition of his soul deteriorates, his spiritual powers become weak, and his purity of mind and psychic forces decrease, and correspondingly his spiritual darkness thickens and his peace of mind disappears. After understanding this way of God, and this perfect wisdom of the All-Wise, those who live in the presence of the ideal, regard austerity, striving and self-abnegation as the essential conditions of Tariqa—the way of life. They hold that breaking the clinging bonds of self, or forsaking the world is this perquisite of Tariqa.

In the foregoing paragraphs I have made explicit the meaning of striving, austerity and self abnegation in modern terms, which is, changing vices by virtues. Forsaking the world is the same as "Journeying in one's homeland"; a journey, as it were, in the human nature itself; it is transference from vices of virtues. Dissociation with everything except God means keeping the same ideal always in view. Seemingly, one should associate with created beings, but at heart he should be with God Almighty, who is his Supreme Ideal.

This Divine law, or the practice approved by God, has been explained by a sage in the following couplets:

> "If you follow the path that leads to the nurture of your body, blazing fire is ready for you!
>
> And if you tread the path of heart, paradise would be your abode!
>
> If you walk on the path of spirit, then my dear,
>
> I shall cut my speech short and tell you that you will have a glimpse of your Beloved."

Peace of mind, felicity and the pleasures of Heaven on earth are enjoyed by those alone who, being contented with frugal eatables and drinks, spend all their energy in invigorating their mind and heart, never overlook their ideal, or in the words of pure-hearted Sufis, who live perpetually in the presence of God! Their gaze is turned away from this world and their spirit, in a state of abstraction and ecstasy, always enjoys an indescribable bliss, being inwardly separated from all but God, seeing inwardly none but God, listening to none but God! In other words, their heart gets released from the captivity of the world, it gets emptied of the thoughts of what is not God. Thus it forms a complete contact with God and is totally disconnected with what is not God! Now there remains for them only one object of knowledge, and no other, and that is God! The perceptive faculty is completely purified and abstracted in the terminology of the Sufis. The alone is called "absolute annihilation" or "Passing away".

> "Humble your being and accept that which has been prescribed for you by your friend, Whether sorrow or joy.
>
> If anything else save God—even an atom—be your object,
> Destroy it, for it would become the object of your worship,
> In both the worlds there is no other save the One.
> So, do not yearn for any other in your heart!

The acquisition of such a state is, in the language of the Sufi, Takhlia-i-Sir. In such a state, as I have pointed our earlier, the mental faculty of man gets rid of the thought of everything save God and is totally captivated by God. It may be illustrated by the example of the thirsty person whose prime desire is nothing save water. This state cannot be acquired without the faculty of love and devotion which is termed "Jadhba-i-Hahia"

> "To acquire this bliss,
> A thousand lives may willingly be staked"

Further elaboration may not be justifiable, for the object in view is hardly gained by mere talk. It is acquired by inward search and striving:

> "This much may we speak, the rest is meant for reflection."

Revised and edited; originally published in Islam and the Modern Age, Feb.1978.

5

A Muslim's Devotions

S VAHIDUDDIN

(Abstract: Prayer, or dialog with the God Almighty, is a communication process, and it is done in different ways, and in different context. Presents the experiences and interactions in the process of fulfilling a desire of the inner self for a direct link with the Creator).

When I think of prayer, I think of it as a kind of dialogue, as a kind of communication with God. What is generally called *tawajjuh* is I think, the greatest moment is the experience of prayer. That is to say, my attention should be directed towards God all the time. I do not conceive of prayer in terms of certain moments, in terms of certain fixed texts, in terms of certain repetitions or certain known formulas but in terms of the total attitude, in terms of my whole response to what I feel about God, in adversity, in thankfulness. Prayer for me is an uninterrupted dialogue. What is called interruption is only due to our finitude. I consider my whole existence as a kind of attunement to God.

From the very beginning I had a deep religious feeling. This deep religious feeling came to me from my family background. My paternal grandmother was a very devout woman. and her life and experience influenced me deeply. My father died when I was about three years old. He was the only son of his mother. She was married early in life, but she was widowed after only two years of her marriage. These two experiences moulded her life and thus influenced me too. Why? because I found that in out day to day experience, especially in these our times, man becomes totally dissatisfied with the order of the universe the moment he is frustrated, the moment he loses something he thinks everything is lost. She reacted differently. She lost what was most important and precious to her, and she had nothing else to rely upon, She lost her husband, she lost her only son and yet I did not perceive in her any resentment against the order of the universe. This total acceptance moved me very much, and I found in her really an example of what Islam means or should mean: a total resignation and submission to the divine order. I still remember how, even in her old age, she used to recite in the morning the Qur'anic verses from the sura *al-Rahman*: "Which is it, of the favours of your Lord, that ye deny?" This still haunts my memory. This woman, in her life, in her contentment, in her peace, in her grief influenced me deeply. She lost her husband, she lost her son but still she retained that which comes from our total submission to God. This is how I was introduced to Islam from the very early years of my life.

Then, from the very beginning, I had a very deep sense of the unknown, *al-ghayb*. This felling for the unknown, I think, is the very essence of religion. It means that I do not only accept what is given to me but I also have a feeling for what is not given, for what is not known to me and what cannot be known to me. I feel that in this world I am just overshadowed and overpowered by the unknown. The unknown is much vaster, infinitely more than what is perceptible and what can be known. This felling for *al-ghayb* has always been a characteristic of my personal experience. And I do not think that there can be any *du'a* or any worship or any *salat* which excludes this experience of *al-ghayb* and which does not give weight to this experience of the un-known. I think it very characteristic of the *Qur'an* that it insists on the *ghayb* as a constituent of faith. Without faith in the *ghayb* there cannot be any Islam and I think there cannot be any religion whatsoever. Whether we think of God in personal terms or in impersonal terms, the feeling of the *ghayb* must be there.

It follows from what I mentioned that I grew up as an orphan. The whole atmosphere at home was rather gloomy and sad. My grandmother had not enough means to provide for the education of her grandchildren. And my mother on her part could not get any pension or sustenance from the government because her husband died so early in life. She depended on her parents for the sustenance. This double bereavement, the agony of my grandmother and the anguish of my mother, had a deep impact on my own personal experience and on the development of my religious consciousness. Yet, I never thought of denying God simply because there was anguish, agony. Man had to pass through suffering. I thought suffering had a meaning and that there is an element of compensation whether we think of compensation in a low or cheap way, or in more spiritual terms. Our suffering and what we are deprived of are somehow atoned and compensated for whether in life here or in the life to come, in ways which we do not or may not understand until the last moment of our life or only when we have crossed its threshold. That suffering has a meaning, an import, had always been my conviction.

I have not much to say about my earliest education, the Qur'an came first, and then western school education. Only •when I grew older, during my time at college and university, the new factors began to appear. I read the sceptics. I still remember reading some essays and books by Bertrand Russell. They impressed me and I became rather in different to religion and doubts began to creep into my mind about the validity of religious values and norms. But this period lasted only a short while because I found that in spite of all scepticism I could not evade the overpowering consciousness of the *ghayb* which I never lost in my life.

Somehow or other this persisted in me and even now persists; this terrible consciousness that I am surrounded, overwhelmed or enveloped by forces which I do not understand. This world is only a very small segment of reality, of what we call the world. Astronomers think of worlds without number. This also does not impress me very much. Because I think apart from the world which are without number there are other worlds of a totally different kind. They exceed by far those worlds without number of which the astronomers speak. Reality may indeed by hierarchical; there may be different segments of reality. When I read the *sura al-Fatihah* where God is refferred to as *rabb-al-alamin*, I am very much taken because I think of the worlds, spiritual worlds, world of which we cannot have any idea and I think of man as just a part of this universe which is inexhaustible. The concept of the inexhaustible is in fact the other concept (in addition to that of *al-ghayb*) which I find very important in my consideration of the philosophy of religion. That is to say: reality in inexhaustible, conceptually, because whatever we think of reality, we cannot grasp it.

God, as reality, is unapproachable. Some so-called mystics teach that by intuiton or whatever other name given to it, they can take hold of God. I think this is a great illusion. No intuition, no form of knowledge is able to fathom what is unfathomble, ineffable. This is one of the constituent parts of my experience.

Now a few words about how I pray. I have different kinds of prayer. At one time, formerly, I did not bother much about ritual prayer, especially when I was very young, in my school days. But I respect those who pray and lay great emphasis on ritual prayer because I think that in ritual prayer we participate in his history of our community, the *ummah*. When I offer my *salat* at fixed times which I generally do these days, I find that I have been somehow or other associated with the history of Islam and especially with the person of the Prophet. Ritual prayer forges an association with the life of the Prophet which we cannot have otherwise. And then I also go for congregational prayer, although not regularly. There also I find the same collective consciousness aroused which makes me think of Islam as a kind of a global and open brotherhood. This feeling of brotherhood, this feeling of participation, this awakening of historical consciousness helps me and moves me to observe ritual prayer. But I do not make a fetish out of it. If I miss one prayer, I do not feel very upset. I think that ritual prayer is part and parcel of the Islamic way of life, and no doubt it somebody feels strongly about it he should not miss it by any means. But that does not make me very much concerned about its strict observance.

I give most emphasis to prayer in solitude, especially at night. I mean these nightly vigils: to wake up at night and to think of God and to pray and to turn towards Him in my own way. Occasionally it may be through reciting Qur'anic phrase in the context of some wordly troubles and problems. I seek the support in patience and prayer repeating many times that God is sufficient unto us, and that he is the best of protectors. To think of him and to seek His help: that gives me great consolation. I am reminded of what Hafiz says. He said that what made him what he was, was nightly vigils, to wake up at night, to think of God and to cry. It is this tenderness the Qur'an also speaks of, mentioning those who when they read the Qur'an their hearts shake and their eyes brim over with tears." This kind of tenderness is very precious to me. Baba Farid, the Indian mystic, used to say whenever he was pleased with somebody: May God give you *soz* !; that is to say, that kind to anguish. You may be surprised that Baba Farid was praying for something which may not be very agreeable to most of us. But what is meant is that sensitivity for the unknown which is accompanied by a peculiar type of emotion which can only be characterized as a subtle agitation of mind and body.

So when I wake up early in the morning I just think of God in whatever way I like. This thinking of God, especially at night, I think, is very useful for out spiritual development. Apart from this prayer at night I also think of God whenever I can and wherever I am, even in society which may seem to be very worldly and to have nothing to do with religion; in the cinema or in the street, I think of God. This uninterrupted turning of my attention to God I find very heartening. It brings great spiritual elation. What impresses me most is the Qur'anic attitude when it says: "*La takhaf wa la tahzan*" i.e. "Don't be afraid and don't grieve', God indeed is with us. This feeling of the proximity of God, this nearness to Him, this association with God, the feeling that God never leaves me, this His total presence, I find very characteristic of my own religious life. That is why I think of God always, not at certain periods of time only. The continuous, uninterrupted rapport with the divine is what has made me a very religious man.

A Muslim's Prayer

Allah, My Lord! Hidden and manifest, Creator Supreme and fashioner superb! Thine is the world I know and Thine the worlds I know not. Thy mercy envelops creation and Thy light dispels gloom. Burden me not with what I cannot bear and forgive me when I err. My life is a waste: let me not squander Thy bounty and lose hope in Thy loving beneficence. Unto Thee I flee and cry in anguish. Hold me close when my feet fail and lead me with the righteous to victory. Why should I grieve and fear when Thou art night and why should I complain against Thy decrees when I know not what Thou hast prepared for me? Ignorant as I am I know not the joy that may lie hidden in sorrow and the sorrow that may lurk in joy. I pray for those who have gone before me and beseech Thy forgiveness for my parents, in whose loving care I grew. Informed with wisdom let me grow in knowledge that comes of Thee. Suffer me not to envy the pleasures that others have and to languish in grief at the loss of what I have. Guard me against pride and lust and make me not vain and hypocrite. Let not passion make me wild and let not power blind me to the transient state of all that life offers. Blessed is he who has surrendered his all unto Thee and who has won his peace in. Thy pleasure. May my tears in constant remembrance of Thee sustain the heart and bring deliverance; Bless me with the fullness of life on earth and when the time comes make me return unto Thee united in the fellowship of Thy loving ones. Lord; Grant me above all, I pray, the vision of Thy countenance that Thou hast promised for those who are Thine.

Revised and edited; originally published in Islam and the Modern Age, Nov. 1979, and in Encounter

6

The Path of God

DAYANG MUDA OF SARAWAK

(Abstract: "The Universe is only Man on a large scale, as Man is a small Universe," says the Islamic tradition which is in accordance of this point with philosophers and the Initiated of all times, just as it conforms with the verdict of science... Our fidelity to God will assure us the help of His kindness and mercy).

All the elements of Creation visible and invisible exist in Man and establish a real link between him and the whole of the Universe. Every element in nature is in harmony with a corresponding order of elements in the Universe and subject to laws and rhythms appropriate to its to nature. A man therefore is not an isolated individual and has no personal Existence unless as a temporary combination of eternal elements. When a man is born these elements already exist in a different form, and after his death they still exist in another form.

Modern science, studying the constitution of the atom, has formally established that it is a solar system in reduction, composed of small particles evolving in a rotary manner around a fixed point. These particles are governed by the same magnetic and dynamic laws as well as by the same laws of gravity, as the planetary system.

This confirms the old theories which come to us in the form of Tradition, whose origin is lost in the mist of Time.

We would wander from our subject were we to establish

strange analogies, connected with this question by examining the philosophical consequences which it embodies. We will only endeavour to establish the intimate connection of the Universe and Man in order to ascertain another side of the question.

When one observes the evolution of humanity, one is bound to notice that in all its spheres it can be compared to the individual evolution of Man.

Taking into consideration the difference of the scale which touches not only the innumerable elements but also time and space, we may deduce from this knowledge the laws which rule the Universe. And this comparison extends to all the conditions which make Man one of the links of a chain.

Humanity in its evolution is undergoing all the stages of the normal growth of an individual passing through different phases of life. This has been determined by the Indian doctrines. These theories applied to Man establish his evolution in a parallel manner and have enabled prophets to foretell the future of the human race.

These prophecies are infallible when they emanate from those who have studied the moral and physical laws governing the Universe (or, in other words, the Divine Laws). They can then trace by analogy the future stages through which humanity must pass. As in the case of the body, cells which die are imperceptibly renewed by fresh ones without affecting the life and functions of the whole, so men are born, fulfil their allotted part in the scheme of evolution, die and are replaced.

Humanity has a soul composed of the embodiment of human souls. And as this collective soul is subject to evolution like the soul of the individual, it is attached to God.

Humanity has a Conscience whose standard is dependent on the spiritual evolution of Men, and as an obvious repercussion the Soul and Conscience of the Universe reflects on each individual who at the same time participates in and benefits by it.

This conception allows us to understand the part played by the higher elements of humanity. Their elevation is not limited to themselves; they share in the general elevation. What they acquire does not perish with them. They leave after their death seeds of fresh progress and sometimes, as in the case of the Prophets of God, they give to Men an imperishable impetus. What can be said about the soul applies equally to the brain. Humanity has at each succeeding stage a definite spiritual level, the reflection of the intellectual value of Men, especially of the Elite. But here social laws differ from spiritual laws because they are founded on a more concrete basis. It is important to distinguish between social and spiritual evolution. This latter point of view is generally taken into consideration and has been comprehensibly treated by sociologists and historians. There is no doubt that spiritual evolution influences social evolution and in a lesser degree the reverse is true. But one has to admit that the two evolutions do not run on parallel lines. As far as the social point of view is concerned, we notice not a continued rise but alternate periods of progress and decadence. Material progress, conquests, great undertakings, all works that are purely human, are not necessarily indications of a high spiritual standard. In this one finds the reason which causes epochs of great civilisation to be followed by destruction and regress. Human elevation is not to be sought in civilisation, in the perfection of human institutions, but in the spiritual development of Men.

Social life is necessary for the continuation of the race, for the support of those of inferior spiritual attainments, and also to enable the more highly developed to find means of self-expression, just as the difficulties and struggles of life are necessary to Man in his evolution towards good. The social vicissitudes, of humanity, its periods of prosperity and distress, are ways designed by the Creator, successive stages of a long and continued spiritual evolution, which leads towards a fuller comprehension of His laws.

Humanity must progress according to a plan fixed by God and known by Him only. It must progress painfully towards a state which grows gradually nearer perfection until it becomes, as the

Scripture says, the Kingdom of God. This ideal is expressed in the Tradition of the Patriarch, the idea which has animated since all Time the Prophets of God. It suffices to study the spiritual development of humanity without going back further than the Hebrew Tradition to see confirmed by historical facts the first stages of the realisation of this ideal, and to know that Humanity is progressing.

Towards what end? We do not know. Some have built round this subject hypotheses which themselves rest on hypotheses. We can base our conjectures on the similarity between atomic and molecular systems and the solar system, link between elements of the same nature throughout Creation.

Extending these analogies to Men, we arrive at conclusions. We cannot claim any value for them. The End, the great End, passes our comprehension, but we are nevertheless obliged to admit them, whilst remembering our imperfection and our limited understanding. We can only reason by our senses. Our most exalted thoughts and convictions, if we analyse them, are always based on tangible analogies. Few people will deny the statement that in the course of his life, Man evolves towards good. Those of a religious and philosophic frame of mind know that their trials are destined to make them see their failings and their ignorance. But can we explain only by our intelligence the irresistible impulse which draws us towards good?

Can we define conscience, that bridge between God and ourselves, the link by which God leads us in the way which we should follow, in accordance with our evolution?

Why are Men evolving towards the divine? What is the aim of it all? To enable us to understand it, we have to take up again our comparison of the Man and the cells of his body.

The cells are living by reciprocity. They could not exist one without another. Every one of them takes a part in the life of all the others and could not itself live without the work of the others.

Everyone of them takes its life from the life of the body and is itself necessary to that life.

Thus we have the image of Man in Humanity. But this analogy is more important when considered philosophically. The cell has a very short existence when compared with the life of the body. It is accomplishing a very limited function, very simple compared with the multiple functions of the body. Its part considered in itself is without significance, but nevertheless it has contributed not only towards the life of the body, but also towards its actions. But the body is the receptacle of the intelligence and the Soul. Thus the infinitely small cell participates through its existence in a work which outlasts the body. Let us suppose that for a brief moment one of these cells has separate intelligence. It will find itself surrounded by inexplicable mysteries, just as we are unable to explain our own use in the work of the Universe.

Let us go further. We will suppose that certain cells are not working or are moving in a direction opposed to the harmonious working of the whole, the result of this will be trouble for the whole body. Therefore all its vital forces and nerve centres will unite themselves in setting up a counter-action in opposition to the rebellious or harmful cells. The whole body will suffer while this war is going on, and this suffering will entail illness for the individual; although as a rule he will triumph since all his vital forces will rally to his aid to restore him to his normal state of health.

Now let us suppose once more that the cell has some intelligence of its own. It will still be unaware of the functions of the body, unaware of the process of its evolution. It does not know what controls its health and its progress from childhood to old age. It is the same in the case of Man. We offer this analogy to the reader. He will realise two things: the first is that all those whose lives are in harmony with the true meaning of the Universe, are aided by favourable forces, whereas those who are opposed to the higher laws and aims have all these same forces against them; the second, that we have a definite plan, an appointed path and a reason for our existence. We may not know to what purpose we live. We are in the same position as the human cell, not knowing that it is a part of a man who has thought and action. The Evolution of the world is inseparable from the evolution of every human being.

One can realise therefore the importance which rests on the perfection of every individual and the necessity for his working in harmony with the rest, animated by the same purpose in accord with the divine aim.

The Spirit of the Universe influences the individual for it reflects his own soul.

We can realise the meaning of divine forces which can be divided into forces of Progress and forces of Order, the latter chastising Men to bring them to God when they go astray. We can realise the necessity of human effort to achieve spiritual perfection.

We know thus the existence of a divine will, to which we have to submit. We realise the existence of divine laws which we are not allowed to transgress without being punished. Harmony with the Divine Will, Divine Aims, Divine Laws will keep us in the path of God, the path we have to follow to give the full meaning to our life, and please God.

This question, so rich in possibilities, can be carried still further.

> We will find in it the conflict between good and evil, the explanation of what we call the struggle between devils and angels. We will also find the explanation of the idea of punishment for sin and expiation as the proof of their evitable triumph of good. These considerations are necessary to understand the linking up, superposition and interpenetration of different elements of the Universe and their mutual dependence. The system which shows us the Unity of the Universe leads to the comprehension of the Unity of God.

Dayang Muda of Sarawak.

We will then live in conformity with all that the Prophets have taught us and find the secret of a harmonious and fruitful life. Our fidelity to God will assure us the help of His kindness and mercy.

(Revised and edited; originally published in Islamic Culture, Oct. 1933.)

7

Hadith Literature: Influence on Arabic Linguistics and Lexicography

M Z SIDDIQI

(Abstract: Study of Traditions, or Hadith, is a science, which requires a fairly good knowledge of linguistics, vocabulary, lexicography, etc.The growth and development of Hadith related literature influenced directly on the growth of the Arabic language and literature).

Interest in the linguistics among most of the nations developed out of the study of their religious literature. Among the Chinese, it was due to the study of the Buddhist and Taoist texts; among the Hindus, it was essential for the study of Vedas; for the Greeks, it was the study of the ancient epics which had quasi-religious importance. Similarly, among the Arabs, it was the study of the *Qur'an* and the *Hadith* which led, like many other branches of Arabic literature, to the origin and early development of linguistic studies.

The earliest treatise on Arabic grammar by 'Ali, the fourth Caliph, or by his disciple Abu'l-Aswad al-Du'ali (d. 69/688) was composed in order to keep up the purity of the *Qur'an* and of the Arabic language. The personality and character of Abu'l-Aswad, as well as the circumstances which led him to the composition of the book, have been discussed by Haywood in detail. As a matter of fact, the period in which the treatise is said to have been composed was the most suitable for such a work. The treatise was seen by Ibn al-Nadim and his opinion is upheld by later Arabic writers like al-Zubaidi (d. 379/989), al-Qifti (d. 646/1248) and Ibn.

About a century after the composition of the earliest treatise on Arabic grammar, al-Khalil *b.* Ahmad (d. *circa* 170/786) wrote the *Kitab al-'ain,* the earliest book on Arabic lexicography. Being an extremely religious and godly man, brought up and educated at Basra, an important centre of islamic learning, and being well-versed in the *Hadith,* it cannot be doubted that al-Khalil's main object in composing the *Kitab al-'ain* was to serve religious literature.

It was not long after the composition of the *Kitab al-'ain* that treatises and books on *gharib al-Hadith* (vocabulary of the Tradition) began to be compiled. A short critical account of the origin and development of this branch of Arabic literature, till about the end of the 6th century of the *hijra*, has been given by al-Mubarak *b.* al-Athir in the introduction to *al-Nihaya fi gharib al-Hadith wa'l-athar* Hajji Khalifa has, after having summarized it, described partly its later development also. All these treatises and books explain the rare expressions found in the Traditions of the Prophet of Islam as well as those in the remarks of his 'companions' and the 'followers' and illustrate them with the help of early Arabic poetry, proverbs and idioms.

The earliest of these treatises was compiled by Abu 'Ubaida Ma'mar *b.* al-Muthanna (d. 208-13/823-28). He descended from a Jewish family of Bajarwan, a small place in Armenia. His father, al-Muthanna, was converted to Islam and settled down at Basra. Here Ma'mar learnt Arabic linguistics and Islamic Traditions and became thoroughly conversant with these subjects as well as with the history and genealogy of the Arabs. Al-Jahiz considered him to be the greatest master of all the branches of Arabic literature during his time. Ibn Qutaiba and al-Mubarrad held that Ma'mar excelled specially in the history and the geneology of the Arabs. Among his eminent students were Abu Nuwas the poet, Qasim *b.* Sallam, the biographer, and Abu Hatim of Sijistan, the Traditionist. In spite of wide knowledge of Arabic poetry, Ma'mar, however, could not recite it correctly, nor could he read the *Qur'an* properly.

Hammad, the son of Ishaq al-Mausili, one of the friends of

Ma'amr, spoke of his high attainments and generosity in communicating his knowledge to others, to Fadl b Rabi, the minister of Harun al-Rashi. Hammad did this because he had felt offended by the behaviour of al-Asma'i (d. 216/831) towards him in the presence of the minister, and wanted that a rival of al-Asma'i might be introduced in the court of the Caliph.

Fadl *b.* Rabi' called Ma'mar from Basra to Baghdad, honoured and respected him and asked him to recite some poems, and enjoyed and appreciated what was recited. Ibrahim *b.* Isma'il, the secretary to the minister, who was present, asked Ma'mar to explain the use of such expression in the *Qur'an* the exact significance of which was not known to the Arabs, *e.g., ru'us al-shayatin* (the heads of the Satans). Ma'mar replied that the *Qur'an* had followed the usage of the Arab poets in this respect. Imru' al-Qais, for example, he said, referred to the tusks of demons (*anyab al-aghwal*) in one of his poems. The reply way highly appreciated by all those who were present and led Ma'mar to the composition of *Kitab majaz al-Qur'an*, in which he explained the uses of all similar expressions in the *Qur'an*.

According to al-Farra', the grammarian, and al-Asma'i, the philologist, this book contained many mistakes. Al-Asma'I had remarked that Abu 'Ubaida had interpreted the *Qur'an* on the basis of his personal opinion. Ma'mar, on being told of it, went straight to al-Asma'i, talked to him for a while and then asked him was was meant by *khubz*. Al-Asma'i replied: "What you baked and ate." Ma'mar at once recited verse 36 of *sura* XII in which the word *khubz* occurs, and said to him that he was interpreting the *Qur'an* according to his own personal opinion.

There was strong rivalry between Ma'mar and al-Asma'i. Both of them were great scholars. Each of them made distinct contribution to Arabic literature as is evident from the list of their books given by Ibn al-Nadim, Al-Asma'i was more cultured and better equipped in the art of discussion, but Ma'mar possessed more sarcastic humor and a sharper tongue than his rival and therefore, was dreaded and avoided by him. It has been related that once the servant of one of Ma'mar's host dropped soup on his clothes. The host apologized for it, saying that he would replace his clothes by ten garments. But Ma'mar replied that it did not matter because the soup contained no grease.

Ma'mur suffered from weak memory and held the view of *Shu'ubiya* and perhaps also Kharijite views. The Traditionists did not, therefore, accept the traditions related by him. People is general also disliked him because of his offensive tongue. His funeral was not attended by any one.

He was the first author to compose a vocabulary of the Traditions. It was very short, because when it was composed, the Traditionists were conversant with the significance of most of the expressions used by the Prophet of Islam. But it served as a model for the works on the subject for more than two centuries. Ma'mar composed about two hundred other treatises, on Arabic linguistics and the history of the Arab tribes and their battles. A list of some of his works is given by Ibn al-Nadim and Yaqut (*op. cit*).

Almost simultaneously with Ma'mur, another linguist of Basra school, Nadr *b.* Shumail (d. 203-4/818-9) composed another vocabulary of the Traditions. Unlike Ma'mar, Nadr was an Arab and belonged to the Banu Mazin branch of the tribe of Tamim. Some of the members of this tribe had settled down at Marw after its conquest by the Arabs and Nadr was born there. During the rise of Abu Muslim in Khurasan in 118/736, when al-Nadr was a mere child, he was taken out by his father to Basra. Here he was brought up and educated. He also lived with the Bedouins in the desert for a long time. There he acquired mastery of the Arabic language and poetry. He studied Traditions with the competent Traditionists of his time. At Basra he acquired good reputation as a master and teacher of these subjects. Among his students were such reputed Traditionists as Yahya *b.* Ma'in and al-Madini.

Reduced to extreme poverty, Nadr had to migrate from basra to Marw, when he settled down. He carried the *Sunna* to Khurasan for the first time, and was appointed a judge. He became friendly with al-Ma'mun and received from him the reward of fifty thousand *dirhams*, for pointing out to him the correct reading of a Tradition and the meaning of some Arabic expression. Fadl *b.* Sahl also rewarded him thirty thousand *dirhams* when he related to him what passed between him and al-Ma'mun. At Marw he became rich. But he always lived like a poor man.

He was respected by the scholars on account of his learning and unimpeachable character. When he was leaving Basra for Marw, three thousand scholars, including Traditionists, lawyers and linguists came to bid him farewell. He was considered to be a perfectly reliable transmitter of the traditions. Several of the traditions related by him are included in canonical collections.

Almost simultaneously with Ma'mur and al-nadr, al-Asma'i and some other linguists also compiled small vocabularies of the *Hadith.* Each of them made some additions to the work of his predecessor and all of them, except Abi 'Adnan, quoted the complete texts of the *Hadith*, leaving out the *isnads*, and explained, illustrated and commented upon the rare expressions found in them. They included in their treatises and saying of the 'companions' and of the 'followers' and commented upon the unusual expressions in them also. But Abu 'Adnan added to the text of the traditions their *isnands* also and arranged them according to their subject matter like the *Musannaf* works.

Far more important and comprehensive than all the *hadith* vocabularies mentioned above is the vocabulary compiled by Abu 'Ubaid Qasim *b.* Sallam who worked on it for forty years. He collected his materials for it from all the available sources, written as well as oral. In it he put together 526 traditions of the Prophet, added to them their *isnads*, arranged them under the names of the 'companions', who narrated them, like the collection of the traditions called *Musnad*, explained the rare expressions in them and illustrated them with the early Arabic poems, proverbs and idioms. He also included in the book the important sayings and remarks of about forty-seven 'companions' and of more than forty 'followers', and explained and illustrated the rare expressions in them in the same way as he explained those in the tradition. It is one of the most important work on *Hadith*-vocabulary. For a long time it was utilized and relied upon by the Traditionists, as well as the jurisconsults and biographers.

Abu 'Ubaid was the son of a Greek slave of an Azdire Arab of Herat, with whom his father worked as a porter. He was born between 154 and 160 A.H. He received his education in Arabic linguistics, *Hadith* and *fiqh* at basra and Kufa. He lived at Baghdad for some time, where he worked as a *mu'adhdhin* in a mosque and as a teacher, and delivered lectures on some of his books, which were attended by eminent Traditionists like Yahya *b.* Ma'in and al-Madini.

He was at first appointed by Harthama, the governor of Khurasan, as a tutor of his sons, and later on by Thabit *b.* Malik, the governor of Tarsus, to teach his sons. Thabit also appointed him as a judge in Tarsus. He held this post for eighteen years. After this he attached himself to 'abdallah *b.* Tahir, the governor of Khurasan, who recognized his scholarly attainments and encouraged him in his literary activities. He gave him handsome rewards and a large permanent pension for the books which he composed and presented to him. Once 'Abdallah was asked by his friend, Abu Dulaf, an eminent general and *amir* and also a scholar of some merit, to send Abu 'Ubaid to his newly-founded town, al-Karaj, to keep his company for two months. Abu 'Ubaid went to Abu Dulaf who enjoyed his company very much and offered him thirty thousand *dirhams* at the time of his departure. But Abu 'Ubaid refused it, saying that he lived in the company of a man who had made him free from the need of any help from any other quarter. When he returned to 'abdallah, he granted him thirty thousand *dinars*. Abu 'Ubaid accepted the gift and said: "O Prince, you have already made me so rich by your munificence that with this money I would purchase weapons and horses and send them to the border area, so that you might get rich reward from God." In 214/829 Abu 'Ubaid went to Mecca to perform *hajj*, and stayed there till he died at Mecca, or at Madina, in 223-224/837-838.

He composed more than twenty big and small books and treatises. Ibn al-nadim has mentioned twenty of them, and I.A. 'Arshi has mentioned twenty-five of them in the introduction to the *Kitab al-ajnas*. All his books are valuable. But perhaps the most valuable of them is *al-Gharib al-musannaf*, to which he attached great importance. It was probably his earliest work. According to al-zubaidi, it contained Abu 'Ubaid's comments on seventeen thousand nine hundred and seventy unusual Arabic expressions. His *Kitab al-amwal*, according to Ibrahim al-Harbi (198-285/813-898), is the weakest of his works. But according to others, it is the best book on Islamic law of taxation. It is a mine of information concerning the Islamic system of taxation on various kinds of commodities and shows Abu 'Ubaid's wide and deep knowledge of the subject.

He based all his works on some earlier books which he greatly enlarged and improved upon. He based his *al-Gharib al-musannaf* on the work of a Hashimite author, and his *Gharib al-hadith* and *Gharib al-Qur'an* on the works of Ma'mar,. In his *Ma'ani al-Qur'an*, he brought together what was compiled by Ma'mar, Qutrub and others, and added to them their *isnads* and a good deal of his own researches. In his *Kitab al-amthal* also he put together what was collected by previous writers on the subject, and re-arranged the materials more systematically. His main object is all his works was to bring together all the materials on their subjects scattered in various treatises, to add to them whatever could be available from other sources, and to explain and arrange them in a systematic form.

But this peculiar feature of his works did not affect his reputation either as a scholar or as a compiler and author. On the other hand, he was considered to be the greatest master of all the branches of Islamic literature during his time and was described to be a good compiler and the most authentic and useful writer.

Ishaq *b*. Rahuya (Rahawaih) observed: "Abu 'Ubaid was a greater scholar than I, Ahmad *b*. Hanbal and al-Shafi'i." Hital *b*. al-'Ala of al-Raqqa is said to have remarked: "God showed his greatest kindness to us through four scholar: (i) through al-Shafi'i, who laid down the foundation of Islamic law on the basis of the traditions of the Prophet; (ii) through Ahmad *b.* Hanbal, who held out till the end against the cruelty of al-Ma'mun; (iii) through Yahya *b.* Ma'in, who protected the traditions of the Prophet against forgery, and (iv) through abu 'Ubaid, who explained the difficult expressions in the traditions and without whom people would have committed mistakes with regard to them." His command over all the branches of Islamic literature has been generally acknowledged. His zeal for literary work cannot be denied. He divided his nights is three parts. In the first part he offered prayer, in the second part he slept and in the third part he did literary work. His piety and truthfulness have been admired by all those who have written about him. He was neither vain nor irritable. When he was told that he had committed more than one hundred and twenty mistakes in his *al-Gharib al-musannaf*, he calmly replied that it was not much in a book in which ten thousand errors were explained, and added that perhaps if he and the critic discussed these mistakes together, he might be able to justify some of his statements. The traditions related by Abu 'Ubaid are included in the *Sahih* of al-Bukhari and in the *Sunan* of Abu Da'ud and al-Tirmidhi.

Abu'l-Tayyib 'Abd al-Wahid (d. 351/962) and al-Suyuti are of the opinion that Abu 'Ubaid was weak in grammar, and the former also asserted that he was a weak narrator. Ibrahim *b.* al-Harbi remarked that fifty-three traditions in the *Gharib al-Hadith* were baseless.

But M.J. de Goeje, in his learned article on the *Gharib al-Hadith*, says that abu 'Ubaid's memory was as good as that of any Arab narrator which was a matter of wonder. "Of his knowledge of Arabic grammar," writes de Goeje, "he could not be a judge. But as a grammarian he followed the school of Kufa." *The Gharib al-hadith*, the only book of Abu 'Ubaid which he had read, he adds, "certainly showed his exactitude as well his learning; but it did not show his originality." Shaikh Kurd 'Ali says that the *Kitab al-amwal* shows Abu 'Ubaid's wisdom, his deep insight into the subject as well as his wide knowledge of it.

The *Gharib al-Hadith* of Abu 'Ubaid, however, did not deal with the whole of the wide range of its subject. Abu 'Abdallah Muslim *b.* Qutaiba (213-276/828-889) wrote, therefore, a large supplement to Abu 'Ubaid's work, followed his general plan and explained a large number of such traditions as were missed by him. Ibn Qutaiba wrote in the introduction to his book that for a long time he was under the impression that Abu 'Ubaid's work completely satisfied the requirements of the Traditionists. But its deeper critical study convinced him that he had missed a large number of the traditions. He compiled, therefore, its supplement, in which he explained such traditions as were missed by Abu 'Ubaid, on the lines adopted by him. He explained the traditions more thoroughly and supported his interpretations by a larger number of authorities than his predecessor, and pointed out many of his mistakes. He also wrote an independent treatise on them. But he himself also committed many mistakes. He expected, however, that after these two books there would be no more room for further investigation on the subject. But actually he had also missed a large number of such traditions as needed explanation.

This was realized by Abu Sulaiman Ahmad al-Khattabi (319-388/931-998). He brought together such of the traditions as were missed by both Abu 'Ubaid and Ibn Qutaiba, and commented on the rare expression in them according to their plan and standard. In the introduction to his book, he praised the work of his two predecessors and remarked, like Ibn Qutaiba, that for a long time he had held that after their works there was no need for any other vocabulary of the traditions. But on actual study of the traditions he found that both of his predecessors had missed a large number of such of them as needed explanation. He compiled, therefore, a supplement of their works according to their plans and standards. But, unlike Ibn Qutaiba, he confessed that there still remained many traditions which he could not explain, and hoped that they might be collected and explained by someone who might be favoured by God with the ability to do so.

The book of Abu 'Ubaid and its two supplements were recognized as standard vocabularies of the traditions and were depended upon by the Traditionists for centuries in spite of the fact that several authoritative linguists and Traditionists after them, like al-Mubarrad and Ibrahim al-Harbi and others, compiled many small or big vocabularies of the traditions. This was because most of them added little to what was collected by their predecessors and some of them were too voluminous to be easily available.

Abu 'Ubaid and his followers, however, had collected the texts of such traditions as contained unusual expressions, gave their complete *isnads* and explained under each traditions such words as were generally unknown, *without following any system* in arranging their materials. They also did not mention the sources of the traditions quoted by them. None of these vocabularies, therefore, could be utilized without due care and deep and through study.

These defects were realized by Abu 'Ubaid Ahmad *b.* Muhammad of Herat (d. 401/1010). He left out, therefore, the texts as well as the *isnads* of the traditions while compiling his *Kitab al-gharibain* and collected and explained the rare expression occurring in the *Qur'an* and the *Hadith* out of the works of the previous writers, added to them many more by his own investigation and arranged them in alphabetical order. This book is more comprehensive and easier to consult than all the previous vocabularies. Therefore, it became more popular than all the previous works on the subject. *Al-Fa'iq* of Al-Zamakhshari also lost its position after it. For al-Zamakhshari had arranged the whole or part of the traditions alphabetically and explained all the rare expressions in them, under the root of *one* of them, Many of them were, therefore, included under entirely different roots. In fact, the arrangement of the various roots of words in *al-Fa'iq* is extremely confusing.

Al-Harawi, had, however, also missed a large number of such of the rare expression found in the *Qur'an* and the traditions as needed explanation. Abu Musa Muhammad *b.* Abu Bakr of Isfahan (d. 581/1185) compiled, therefore, a supplement to the book of al-Harawi. These two books supplied a very large part of the needs of the students of the *Qur'an* and *Hadith.* But they did not include any of the rare expressions used in many of the traditions included in the *Sahih* of al-Bukhari and of Muslim and many of those in other important *Hadith*-collections.

Abu'l-Sa'adat Majd al-Din al Mubarak *b.* al-Athir extracted, therefore, the vocabulary of the traditions only out of the works of al-Harawi and al-isfahani, made considerable additions to them by his own study of the various important collections of the traditions, explained them on the lines of his two main sources, and compiled them in his book *al-Nihaya fi gharib al-hadith wa'l-athar*. In its introduction, he gave a short critical account of all the important previous works on the subject. It is on this book that the above remarks are mainly based.

Al-Mubarak *b.* al-Athir was an excellent scholar. He combined the wide knowledge of Arabic literature and linguistics with that of the *Qur'an*, the traditions and Islamic law. He was well-versed in the biographies and the character of the Traditionists. He possessed critical knowledge of the genuinness and the defects of the traditions. He wrote books on all these subjects. These books were well-known in al-Mausil and other places.

Al-Mubarak *b.* al-Athir was born at al-Jazira in 544/1149. He studied the various branches of Arabic literature with the reputed masters of them at the various centres of learning and settled down in 565 A.H. at Mausil where, at first, he delivered lectures on Islamic subjects, and afterwards was appointed to responsible posts at al-Jazira and at Mausil by the Zanji Chiefs and Sultans. During the reign of Nur al-Din Arsalan Shah I, he rose to an important position in the Zanji-Sultanate. The sultan frequently visited him at his residence and consulted him about important affairs of the state. He offered him several times the post of the minister of the state. But he always refused it in spite of protests by his father and brother. Indeed, once he was actually appointed a minister. But when he came to know of it, he wept bitterly. The Sultan having come to know of his grief, went to his residence, excused him from the post and consoled him. About the end of his life he became invalid and was unable to move about. It was during this period that he composed most of his books. He endowed his house and all his properties for the use of the mystics. He died in 606/1210.

He was a versatile writer. He wrote several books not only on Islamic subjects but also on arithmetic. His most important books are *Jami' al-usul li ahadith al-rasul and al-Nihaya fi gharib al-Hadith wa'l-athar.*

In the *Jami' al-usul,* which is in ten volumes, he collected the traditions contained in the six canonical works, in the alphabetical order of their subject mater, explained the rare expression found in them gave critical accounts of their transmitters and pointed out all that was necessary in connexion with the particular traditions. Yaqut has remarked that "he was absolutely certain that on *Hadith* no book like it was ever written nor shall it be ever written".

In *al-Nihaya,* which is in four volumes, he arranged about four thousand and fifty rare expressions found in the traditions, in alphabetical order of the first, second and third radica Is, as was done by al-Harawi and al-Isfahani in their works. He put the letter of increase under the letter to which they are added, as it has been explained by him at the end of the introduction to the book.

Al-Nihaya is the most important, most useful and most popular vocabulary of the traditions. It was versified by *b.* Bardis (720-786/ 1320-1383). Al-Suyuti prepared a synopsis of it, in which he also added what was missed by al-Mubarak *b.* al-Athir. Mahmud *b.* Abu Bakr Muhammad al-Urmawi (d. 723/1323) also wrote a supplement to it. Ibn Manzur, who has criticized it in the introduction to his *Lisan al-'arab*, has also admired it, saying that its author illustrated excellently the rare expressions contained in the *Qur'an* and *Hadith* and surpassed all the limits in this respect. J.A. Haywood remarks: "All in all, al*Nihaya* is a most efficient book within its limited scope."

Simultaneously with the works mentioned above, as well as after them, were composed a large number of other books on the *gharib al-Hadith*. But the works mentioned above form the landmarks in the history of its development. It is on the one or the other of them that the general plan as well as a large part of the contents of the later works on the *gharib al-Hadith* are based. They influenced the Arabic lexicographical works in general, in their plans as well as in the arrangement of their contents. The arrangement of the roots of the words according to their subject matters followed by Ibn Sida in his *al-Mukhassas* at a much later date was first introduced in the vocabulary of the traditions. Similarly, the alphabetical arrangement of the roots of words was first introduced by Abu Bakr Muhammad *b.* 'Umar (d. 330/941) in his *gharib al-Qur'an* and was followed by Ahmad *b.* Muhammad al-Harawi in his vocabulary of the *Qur'an* and the *Hadith* and thoroughly utilized by al-Raghib al-Isfahani (d. 501/1108) in his vocabulary of the *Qur'an* before being consistently taken over by the Arabic lexicographers. "It is perhaps significant that almost all dictionaries so arranged were restricted to religious vocabularies. The system did not, then, affect the mainstream of Arabic lexicography, says Haywood. Of course, the alphabetical method was used by some vocabulary writers as well as lexicographers, like Ibn Duraid (d. 321/934), before al-Harawi and al-Isfahani also. But they used it only partially. The earliest lexicography in which alphabetical order was used in its entirety in *Asas al-balagha* of al-Zamakhshari (*b.* 538/1144).

Arabic linguistics and lexicography, as has been already remarked, originated and developed in connexion with the Islamic religion and its original sources. All the important philologists have emphasized the religious importance of the subject. Ibn Manzur has remarked that round the lexicography revolve the commandments of the *Qur'an* and *Hadith*. al-Suyuti has said that lexicography is a part of religion. He has applied in *al-Mazhir* the whole method and technique of the tradition to lexicography.

The Arabs, however, gave serious consideration to the application of the alphabetical method to the lexicographies and vocabularies in the early period of Islamic culture. Khalil *b.* Ahmad (*d.* 175/791) discussed the importance of the alphabetical method in the introduction to his *Kitab al-'ain*. But he changed the order of the Arabic alphabets on account of philological considerations. After him, Abu Bakr Muhammad *b.* al-hasan *b.* Duraid discussed the matter further. He confessed the greatness of khalil as a lexicographer, but he discarded his theory, introduced certain other changes in the order of the alphabets and compiled his *al-Jamhara,* mainly on the basis of the alphabetical order of the radical letters in the words. Al-Zamakhshari also composed his *Asas al-balagha* entirely on the basis of the commonly accepted order of the radical letters.

Among the compilers of the vocabularies, Abu Bakr Muhammad *b.* Udhyr (*d.* 330/941), Abu 'Ubaid Ahmad *b.* Muhammad of Herat, Abu Musa Muhammad *b.* Abu Bakr of Isfahan and Majd al-Din Mubarak *b.* al-Athir used alphabetical method in their works. In fact, the alphabetical methods had been in use among the Arabic writers since the 9th century. Imam Bukhari (*d.* 256/873) used it in a part of his *Sahih* and in his *Kitab al-du'afa' al-saghir.* (*d.* 303/915) used it in his *Kitab al-du'afa' wa'l-matrukin* and after them a large number of biographers used it in their works.

It is not correct to say that the European scholars began to use the alphabetical method long after the Arabs, for it has been shown that in the *Corpus glossary* which is believed to have been written about 725 A.D. and has over 2,000 entries, alphabetical order has been observed upto two initial letters. And in a glossary of the 10th century (British Museum 3376) the alphabetical arrangement has been carried as far as the third letter. It cannot be said with certainty whether the Arabs or the Europeans were the first to use the alphabetical arrangement in their vocabularies and lexicographical works. But there is no doubt that Haywood has rightly remarked that "the truth is that in lexicography—as in may other fields—the Arabs occupy a central position both in time and space, between the Ancient Word and the Modern, between the East and the West."

The influence of Arabic linguistics and lexicography on Hebrew and Syriac linguistic and lexicography cannot, however, be doubted. The earliest Hebrew lexicographer, Sadiya *b.* Yusuf (892-942 A.D.), who was the founder of the scientific activities in Judaism, wrote in the introduction to his dictionary that the works of the Arabic authors served him as models for his book. "It is significant," says Haywood, "that the terminology of Hebrew grammar—even to the vowed names—is to a great extent borrowed for Arabic." In Syriac grammar and lexicography also there are unmistakable signs of indebtedness to Arabic grammars and lexicography.

REFERENCES

1. John A Haywood, Arabic lexicography, p. 6, London, 1960.
2. Brockelmann, Geschichte der arabischen litteratur, vol. I, p. 119.
3. Al-Tirmidhi, Sunan, ed, Ahmad Muhammad Shakir, Cairo, 1938.

Revised and edited; originally published in Studies in Islam, October 1968.

8

Origins and Development of the Hadith Literature

M Z SIDDIQI

(Abstract: Discusses the nature of the Hadith, roots of ijma, and the development of the exegesis of Hadith. Shows a positive picture of the methodology of religious discipline in the earliest period of Islamic history, which proved decisive for the subsequent religious development of Islam, with a brief critical review of the treatment of the subject of Hadith by the leaders of modern Western scholarship in the field, the nature of the Prophet's authority, and the process of the development of the Hadith related literature).

Introduction

So long as the Prophet was alive, he provided the sole religious and political guide for Muslims both through the Qur'anic revelation and by his words and behaviour. With his death the Qur'an remained, but his religiously authoritative personal guidance was cut off. The first four Caliphs met the ever-arising new situations by applying to these their judgments in the light of the Qur'an and what the Prophet had taught them.

The next century (from about 50-150/670-767), which saw the rise of early theological sects, and the first stage of development of law was most remarkable for the growth a of phenomenon which may perhaps best be described as religious methodology in the absence of the living guidance of the Prophet and of the earliest generation of his Companions. The first manifestation of this phenomenon is known as the Hadith or the Apostolic Tradition, subsequently compiled in a series of works six of which, composed in the 3rd/9th century, came to be accepted as the authoritative second source of the content of Islam besides the Qur'an. Whereas the vast majority of Muslims still uphold the view that the Hadith genuinely represents the sayings and deeds of the Prophet, Western Islamists are generally sceptical; some indeed have recommended a wholesale rejection of the Hadith as an index not only of the Prophetic example but also of the religious attitudes and practices of the Companions. We shall subsequently note the existence of a small group of contemporary Muslims who also seek to reject the Hadith, but not on the grounds of any scholarly study of the development of the discipline.

Orientalists and the Hadith Literature

In his *Muhammedanische Studien,* until now the most fundamental work on the subject, I. Goldziher declares that it is hardly possible to sift, with any confidence, from the vast material of the Hadith, a portion that may genuinely be referred either to the Prophet or to the early generation of his Companions and that the Hadith is to be regarded rather as a record of the views and attitudes of early generations of Muslims than of the life and teaching of the Prophet or even of his Companions. Goldziher, however, maintained that the phenomenon of the Hadith goes back to the earliest times of Islam and even conceded the possibility of the existence of 'informal' Hadith records contemporaneous with the Prophet, although he voiced his scepticism about some of the alleged records *(sahifa)* of that period. But, his argument runs, since the corpus of the Hadith continued to swell in each succeeding generation, and since, in each generation, the material runs parallel to and reflects various and often contradictory doctrines of Muslim theological and legal schools, the final recorded products of the Hadith, which date from the 3rd/9th century must be regarded as being *on the whole* unreliable as a source for the Prophet's own teaching and conduct.

A concept the understanding of which is fundamentally

important for our understanding of the development of the Hadith and which, at least throughout medieval Islam, has been identified with the practical norms or the model behaviour contained in the Hadith, is the concept of the Sunna. Sunna literally means the 'trodden path' and was used by the pre-Islamic Arabs to denote the model behaviour established by the forefathers of a tribe. The concept in this context has therefore two constituents, (a) an (alleged) historical fact of conduct and (b) its normativeness for the succeeding generations. In the Qur'an the word 'Sunna' is applied in the same sense where the opponents of Islam are rebukingly referred to as upholders of the exemplary behaviour of their forefathers as against the new teaching. The Qur'an also speaks of the Sunna of God, i.e. the behaviour of God with reference to the pattern or fate of societies—a behaviour which is unalterable. Here the same two constituents are to be found, i.e. past conduct (in this case of one Being only) which ought to (here 'shall') be operative in the future.

Goldziher holds that, with the advent of Islam, the content of the concept Sunna changed for Muslims into the model behaviour of the prophet, i.e. the practical norms that flow from his reported actions and sayings. This is in line with medieval Muslim theory itself. For Goldziher, therefore, as for medieval Muslim theory, the Hadith and the Sunna (in its Islamic, as opposed to the pre-Islamic usage) are not only coeval but also consubstantial (i.e. they are not two separate things but one). The difference between the two is that whereas a Hadith as such is a mere report and something theoretical, the Sunna is the very same report when it acquire a normative quality and becomes a practical principle for the Muslim. But Goldziher notices at the same time that in early Muslim literature there is evidence of a difference between the two, such that they can sometimes even mutually clash and are admitted to do so. Hence Goldziher also defines the Sunna as the *actual (as opposed to the normative)* living practice of the early Muslim Community.

But this raises a grave issue of which Goldziher does not show a full awareness. How could the Sunna be both normative and actual when the normative and the actual conflict? Or, how could the Hadith and the Sunna conflict if they are coeval and consubstantial although one Hadith may contradict another or, one Sunna another Sunna? No systematic attempt has been made since Goldziher to explore the various possible methods of resolving so fundamental an issue for an understanding of the development of Islam in this early period. Indeed, even the issue has not been clearly formulated by subsequent specialized scholarship and much ingenuity has been directed to discrediting the totality of the Hadith corpus as it finally took shape in the 3rd/9th century. We shall presently essay a plausible picture of this obscure period for which there are very scanty records and hardly any direct source.

After Goldziher a series of scholars developed one of the two lines of thought put in juxtaposition by him, but since the issue was not clearly kept in mind, both sides of the contradiction noted above suffered violence. D.S. Margoliouth, in his *Early Development of islam,* maintained (1) that the Prophet had left no precepts or religious decisions i.e. had left no Sunna or Hadith outside the Qur'an; (2) that the Sunna as practised by the early Muslim Community after Muhammad was not at all the Sunna of the Prophet but was the pre-Islamic Arabian usage as it stood modified through the Qur'an; and (3) that later generations, in the 2nd/8th century, in order to give authority and normativity to this usage, developed the concept of the Sunna of the Prophet and forged the mechanism of the Hadith to realize this concept. H. Lammens, in his *Islam: Beliefs and Institutions,* expresses the same view and declares tersely that the practice (Sunna) must have preceded its formulation in the Hadith.

Neither of these two writers asks, or decides the question whether this early Sunna of the Islamic Community was regarded as Sunna because of its status as pre-Islamic Arabian usage or because the Qur'an, after introducing modifications in to it, approved the rest tacitly. For, if the latter be the case, it, in religious theory (and it is the theory that is here in question), cuts the connection between the pre-Islamic usage and the Islamic Sunna. Further, there are two objections to this account of the Sunna, one logical, the other historical The logical objection is that, as we have seen, the notion of normativeness is an integral part of the concept of the Sunna and, indeed, these authors define the Sunna as 'the normative practice' of the early Muslim Community. We see here that the two juxtaposed but inconsistent descriptions of the Sunna given by Goldziher, i.e. the 'normative conduct' on the one hand and 'actual, living practice' on the other, have been blended in a self-contradictory whole. Now, if the actual practice of the Community was the Sunna i.e., the normative practice, what sense does it make to say that the normative quality was sought to be conferred on the actual practice by *making* it the Sunna of the Prophet? The historical objection, which shall be elaborated presently, is against the thesis put forward explicitly and at some length by Margoliouth and assumed by Professor J. Schacht, whose view we shall discuss next, that there was hardly any extra-Qur'anic legacy of the Prophet.

Professor J. Schacht has been led to assess the general character of the Hadith more systematically through his scholarly studies in Muslim law and the development of legal theory in Islam. But his views on the character of traditions in general are essentially the same as those on legal traditions. We are not concerned in this chapter with the development of law in Islam but only with the findings of Schacht on the character of the Hadith, which occupy the author in a major part of his *Origins of Muhammadan Jurisprudence.* Schacht claims that his enquiry fundamentally confirms what his predecessors, Goldziher and Margo-liouth, had concluded concerning the concepts Hadith and Sunna in the first century and a half of the Islamic era, and that he goes beyond them only in finding that when for the first time the Traditions began to find currency they were referred not to the Prophet but, in the first instance, to the 'Successors' (i.e., the generation after the Companions), then, in the next stage, to the Companions and finally, after a time, to the Prophet himself. His views are fairly summarized in the following quotation:

> One of the main conclusions to be drawn from Part I of this book is that, generally speaking, the 'living tradition' of the ancient schools of law, based to a great extent on individual reasoning, came first, that in the second stage it was put under the aegis of Companions (i.e. after the Successors more or less), that traditions from the Prophet himself, put in to circulation by traditionists towards the middle of the second century AH, disturbed and influenced this living tradition, and that only Shafi'i (150-204 A.H.) secured to the traditions from the prophet supreme authority.

Schacht in fact follows and seeks to complement the views of Margo-liouth and Lammens and does not seem to realize that, as we have endeavoured to make clear above, there is a fundamental difference between Goldziher on the one hand and these two authors on the other: the former maintains that essentially the Traditions and the Sunna (in Islamic time) were of common origin and consubstantial whereas, according to the latter, the Sunna or the practice (of the Muslim Community, based on pre-Islamic usage) was temporally anterior to the Traditions by nearly a century. Schacht has also taken over from these authors the expression 'Normative practice of the Community' to characterize the Sunna or living usage, and we have seen in connection with our criticism of Margoliouth and Lammens the logical contradiction that this concept contains.

Schacht's argument about the character of the Hadith is in two parts. First, on the basis of evidence he finds in the works of Muhammad ibn Idris at-Shafi 'i (150-204/767-819), he concludes that Traditions from the Prophet did not exist at all until about the middle of the 2nd/8th century; that the usage or the Sunna until that time was regarded not as the Sunna of the Prophet but as the Sunna of the Community (although the Sunna in Medina, for example, differed from that in Iraq), for it was mainly the product of the free reasoning of individual lawyers; and, finally, that the natural resistance of the lawyers to the Traditions form the Prophet was broken by the efforts of al-Shafi'i who for the first time, systematically introduced into the legal theory of Islam the concept of the Sunna of the Prophet. Secondly, by a comparison of some earlier and later versions of Traditions, he finds that either in the succeeding period there exist Traditions which did not exist in the preceding period and hence that these are forged, or that the succeeding versions are fuller than the earlier ones and that therefore the later ones had been expanded by forgeries. As regards the first part of the argument, which constitutes a more detailed and scholarly corroboration of Margoliouth's hypotheses (which for the first time used al-Shafi'i), we shall, in constructing our own thesis, endeavour to show that it gives too simple an account of the situation and instead of illuminating the early development of Islam makes it more obscure by unnecessarily creating insoluble problems for the religious history of Islam.

The second part where Professor Schacht is the first scholar to have undertaken an extensive and systematic comparison of legal traditions in their historical sequence, is unassailably scientific and sound in method and one only wishes that it were practised thoroughly in all fields of the Hadith. But it is equally important that the method be used carefully and that we must be quite clear as to what precisely it can accomplish, Prove or disprove. Thus Professor Schacht *(Origins,*p. 141) contends that no Traditions of a dogmatic nature existed in the time of Hasan al-Basri's compositions of a dogmatic treatise which will be discussed later in this chapter. This he seeks to prove by the fact that Hasan does not mention any Traditions. Now, as we shall see later, Hasan explicitly speaks of the Sunna of the Prophet in this connection. But he says expressly that there is no *actual transmission (riwaya)* from the Prophet or his Companions *about the question under discussion,* viz., the problem of the freedom of the human will and action *vis-a-vis* theistic determinism, and that he himself (and probably others who had similar views) has *originated* discussions concerning the thesis of human freedom. The Sunna here simply means that neither the Prophet nor the Companions *behaved* in a way that could be compatible with the doctrine of divine determinism which, Hasan also tells us, 'is a new invention of the people'. In this connection, therefore, the question of an explicit verbal Hadith does not arise although the term Sunna has a vilid meaning as Hasan has employed it. what this proves is that, *on this problem* what later Tradition attributes to the Prophet does not verbally belong to the Prophet and must be considered a later formulation, although it will still be perfectly legitimate to say that the anti-deterministic Hadith represents the Sunna of the Prophet and of the early Companions. But to say that there was no dogmatic Hadith *of any kind* is quite a different proposition. How can we assume that there was *no* tradition, e.g. about the importance of the Unity of God and about a hundred other matters?

Other cases of such historical comparative study may be cited but we have given only one example to illustrate to point at issue. Another fundamentally inalienable difficulty that besets the historical critic in this field is to assume the truth of certain statements and on their strength to try to judge others. This difficulty becomes accentuated beyond all proportion both in the case of a naive and credulous historian and in that of an excessively sceptical mind. An inevitable subjectivity follows which may lead to a contrary conclusion. A person with a sympathetic understanding may challenge both the credulous and the aggressive sceptic by his conclusions. Let us illustrate this with an example. There is a story that the Umayyad Ibrahim ibn al-Walid came once to the famous Traditionist Ibn Shihab al-Zuhri with a book and asked the latter that he transmit as Hadith on his authority the statements contained in this work. All-Zuhri (d. 124/742) thereupon, without any scruple, said to Ibrahim: 'But who else (besides me) could have related to you these Tradtions?' The image of al-Zuhri in the Muslim Tradition is that of a very pious man and a reliable Traditionist. But unlike most other pious men of the day, he had good relations with the Umayyad rulers. Can this story be true? Goldziher accepts it as true and regards it as one of his major proofs to show that the Umayyads influenced the Tradition in their own interest. Goldziher also admits that al-Zuhri was a pious man but explains that al-Zuhri did not collaborate with the Umayyads in the forgery of Hadith from any impious motive but for reasons of the stability of the state and that although 'sometimes he did have qualms about this he could not gainsay the official circles' pressure indefinitely' *(Muhammedanische Studies,* II, p.38).

That opposing political parties tried to influence public opinion through the medium of the Hadith and used the names of great authorities of Tradition is a fact no one conversant with the early history of Islam may deny. That al-Zuhri may have even given his support to such official views, out of 'consideration for the State', as he might have considered in keeping with the spirit of Islam, may well also be admitted. The piety of al-Zuhri and his reliable knowledge of the Hadith is not an image built up over the years, but a man of the stature of Malik ibn Anas (b. between 90-97/709-15, d. 179/795) quotes Traditions directly from him. Under these circumstances one is more tempted to believe that the above story about his unscrupulous circulation of the Umayyad Hadith is a legend put out under 'Abbasid rule to blacken the Umayyads. Or, what is perhaps even more likely, that certain pupils of al-Zuhri (the story actually goes back to a pupil of al-Zuhri) put this anecdote in to circulation in order to enhance the prestige of al-Zuhri as the pan-Traditionist without whose authority no Hadith was regarded as valid in his time.

On similar considerations we must use with some caution and reserve the fundamentally sound principle that an earlier report must by true or at least truer than a slightly later version of it, thus condemning the relative fullness of the later versions as being necessarily forged additions. Our reserve about the validity of this principle should apply more especially to the very early period when the Hadith was being 'gathered' and put together. It is perfectly possible and indeed logical that in this earlier period the first reports of a given Hadith had not been able to mention all the relevant facts and details and that these were supplied by wider contacts with the Companions and their immediate followers. On the whole, a healthy caution rather than out -right scepticism is likely to lead to reliable and constructive results.

The Nature of Prophet's Authority

The Qur'an incessantly couples Muhammad with Allah when speaking of authority, and in a large number of verses the Faithful are commanded to obey Him and the Prophet. Muslims, *at least* since the turn of the Ist/7th century, and majority of orientalists, take this to mean that this authority of Muhammad refers to the verbal and preformative behaviour of the Prophet outside the Qur'an. In fact, for Muslims, the Qur'anic authority is something above the authority of the Prophet himself, who, standing under its commands and judgments, is himself only its transmitter. There is also little doubt that the Prophet himself carefully disitinguished between Qur'anic pronouncements and his own quotidian speech and action, even though the Qur'an itself appeared in a historical context and considerable part of it is related to specific events.

Margoliouth, however, has contended that wherever the Prophet has been coupled with Allah in the Qur'an, this refers only to the context of the Qur'an itself: that the authority of God and the authority of Muhammad, the human instrument of divine revelation, are both indistinguishable and one and the same, and have only an intra-Qur'anic reference. From this it follows that Muhammad had no extra-Qur'anic Sunna which *could* have been recorded in any 'tradition'. This view seems untenable on the basis of the Qur'an itself. While in many casesd, where the Qur'an speaks of the authority of God and the Prophet, this may be interpreted in general terms as referring to the injunctions of the Qur'an itself, there are cases where this is obviously not so. There is, for example, the case where the Qur'an refers to a dispute (which, the commentators say, arose over a decision of the Prophet with regard to the distribution of booty after a certain expedition) and says, 'And what the Prophet giveth unto you take it, and what he prohibiteth desist from it'. In another verse the Qur'an says, 'Nay, by thy Lord, they shall not have faith, until they bring their disputes under thy judgment and then feel no misgiving in their souls about thy judgment but submit (to it) completely. This warning also refers to a specific case of an internal dispute in the Community, and there are other similar instances in the Qur'an. The point here is that these and other specific cases have been dealt with in the Qur'an only because certain acute troubles arose in the Community threatening above all the authority of the Prophet as the judge. If, as in normal cases, the Prophet's authority had been accepted willingly by all people without bickerings in certain quarters, the Qur'an would not have intervened. It follows necessarily from this that the Prophet had, and, indeed, normally exercised, an unchallenged authority outside the Qur'an in giving judgments and moral and legal precepts. The Qur'an, indeed, also speaks of the 'exemplary conduct of the Prophet of God'. There was, Therefore, an exemplary conduct, i.e., a Sunna of the Prophet, besides the Qur'anic revelation. Obviously, the basis for Margoliouth's thinking that the only moral and legal precepts and precedents left by the Prophet were those recorded in the Qur'an is the conversation recorded by al-Shafi'i in his works between himself and certain Mu'tazilite ('neutralist') adversaries of the Hadith who claimed to accept only the Qur'an as authoritative. But we shall show in the next section the true character of this controversy and bring out the fact that the *Ahl al-Kalam* ('rationalists') or the Mu'tazila in fact accepted much more than the Qur'an.

But if our reasoning has been at all correct, another conclusion follows from this argument to make the situation intelligible. This is that the Prophetic Sunna, outside the fundamental matters touching the religious and the social and moral life of the Community, could not have been very large, let alone being of such titanic inclusiveness of all the details of daily life as medieval law and Hadith literature make out to be the case. The evidence as a whole strongly suggests that the situations where the Prophet was called upon to decide or pronounce authoritatively, or where he felt compelled to do do, were *ad hoc* situations. Normally, the Muslims carried on the business and social transactions of daily life by settling their minor differences among themselves. This view is also in accord with the general character of Muhammad as Prophet-statesman: he was not primarily a lawyer but a religious and political reformer. Indeed, nobody who reads the Qur'an itself carefully can fail to notice the gradual character of Islamic reform. Wine-drinking, for example, was allowed for a period of many years after the opening of the Prophet's mission. Then came measures introducing restraint in drinking, and finally a ban on all consumption of alcohol. Further, on most, perhaps all, measures of important political and legal action and reform, the Prophet consulted informally with his senior Companions and sometimes consulted the Community publicly. The Qur'an bears unequivocal testimony to this. Sometimes the advice that was forthcoming conflicted, and indeed at points it conflicted so much that (since it had the character of group-functions) it culminated in challenging the Prophet himself. In the Prophetic Sunna indeed democracy and religious authority were balanced with a *finesse* that defies description.

But as to the religious and religiously binding character of the out-come of the process of the arrival by the Prophet at a decision, the Qur'an repelled every shadow of doubt for the potential dissident. Further, the life and character of the Prophet himself were permeated with a religious spirit. Even if we may *theoretically* suspect each individual statement in the medieval Muslim records about him, the nature of the case forbids us concluding otherwise than that to his Companions his life was a religious paradigm and as such normative. Any suggestion that this was not the case until about nine or even fifteen decades later, when formal Hadith was developed as a neat and perfected medium of transmitting information about the Prophet, must be rejected as a shallow and irrational 'scientific' myth of contemporary historiography. But the myth itself arises from and singles out a crucial enigma in the situation. If the Prophet's speech and conduct were regarded as religiously normative for the muslims, it is extraordinary that there should be no contemporary records of these Sunnas preserved as the Qur'an has been recorded and preserved, except for certain documents relating to pacts, etc. Besides, despite agreement on general and fundamental points of law, we find that the practice in detail differed in the early schools on most points and each regional school, for example, the Medinese and the Iraqi, defended its practice by calling it 'Sunna'. If the ultimate reference of the Sunna is the Prophet's example then, so the argument runs differing Sunnas cannot be called '*the* Sunna' and must, therefore be regarded as the practice of the local Muslim communities. As for the prophet, it follows either that he had left hardly any precedents relating to such points in his conduct, or that if he had, they were not regarded as Sunna or as binding.

As for the 'practice' of the Muslims in the early post-Prophetic period and the concepts with which they worked out this practice, we shall analyse these more closely in the next section of this chapter. As regards the two alternatives offered theoretically about the Prophet which have been partly tacitly, partly expressly accepted by modern writers on the Hadith and the Sunna, out investigation so far has led us to reject them both. This must be done in order to bring the requisite reasonableness into the situation. To solve the enigma, however, two important points must be made. First, there must have been the fear that if the extra-Qur'anic speech of the Prophet were formally recorded, it could easily have been confused with the text of the Qur'an which was also delivered by the Prophet. Confusion could have worked in both directions. Either the Qur'an, in the course of time, might pass as the word of the Prophet and not as the Word of God, in whole or in appreciable part; or, the word of the Prophet might have passed as the Word of God. Historical evidence suggests that some confusion in certain quarters did nevertheless take place. There is, for example, the report that the famous Companion of the Prophet, 'Abd Allah ibn mas'ud (d. circa 32/653) did not regard the first and the last two Suras of the Qur'an as part of it. Ibn Qutayba (d. 276/889) explains that since the Prophet often recited the last two Suras over his grandsons as prayers and that Ibn Mas'ud frequently saw him do this, he concluded that these were not part of the Qur'anic text. We have already mentioned that the Prophet himself distinguished between his own utterance and that of the Qur'an and that it was only at special critical points that his decisions had to be supported by the Qur'an itself.

Secondly, we have already referred to the *ad hoc* character of the Prophetic decisions and precepts. As for the precepts, they were usually occasioned by a particular situation and were informally proclaimed in the presence of such Companions as happened to be there. The most formal pronouncements were made in a sermon *(khutba)*but these also usually grew out of immediate phenomena and situations, religious or political. The same holds true of decisions legal or otherwise. Each case was decided as it presented itself, taking into account both general and specific factors. Now, the informal and *ad hoc* nature of these procedures naturally argued for not being formally recorded. It also meant that similar but always somewhat different cases were decided in a similar but at the same time somewhat different manner, and there is little doubt that the Prophet used his discretion, even though on major issues he consulted his senior Companions. Let us illustrate this variation from the case of the religious rite of prayer, the most fundamental of all obligatory religious duties. Among other minor details, controversies raged in the early Muslim legal schools about certain physical postures, for instance, the position of the hands — are these to be left loose in the standing posture or are they to be folded? If folded, whether on the breast or below the breast? Similarly, controversies existed about variations in the exact times of prayers. Those who reject the Sunna-tradition from the Prophet will have to say that this reflects variations in a generation after the Prophet. But this is surely ridiculous - for the Prophet regularly offered prayers in public for a good many years, and the only explanation that would make sense is that he used slightly different postures at different times and that those who happened to observe a particular posture regarded it as normative. Just as in the ritual sphere, so variations in the field of positive legal decisions of the Prophet probably explain in part the differences in the legal schools of Islam, although here, in view of the ever-increasing complexity of the legal situation in a rapidly expanding empire, the individual interpretations of legists played a fundamental role.

Hadith and Sunna, or the Verbal and Practical Tradition

Hadith (which literally means a story, a narration, a report) as we know it, being a unit of that discipline which bears the same name, is a narrative, usually very short, purporting to give information about what the Prophet said, did, or approved or disapproved or, of similar information about his Companions, especially the senior Companions and more especially the first four Caliphs. Each Hadith falls into two parts, the text (*matn*) of the Hadith itself and the transmissional chain (*isnad*), giving the names of the narrators, which supports the text. Both the classical and the modern historians agree that at first Hadith existed without the supporting *isnad* which probably appeared at the turn of the Ist/7th century. This is also roughly the date when the wholesale appearance of the Hadith as a formalized written discipline begins. There is, however, strong direct and indirect evidence that before becoming a formal *discipline* in the 2nd/8th century, the phenomenon had existed at least since about 60-80/680-700.

The first point to be made in this connection is that a highly developed system with two parts, the text and the *isnad,* could not have appeared on the scene all of a sudden without a period of growth in which it had not only developed technically but expanded materially as well. An informal tradition is, indeed, naturally to be postulated during the lifetime of the Prophet himself who was the pivot of the Muslim Community. But after the Prophet's death, the Hadith passed from a purely informal condition into a semi-formal state. Whereas during the lifetime of the Prophet people talked about what he said or did as a matter of course, after his death this talk became a deliberate and conscious phenomenon since a new generation was growing up for whom it was natural to enquire about the Prophet's conduct. But it must be remembered that the natural religious orientation of a Hadith—a verbal transmission— was towards a corresponding Sunna, a religious norm of practice. This practical orientation, rather than primarily intellectual curiosity, especially in a community that was expanding and growing more complex at an astonishing and unprecedented speed with the assimilation of new elements, argued for the fact that the 'transmission' be less of a verbal nature and more of the character of a 'silent' exemplification *in actu.* This non-verbal transmission, the 'silent' or 'living' tradition, was called the 'Sunna.'

We must, therefore, distinguish between the two, but closely allied, meanings of the word Sunna. We said about that to the later generations the Sunna meant (as it originally did mean) the conduct of the Prophet, from whom it acquired its normativeness. But to the extent that the tradition continued to be largely 'silent' and non-verbal, this word was applied to the actual content of the behaviour of each succeeding generation in so far as that behaviour claimed to exemplify the Prophetic pattern. It is clear that the second usage is a derivative from the former and the two are related *secundum prius et posterius.* 'Sunna' literally means 'a trodden path' and just like a path, each part of it is a Sunna whether it be near the starting-point or remote from it. In regard to content, as we shall see, it was not so much like a path as like a river-bed which continuously assimilates new elements; but the *intention* of the term Sunna was always directed towards the Apostolic model. It is this very confusion which has led several modern writers to assert that until well into the 2nd/8th century, the Sunna meant *not* the practice of the Prophet but that of the local Muslim communities in Medina and Iraq.

But the tradition was not entirely 'silent' and non-verbal. This that could not have been the case is in the first place *a priori* deducible from the *fact* of the living tradition itself. Men do not merely act and follow (and innovate) but also talk and report. There was, therefore, at least an informal verbal tradition. But, further, this informal tradition seems to have become a deliberate activity in the hands of the younger generation of the Companions. A letter written by the Umayyad Caliph 'Abd al-Malik (65-8/684-8) to Hasan al-Basri (21-100/642-728) and the latter's answer shed important light on the subject when analysed carefully. This letter from the Caliph, who disapproved of Hasan's views in favour of human freedom and responsibility, states :

> The Commander of the Faithful has been informed of your views on human freedom (*qadar*) such as he never heard before from anyone else from among the bygone generation: the Commander of the Faithful does not know of anyone whom he has met from among the Companions holding any view with regard to this such as he has been told about you...So write to him about it — whether it is a *verbal transmission (riwaya)* from anyone of the Companions of the Prophet of God, or your own considered opinion (*ra'y*) or anything that may be confirmed by the Qur'an...

The essential point here is that the Caliph demands, among alternative forms of evidence, a *verbal transmission* from any one of the Companions. The Caliph could have demanded this only if he thought that verbal transmissions existed and were authoritative. In his reply, Hasan al-Basri refers to the 'Sunna of the Prophet of God', but is unable to quote any verbal transmission from the Prophet or his Companions on *this specific point* (although he goes on to quote the Qur'an profusely). But this is not because there was no verbal transmission or Hadith of any kind—as Professor Schacht holds - but because Hasan al-Basri goes on to admit that the debate about the human freedom of choice versus the theistic determinism is new :

> There was none among our (Muslim) predecessors who rejected this (viz., that human beings are free to choose); nor did anybody dispute with regard to this since they were (tacitly) agreed and unanimous about it. *We have introduced* this theological discourse (*kalam*) on the point since (some) people have *innovated* a rejection of it....

In an enclosed note, the officer who forwarded Hasan al-Basri's letter to the Caliph says, 'None remains among those who learned (*akhadha*) from the bygone generation of the Companions of the Prophet, more versed in knowledge about God...than Hasan'. The word used for 'learning' in this quotation has remained a technical term for formal study with a master.

The conclusions we have arrived at so far are first that the Sunna and the Hadith were coeval and consubstantial in the earliest phase after Muhammad and that both were directed towards and drew their normativity from him. Secondly, we have also noticed that the concept Sunna, since it meant the 'silent' living tradition, came perforce to have the meaning of the living tradition in each succeeding generation. Therefore, although the Sunna as a concept referred to the behaviour of the Prophet, its *content,* nevertheless, was bound to change and derive largely from the *actual* practice of the early Community. But the actual practice of a living community must continuously be subject to modification through additions. In a rapidly expanding society such as the early Islamic one, new moral issues and legal situations, including the almost entirely new administrative system, constantly arose. These moral issues had to be answered and these legal situations resolved. As the legal situations and the consciousness of moral and religious issues became more and more complex, controversies arose on most points, and in the theological and moral sphere especially there were foreign influences. But the concept of an ideal Sunna was retained: whatever new material was thought out or assimilated, it was given as an interpretation of the principles of the Qur'an and the Sunna. The interpretation, as we shall see in the next chapter, was at first based on free and considered individual opinion which was replaced in the second century by the concept of systematic analogy (*qiyas*).

The term Sunna itself was at first probably not formulated as a conscious concept until differences arose over religious issues. The 'silent' living tradition implies that it was not *ab initio* described by any term, and that this description and formulation came only when different and indeed opposed interpretations were put forward. Then one was led to oppose the concept Sunna to innovation (*bid'a*). The occasions of religious controversy had most probably political implications. This is suggested by the controversies between the Shi'a (the followers of 'Ali), the Kharijites and the Umayyads. The above account of Hasan al-Basri illustrates this: it clearly shows that the Sunna was being explicitly formulated not only in respect of its content but also in the concept of Sunna itself, after extreme predestinarian views were put forward. And the ethical controversy about human freedom and determinism had also definite political implications, since the anti-determinists would favour of the reform or displacement of the worldly-minded rule of the Umayyads.

From the fact of individual interpretations of what had been handed down from the Prophet, both through living tradition and through the meagre amount of verbal transmission (Hadith or *riwaya*), there followed a third meaning of the Sunna—that is to say, in relation to the content, because the *intention* of the concept still remained directed to the Prophet, besides the two noted above and again closely allied to these. This is that from a Hadith or a Sunna-report several points of practical norm were *deduced* by interpretation and all these points were called Sunnas because they were seen to be *implicit* in the Sunna. This process of interpretation undoubtedly began both tacitly and explicitly with the Companions themselves. For the generation after the Companions, all the sayings and deeds of the Companions also began to be regarded as Sunna since, it was argued, the Companions, especially when they agreed, but even when they disagreed, were in the most privileged position to know and interpret the Prophet's conduct. After the period of the Companions (and in some cases of the following generation of the 'Successors') the Sunna could not be deduced from actual practice but only from the expressly transmitted Hadith. But it is most significant and remarkable that deductions by interpretation from a Hadith in *any* period were called Sunnas. Thus Abu Da'ud (d. 275/888) after relating a Hadith remarks, 'There are five Sunnas in this Hadith', i.e. five points with the character of practical norms can be deduced from this Hadith.

The three categories of the content of the Sunna outlined above—the Sunna of the Prophet, the living tradition of the earliest generation, and the deductions from these — created a wealth of material, especially through individual interpretation of the law and the dogma, which although it was generally uniform in its essentials, except for certain extreme doctrines of the Kharijites and other sects, conflicted in its details on most points. This material was, in the next step, brought under the concepts of 'the agreed practice' (*'al-'amal*) and the 'consensus' (*ijma'*). These terms were used equivalently and the concept of the 'consensus' was destined, as we shall study more closely in the next chapter, to play the most fundamental part in the paraphernalia of Muslim methodology throughout the religious history of Islam. There is a certain affiliation between the concepts Sunna and *Ijma'* in this early period: just as the former was formulated to check innovations, the latter was formulated against arbitrary individual and sectarian opinions. But there is a conceptual difference as well: the Sunna is the Sunna of the Prophet in its primordial intention and thus innovation is that which contravenes the Prophetic model, while the *Ijma'* is the consensus either of the Community or of the doctors of religion and thus arbitrary opinion is that which contravenes the *communis opinio* of the Community. But since the *materials* of the Sunna, as distinguished from its conceptual intention, included, as we have seen, also the interpretation of the Prophetic model, *in fact* Sunna and *Ijma'* come close to one another, and so do their opposites.

Classical Opposition to the Hadith

We have seen above that verbal transmission (*riwaya*) concerning the Prophetic model of behaviour started early in Islam. The contemporary statement about Hasan al-Basri given above, that 'the most learned surviving person of those who learned from the bygone generation of the Companions of the Prophet', implies that this process of transmission had started earlier than Hasan's career as a student (he was born in 21/642). But as we have seen also, the work of interpretation of the Prophetic Sunna had also begun with the Companions themselves a fact upon which the nature of the case bestows intelligibility of the highest order. This is because the Companions were not 'students' of the Prophet, even though this impression is sometimes created by later Hadith literature, but his followers and disciples. A disciple does not only 'learn' and write from his master but tries to live, and so embody, the master's teaching. It was therefore inevitable that in the minds of the Companions the *actual* dicta and facta of the Prophet were often imperceptibly intertwined, and even more so in the minds of the succeeding generations, with their own behaviour. This fact must be borne in mind because it explains why it became difficult for the formal traditionist at the turn of the century and for subsequent generations to disentangle the strictly prophetic element from the alleged dicta and facta of the Companions. It also explains in part why the Hadith, when it first began to be codified by the traditionists, was referred to the Companions rather than to the Prophet. But only in part, because the major burden of this explanation must be borne by the fact that in this early phase there had not yet developed the technique of the transmissional chain (*isnad*) and thus a Hadith was referred to the immediate reporter in his reportative capacity or to the source of the actual transmission, although the Hadith itself claimed to go back to the Prophet himself. While in the pristine period, as we have seen, the Hadith and the Sunna were coeval and consubstantial, the inevitable expansion we have described of the *content* of the Sunna in the categories of the living tradition and individual interpretation complicated the situation and there emerged a disengagement of the Hadith from the Sunna. The concept of *Ijma'* or consensus was still nebulous and failed in practice to standardize or render normative the actual and conflicting living practice. In order, therefore, to bestow normativity on the actual views or practice, the traditionists launched a wholesale and mass campaign to standardize the living Sunna and to try to codify the practice that would conform to the Prophetic model and to reject the more extreme interpretations of both the dogma and the law. That is how the mass condification of the

Hadith as a discipline began towards the end of the Ist/beginning of the 8th century. This led to the introduction and subsequent perfection of the chains of transmitters. A typical chain of transmitters runs like this: *A* (the last narrator) says he heard it from *B* on the authority of *C* who said this on the authority of *D* that the Prophet of God said..., etc.

The mass introduction of the Hadith in its new formal phase represented a genuine and basic need for some kind of canonization of the earliest interpretative-assimilative experiences of the Community which had undoubtedly derived much of its basic teaching from the Prophet. The process of the living tradition could not go on indefinitely by itself because in the long run the religious ideological fabric of the Community would be endangered by chaos for want of a sufficiently authoritative point of reference. It was indeed against as already emergent extremism and arbitrary interpretation that the Hadith invaded the field on this massive scale. But there were dangers in this process of canonization too, against which warnings, sometimes also couched in extreme terms, came from some law schools and theological circles, warnings which were partly justified by the subsequent development and growth of the Hadith. These anxieties essentially consisted of drawing attention to two undesirable alternative developments that would ensue: first, by referring every theological, dogmatic or legal doctrine to the authority of the Prophet as was demanded by the logic of the Hadith phenomenon, the free and creative process of interpretation would almost come to an end. Or, second, if the creative process is to go on then a massive and incessant fabrication is necessary. In fact, both fears interacted. But the traditionists attempted to safeguard against both extremes by producing two principles, both of which are probably fictions generated by the Hadith itself. According to the first, the Prophet was reported to have said that whatever of good sayings there be, it can be assumed to have been said by him and can be accepted on his authority. According to the second principle, the Prophet was alleged to have pronounced: 'He who tells a deliberate lie about me should be prepared for his seat in Hell'. Up to about the middle of the 3rd/9th century theology and law continued to develop under the aegis of the Hadith and so did the selective activity of the 'genuine' Hadith from the 'weak' and the false. This, as we shall study further in the following chapters, was also the period of the formation and consolidation of the orthodoxy. When the climax of this formulative process was reached, the Hadith was finally codified and accepted and at the same time the activity of creative interpretation in any major sense came almost to an end.

The earliest extant record of the warnings against and opposition to the Hadith is contained in the works of the jurist al-Shafi'i (d. 204/819). These are highly instructive about the situation obtaining in the 2nd/8th century. The opposition varied from that against an individual Hadith to that against almost all Hadith. Al-Shafi'i was the archprotagonist of the acceptance of the Prophetic Hadith in the field of law on a mass scale and *as a principle of law,* while his opponents in the legal schools claimed that the basis of law shall be the Prophetic Sunna as it was living actually in the practical tradition. They did not deny the prophetic Hadith as such but claimed that the Prophetic teaching was to be found in the practice of the Community. By that time the concept of the *Ijma'* or consensus had emerged, and they argued that the agreed practice was more entitled to represent the legacy of the Prophet than an obscure Hadith which claimed to go back to the authority of the Prophet but had in fact no basis in the practice. Such Hadiths, they contended, if accepted would in fact open the door for wholesale fabrication of the Hadith in the name of the Prophet. Their argument ran as follows: 'The Companions of the Prophet generally and *as a whole* knew best and were the only and reliable bearers of the Prophetic tradition. The younger generations of the "Successors" saw the Companions in action and also learned from them, even if they could not have access to the Prophet himself, and therefore, were the best immediate source for the Prophetic teaching. Even if a few of the Companions did not know the Sunna of Prophet on certain points, they could come to know such Sunna from the general practice of the Companions and *so by the time of the next generation of the Prophetic Sunna can be taken to have been firmly established.* This is *Ijma'* or consensus and against this we cannot accept the testimony of one or two stray narrators of a Hadith that may now claim to go back to the Prophet'. This argument is clearly brought out in a conversation between al-Shafi'i and one of his opponents:

Al-Shafi'i: 'If a report reaches us from any of the Caliphs of the Prophet (i.e., the first four Caliphs) and another report reaches us from the Prophet himself contrary to the first, then surely we shall accept the report from the Prophet? For, everything has a final object of pursuit and such object in knowledge is the Book of God (the Qur'an) and the Sunna of the Prophet. Do you agree that the Sunna (of the Prophet) as long as it is with us allows nothing else to take its place?"

The opponent: 'Yes; and I have heard you say—of which I am also not ignorant - that sometimes an opinion is related from more than one of the Companions of the Prophet which is contrary to the Sunna of the Prophet. But if these Companions become aware of this Sunna, they accept it (and reject their own opinions) or if their Successors come to know of the same Sunna, they come back to it (so that by now the Sunna of the Prophet can be assumed to have become accepted)...In Medina there were about thirty thousand, if not more, of the Prophet's Companions, but you transmit perchance a single report not even from six of them but from one of them—or may be from two or three or four, wherein either they agree or disagree—and in most cases they do disagree. What becomes of the *Ijmd'* then?'

Especially cautious towards such solitary Hadiths was the attitude of the lawyers in Medina which claimed a unique position as the depository of the living Sunna. They did not reject the Hadith as such but only solitary Hadiths in certain cases. In such cases , they claimed to rely on the 'agreed practice' even though al-Shafi'i ceaselessly pointed out that their practice was in fact not agreed on all points. But in Medina too were many of the most eminent and prolific of the traditionists and al-Shafi'i accused his fellow jurists of lagging far behind these in relating traditions. Al-Shafi'i's success were, however, ensured by the nature of the controversy itself. Given the need for an anchoring point which would bestow normativity on legal practice and theological opinions, once the name of the Prophet was associated by the Hadith with these, there could hardly be two predictions about the issue of the controversy. Gradually but surely the whole of the living tradition was reflected in the Hadith, and the Hadith and the Sunna once more became completely consubstantial in content. Once the formalized Sunna of Medina was enshrined in the Hadith, most of which also arose out of Medina, the position of that city as the home of the Prophetic Sunna was established beyond question, although Iraq, with its practice interacting with that of Medina but retaining something of its own entity even in tradition, remained the second major region of the Sunna, and independent in law with its Hanafi interpretation.

The emergence of the Hadith as an all-engulfing discipline led some of the Mu'tazila, the rationalistic theologians who will be to take up a sceptical attitude to the Hadith *as a whole*. One should guard against the mistake of regarding the Mu'tazila as a second group of Hadith opponents *separate in kind* from the legists who have been spoken of in the last paragraph. This impression arises from the fact that the Mu'tazila, or rather some part of them, doubted the formal Hadith as a whole and the impression is strengthened by the fact that al-Shafi'i reported about them as a separate category from the normal legists. As a matter of fact, the Mu'tazila were not only theologians, which they were primarily, but also lawyers and jurists as is evident from al-Shafi'i's writings themselves. Their general doubt about the Hadith is rather elliptical and indirect and is fundamentally inspired by the fact that the anthropomorphisms of the Hadith put formidable impediments in the way of their rational understanding of the religion. In actual fact, there was a whole range of warners against the wholesale cultivation of the Hadith, with this wing of the Mu'tazila at the extreme end. The second point to be made in this connection is that *none* of the Mu'tazila in their arguments against the Hadith says that the Hadith is a new-fangled phenomenon appearing in the first half of the 2nd/8th century. Their basic argument was essentially the same as that of the other legal schools noted above, that the Hadith, since its essence is transmission by individuals, cannot be a sure avenue of our knowledge about the Prophetic teaching, unlike the Qur'an about whose transmission there is a universal unanimity among Muslims. Here is what they say to al-Shafi'i:

'You are an Arab and the Qur'an has been revealed in your language. You have preserved it in memory (i.e. verbally). God has deposited in it certain obligatory duties such that, if someone were to doubt about a single item (literally: letter) in it you would ask him to retract from his doubt. If he retracts, well and good, otherwise you would execute him...How then can you permit yourself or someone else to say (on the basis of the Hadith transmissions) with regard to the Qur'anic obligatory duties that these are sometimes general and sometimes specific and sometimes that a certain command therein is clear obligation and sometimes that a certain other command is only an indication (which is to be clearly worked out in the light of the Hadith and does not provide a clear direct obligation). If some person, under the influence of his own whims, were to carry this dissection of the Qur'an further (what would you say?).

'You have a solitary Hadith transmitted to one person from another and to him from another, or may be two Hadiths or three, until you reach the Prophet. But we find that you and other people who are like you (protagonists of the Hadith) do not acquit any one of the transmitters you have met and whom you regard as being foremost in truthfulness and reliability of memory...from (the possibility of) error, forgetfulness and making mistakes in the Hadith....We also find you saying that if someone were to say concerning a Hadith by which you make things lawful and unlawful... "the Prophet did not say such a thing; you either lie or are mistaken or those who have transmitted this to you"—in this case we have found that you do not ask such a person to retract (from his doubt, as you do in the case of one who doubts the Qur'an) and you accuse him of nothing more than saying something bad. Is it permissible that the injunctions of the Qur'an—which is apparently uniform throughout to whomsoever listens to it—be dissected on the basis of reports transmitted by people whose position we have described according to yourselves (i.e., who cannot be absolutely relied upon)?"

While most of the Mu'tazila were originally sceptical of the Hadith on the above grounds, they nevertheless accepted the Sunna and the consensus and indeed they interpreted the Qur'an in the light of both these principles, as is attested by al-Shafi'i. This occurred in the legal field. It may well be that their reluctance to accept the Hadith resulted primarily from theological motives which forbade them to accept anthropomorphisms. This is further corroborated by the fact that when they gradually accepted the Hadith as such they were content either to reject specific Hadiths or even to accept these but to interpret them in rationalizing terms. Ibn Qutayba's work entitled *Ta'wil Mukhtalif al-Hadith* (i.e. 'Intepretation of the apparently inconsistent Traditions') is specifically devoted to answering these *specific* charges of the Mu'tazila against inconsistencies and anthropomorphisms in the body of the Hadith.

Development of the 'Science of the Hadith'

By the middle of the 3rd/9th century the Hadith had taken definite form, had established almost all its detailed content, and had completely, won the field. So far as the content is concerned, it patently reflects the growing and conflicting mass of religious (including political) views and opinions of the Muslims in their first two centuries. In order to collect, sift and systematize this massive and amazing product, a number of eminent scholars began to travel throughout the length and breadth of the then Muslim world. This powerful movement is known as 'Seeking of the Hadith'. Eager seekers went from place to place learning from man to man. By the end of the 3rd/beginning of the 10th century several collections had been produced, six of which have since then been regarded as being especially authoritative and are known as 'The Six Genuine Ones'. Foremost among these is the *Sahih* (the 'Genuine') of Muhammad ibn Isma'il al-Bukhari (194-256/810-70) acclaimed later by Muslims as being next only to the Qur'an in authority. The *Sahih* of Muslim ibn al-Hajjaj (d. 261/875) comes next, close to that of al-Bukhari. The four remaining are the works of Abu Da'ud (d. 275/888), al-Tirmidhi (d. 279/892), al-Nasa'i (d. 303/916) and Ibn Maja (d. 273/886).

By this time also the criticism of the Hadith, such as Muslims have known it, was perfected into the 'Sciene of the Hadith'. This criticism is exclusively directed towards the *isnad* or the transmissional chain of the Hadith. A systematic and complex inquiry was undertaken into the biographies of the transmitters of the tradition and their bona fides and this is known as 'the Science of Justification and Impugnment'. An attempt was made to assess the good character and the reliability of the memory of transmitters. The transmitters were thus divided into different categories such as 'completely trustworthy', 'truthful', 'weak', 'mendacious' and 'unknown', etc., although there remained differences of opinion among scholars about several transmitters. Another classification was adopted concerning the continuity or otherwise of a chain of transmission and as to the stage of transmission at which the link is 'broken'. The third line concerned the *number* of simultaneous transmitters at each stage. On the basis of these investigations, the Hadiths were classified into various categories such as 'genuine', 'good', 'weak', 'not well-known', 'continuous', 'discontinuous', 'discontinuous at the source' (*marfu'*, i.e. where the connection with the Prophet is indirect), etc. The line of criticism intersect: e.g. a Hadith may be regarded as 'genuine' even though a link is missing. A Hadith which at every stage of transmission has found numerous narrators is called *mutawatir* or inductively so certain that doubt is almost *logically* excluded.

A very large proportion of the Hadiths was judged to be spurious and forged by classical Muslim scholars themselves and was excluded from the six canonical collections, and al-Bukhari and Muslim included in their works only those Hadiths which they judged to be 'genuine'. These men sifted out only a few thousand from hundreds of thousands of current Hadiths and some self-confessed forgers are reported to have been executed. Al-Bukhari especially, the ablest and most acute of Hadith critics, showed extraordinary scrupulousness in judging traditions. But it must be remembered that this historical criticism was not the only principle of selectivity used by canonical collectors. This very period in which the Hadith discipline reached its full fruition was also the period during which, from a massive interaction of different and indeed often opposed religious doctrines and views, an 'orthodoxy' was emerging and coming to the surface. The 'people of the Hadith' (*Ahl al-Hadith*) were actively involved in this great drama. They were indeed the vanguard of this orthodoxy, people who *crystallized* it in their works even though its *formulation* was to be achieved by men like al-Ash'ari (c. 300/913). There was indeed, as we have shown in the last section, a fierce battle between the rationalist *Ahl al-Kalam* and the traditionists from the very beginning, a battle in which the former relied, besides their rationalism, on the living tradition. By the middle of the 3rd/9th century the ground had slipped from beneath their feet because the living tradition had by that time been translated into the Hadith form. But they continued to attack individual Hadiths on the grounds of inconsistency and on the basis of reason. The extent of the intensity of this struggle may be gathered from an example. According to a Hadith, 'A'isha, the Prophet's wife, is reported to have said that just before his death a verse of the Qur'an was revealed ordering the stoning to death of adulterers. During the shock and the disturbance at the Prophet's death, so the report goes, the piece of paper containing this verse was devoured by a stray goat. The *Ahl al-Kalam* are shocked at the suggestion that a part of the Qur'an—the consummate World of God—be obliterated in this manner. Ibn Qutayba replies to this by saying that there is nothing astonishing in the fact that a part of the Qur'an be verbally destroyed provided it survives in the living practice (*al-'amal*).

Thus, quite apart from the historical criticism of the transmissional chains, and much more fundamentally than this type of criticism, another intuitive principle of selection was at work *e silentio.* This principle was that of conformity to the Sunna. But this intuitive principle of selectivity was not primarily historical, but doctrinal. Its historicity must have been in the first place a very indirect one, dictated by the exigencies of the form of the discipline itself. The justification of this historicity was furnished by the same type of reasoning whereby the content of the living Sunna was earlier regarded as being the Sunna of the Prophet, i.e., as being deduced from it in spirit and hence being entitled to the name Sunna. This makes us realize the full import of the so-called Hadith according to which the Prophet said, 'Whatever of good speech there be, you can take it to have been said by me'. How much truer this dictum should be about a body of teaching which the incessant and prolonged experiences of the earliest generations had established as expressing the spirit of the Prophet's message. On no other hypothesis than this can we explain the fact that palpably post- Prophetic developments —the theological positions with regard to human freedom, Divine Attributes, etc.,—were verbally attributed to the Prophet himself, and indeed the fact that the Shi'a, the major sect of Islam, which differs from orthodoxy *doctrinally,* also has an entirely separate body of Hadith.

But further, between the personality of the Prophet and the Qur'an on the one hand and the development of the Sunna-Hadith phenomenon on the other, there exists a relationship of public historical continuity which is unique in the major religions of the world. The Prophet founded not merely a religion but a developing large-scale Community, and this in the broad daylight of history. Indeed, this public continuity between the prophet and his Community is the real guarantee of the Prophetic Sunna differentiating it from the parallel case of early Christianity. The existence of shadows does not deny but merely confirms this basic fact. Much of its light may *actually* radiate from the media on the historical path, but so long as the media are homogeneous, they do not distort and conceal but illustrate and reveal the source. Surely this is the deeper reason why also the intelligent orientalist regards this major river-bed of Islam as orthodoxy! For this fact cannot be explained merely on the basis of the number of followers or on the latter's claim to be orthodox. It is this double connection, of spirit and of historical continuity, that rendered the Hadith, despite a lack of strict historicity on the part of much of its contents, impregnable to all attacks in classical Islam. In its turn, it bestowed continuity and stability on the career of the Community for centuries, even though this stability was preserved in later medieval times at the expense of fresh creativity and originality.

Modern Islam yearns for creativity and in the interests of new progress certain groups have arisen which, if their utterances are taken at their face value, wish to reject all hadith and rely on the Qur'an. But in these groups there is hardly any awareness of the issues that are at stake. It is not clear whether they wish to deny historical or doctrinal validity to the Hadith. This confused position (and virtually no appreciation of the nature of the Hadith development) is considerably similar to that of the *Ahl al-Kalam* in classical times. But there is one major difference. The *Ahl al-Kalam* wished to reject the verbal tradition (the Hadith) in favour of the living tradition. But now the only tradition is the verbal one, since the living Sunna, is so far as it is there, now derives its validity from the Hadith through which lies the only avenue of our contact with the Prophet and fundamentally also with the Qur'an as it was delivered to and understood by the Community. For, if thc Hadith *as a whole* is cast away, the basis for the historicity of the Qur'an is removed with one stroke. But the present unrest is equally genuine and expresses a vital need.

This need for new vitality and fresh interpretation neither can be nor ought to be suppressed, but the orthodox guardians of the tradition have so far displayed an uncompromisingly conservative attitude and a lack of judgment both of the new situation and of the actual development of the Hadith. They do not realize that this attitude, far from maintaining stability, which was the real reason behind the Hadith system, would destroy it with violence. But the Modernist also must realize that although the Hadith in part does not represent the verbal and pure Prophetic teaching, it has certainly an intimate connection with the Prophet and especially represents the earliest development of the Community's understanding of that teaching. He may certainly reinterpret the Qur'an and the Prophet's Sunna, in so far as it can be disentangled—and in this he would be only following the practice of the earliest generations—but he cannot disregard, even if he tries, the *ethos* of the Hadith and of the institutions which it guaranteed: no interpretation can take place in a vacuum. For the Qur'an did not come in a vacuum. Hence the well-known paradox that even the thoroughgoing sceptics about the Hadith cannot resist supporting their views by it whenever it suits them.

The disentanglement of the historical Prophetic elements is perhaps incapable of complete achievement for want of early enough sources. But a candid and responsible investigation into the development of the Hadith by the Muslims themselves is a desideratum of the first order. Whatever can be achieved in this way will be a sheer gain, for it will reveal the intimate connection between the Community and the Prophet on the one hand, and between the doctrinal and the practical evolution of the Community and the growth of the Hadith on the other. It will illuminate the relationship between these three and will clear the way for proper future development.

Revised and edited; originally published as Chapter three: Origins and Development of the Tradition, in Islam.

9

Al-Harith B. Sa'id Al-Kadhdhab: A Claimant to Prophecy

D M DUNLOP

(Abstract: Deals with his life and claim as a prophet, or false prophet-al-kadhdhab. He hailed from Syria, and laid a claim of prophethood during the reign of Caliph Abd al-Malik).

There is a passage in the *Mu'jam al-Buldan* (*Geographical Dictionary*) of Yaqut (12th century A.D.), where he speaks of two districts (*nahiyatan*) in Syria called al-Hulah . The first of these, says Yaqut, is dependent on Hims, the other is a region between Baniyas and Sur, dependent on Damascus, in which are many villages. From one of these came al-Harith al-Kadhdhab (al-Harith the Liar), who claimed the prophecy in the days of 'Abd al-Malik. Elsewhere in the work there is no mention of al-Harith. Wustenfeld, the editor of the *Mu'jam al-Buldan*, in his elaborate notes, which by themselves fill a volume, gives no information about him, and does not even list him in the index.

Yet in the passage quoted Yaqut refers to al-Harith as if he were well enough known, and it might be expected that more information would be forthcoming about him. There is in fact a good deal on al-Harith in a biographical notice in the *Ta'rikh al-Islam* (*History of Islam*) of al-Dhahabi, a 14th century writer, which is now available at least in part in a good printed edition. Al-Dhahabi's notice of him, headed as in our title 'Al-Harith b. Sa'id al-Kadhdhab, is not marked by any of the *sigla* indicating the sources on which this author depends in a given article, placed after the heading, e.g.*Kitab al-jami' al-Sahih* of al-Bukhari, S=the *Sunan* of Abu Da'ud, etc. This probably means that no account of al-Harith is to be found in these works. In general, information on him is difficult to obtain, and the only other account which I have come across is in the *Ta'rikh Madinah Dimashq* (History of Damascus) of Ibn 'Asakir (died 571/1176), from which I am disposed to think al-Dhahabi took his own somewhat shorter notice. At all events, the two accounts are so close to each other that they may be treated as one, and this Ibn 'Asakir—Dhahabi notice appears at present to be the main source of information concerning a personality who, it would seem, made not a little stir in the world of his time.

We need have no doubt as to the general trustworthiness of the main part of the notice, which is given on the authority of al-Walid b. Muslim. This is the well-known Damascus personality of that name (born 119 A.H., died 195 A.H.), who lived early enough to have met and spoken with contemporaries of al-Harith (see below).

According to al-Walid's account, al-Harith b. Sa'id was a *maula* (freedman) either of Marwan b. al-Hakam (Caliph for a brief time, 64/683—65/685) or of Abu'l-Julas al-'Abdari al-Qurashi. His father lived at the village of al-Hulah already mentioned. (The name still appears on the modern map, a few miles south-west of Baniyas). It was apparently at Damascus, to which he had gone for some unspecified reason, that the son first drew attention to himself. 'It he had worn a *jubbah*, or cloak, of gold', says the source, 'the marks of abstinence would have appeared on him'. He came to be known for his eloquence in *tahmid*, i.e., praising God, and his skill therein, demonstrated in the mosque or elsewhere, was unsurpassed.

At some point, al-Harith became convinced that he was in contact with the supernatural world, and, greatly disturbed by this, wrote to his father in al-Hulah: 'Dear father, hasten to me, for I have seen things (or 'a thing') which I fear Satan has suggested to me'. His father did not attempt to dissuade or help him beyond writing in reply: 'Go forward to what you are commanded. Verily God says (sc. in the Qur'an): The Satans descend, they descent upon every wicked lair (*Surah* 26: *221-222*). But you are not wicked, and not a liar.'

Thus encouraged, al-Harith began to make propaganda for his new revelation in the mosque of Damascus, approaching individuals and informing them under a bond of secrecy of what he had come to believe about himself. He also produced, it is said, such wonders as the cleaving of a block of marble with his hand and the appearance of summer fruits in winter. He even led people out to Dair Murran—earlier, and perhaps still at this time, a Christian monastery on the slopes of Jabal Qasiyun, near Damascus, to which the Caliphs and others resorted—where the proposed to show them a vision of angels. As a result of all this, we are told, many people followed him, and his disciples became numerous.

Several of his attempts at proselytising ended in information being laid before the authorities, and one in particular was disastrous. The traditionist al-Qasim b. Mukhaimarah took the oath of secrecy, but when al-Harith declared that he was a prophet, the other declared: 'You lie, O enemy of God, and there is no compact between us.' Ibn Mukhaimarah then laid the matter before the qadi of Damascus, Abu Idris al-Khaulani, who blamed him for what he had done, and immediately informed the Caliph, 'Abd al-Malik. Search was made for al-Harith, but he managed to escape and found a refuge at Bait al-Maqdis (Jerusalem). Meanwhile 'Abd al-Malik, who suspected the rank and file of the army of sympathy with al-Harith, himself left Damascus and took up his quarters at as-Sinnabrah, a place in the Jordan valley not far from Tabariyah (Tiberias).

The propaganda for al-Harith was continued by his supporters in Jerusalem, who brought people into his presence with a view to winning them over. Among these was a man of Basrah, unnamed, who was invited by a friend of al-Harith to hear a religious disputation (*qala lahu huhuna rajul yatakallam fa-hal laka an tasma min kalamihi*). Al-Walid b. Muslim, the narrator, remarks at this point that the men of Basrah were very fond of such presentations (*qala al-Walid wa-ahl al-basrah yashtahun al-kalam*). The Basran was impressed by the words of al-Harith, and said so, but in regard to his claim to be a prophet indicated that he would have to consider this. He made it his business on repeated visits to find out all he could about al-Harith. After sometime, he requested that he be excused from further attendance in order to return to Basrah, where he would be al-Harith's first propagandist (*da'i*). Having got the required permission he left Jerusalem and travelled with all speed to as-Sinnabrah. In an audience with the Caliph, he gave him an account of what he had seen and heard. 'Abd al-Malik was suitably impressed, and sent the Basran back to Jerusalem with a troop of forty men of Farghanah and full powers to act. The presence of these men from Farghanah in distant Khurasan is interesting. It is particularly mentioned that they were without skill in theological disputation (*la yafqahun al-kalam*), and therefore not likely to be influenced by anything they heard from al-Harith.

Having returned to Jerusalem, the man of the Basrah in concert with the Umayyad governor provided a large body of the inhabitants with candles and stationed them at nightfall throughout the city. Then he went to the house of al-Harith and requested the door-man (*hajib*) to give him admittance to the prophet of God, as al-Harith claimed to be. As soon as the outer gate was opened, he gave a signal. The candles were lit, and the whole city, we are told, became as bright as day. The Basran entered the house accompanied by his men, but the prophet was not at first to be found. The search continued, in spite of protests from the friends of al-Harith, who demanded why they sought to do violence to a prophet who had already ascended to heaven. Finally, he was dragged from a subterranean hiding-place, and taken prisoner. As they led him away, al-Harith repeated the Quranic verse (*Sura* 40:*29*): 'Will you kill a man because he says, My Lord is Allah, and he has brought you the proofs from your Lord?' To this the men of Farghanah replied in words which in Ibn 'Asakir's text are sufficiently incomprehensible: 'this is our *karamah* (miracle), so bring your *karamah*.' The reading in al-Dhahabi is evidently much preferable, and no doubt original: 'This is our Kuran (sic), so bring your Kuran (sic) (i.e. you have just recited a verse from the Qur'an of the Muslims. But you are no Muslim, so bring you own Qur'an) where Kuran for Qur'an evidently represents the incorrect pronunciation of Arabic by the men from Khurasan.

The unfortunate Harith was brought to the Caliph, who at first had him imprisoned. Sometime later, after an attempt by certain *faqihs* and leaned men to make him recant, orders came for his execution. This was carried out in the cruel fashion of the day. As al-Harith hung on the gibbet, an man attempted to pierce him with a hunting-spear. But, striking upon a rib, the spear rebounded. Thereupon the populace began to shout: 'Arms are not permitted against a prophet! It is not right that a man like this should be killed!" One of the guards then seized a lance, and ran the victim through. We hear of no further protest from the crowd.

Thus died al-Harith b. Sa'id. The year is given by al-Dhahabi as A.H. 79 (March 20, 698—March 9, 699). The main narrative is as we have given it. One or two additional anecdotes are mentioned, e.g. we are told that after his capture, when al-Harith and his guards came to the *'aqabah* (ascent and descent) of Jerusalem, he looked out over the country and recited the Quranic verse (*Sura* 34:49): 'Say: If I am in error, I am in error only for myself. And if I am rightly guided, it is by what my Lord reveals to me. Verily He is hearing, near.' His hand had been fixed to his neck by an iron band, which now, as the words of the sacred text were spoken, dropped to the ground leaving him free, to the astonishment of the guards, who speedily replaced the band. At another ascent the same thing happened. The narrator, a certain Abu'r-Rabi', says somewhat naively that he had forgotten what Quranic verse it was that al-Harith recited on the second occasion.

Al-Walid b. Muslim mentions specifically that after al-Harith had been executed, the Umayyad prince Khalid b. Yazid reproached his relative, the Caliph, with the deed. 'If I had been present', said he, 'I should have bidden you not to kill him' 'Why so?' asked 'Abd al-Malik. 'The fit (*muydhhab,* literally 'demon') was upon him', replied the other. 'If you had hungered him, it would have left him'. Another report was that 'Abd al-Malik was admired during his reign for nothing so much as his ordering the killing of al-Harith.

It remains to see what can reasonable be inferred from the account in Ibn'Asakir—Dhahabi as to the character of al-Harith b. Sa'id and the nature of his religious movement, also what general conclusions, if any, may be drawn. In the first place, it would seem that he was young or youngish, since his father was still alive and he turned to him for advice at the critical moment. He was evidently a man of good character, as appears not only from his father's man of good character, as appears not only from his father's testimonial to that effect, but also from the evidence of his saintly appearance and the sympathy of the crowd at the time of his death, and, perhaps more telling than anything else, from the fact that nothing to the contrary was alleged by his enemies.

Further, it is clear that his movement never made much headway. Otherwise the Caliph would not have sent a troop of only forty men to deal with him. The large numbers of his followers (in Damascus only, it appears) and the fears of the Caliph may simply be part of the legend which has embellished the facts with sundry miracles. To get the movement into perspective, we have also to notice that claimants to the prophecy were by no means lacking in the early days of Islam. In addition to Musailimah and others in Arabia within the lifetime of Muhammad, we have to think of al-Mukhtar in Iraq only a few years before al-Harith and sundry claimants later. Al-Harith b. Sa'id evidently cannot be regarded as an isolated phenomenon.

Yet the case has its own special features. Thought in one place he is named al-Harith b. 'Abd al-Rahman b. Sa'd al-Muthanna, I cannot see this as a ground for thinking him to have been of Arabian stock. He is definitely mentioned as a *maula* or freedman. So doubtless was his father, who is represented as a Muslim, familiar with the Qur'an. Al-Harith b. Sa'id no doubt belonged to the class of country-dwellers in Syria, who before the Arab conquest had been Christians of varying confessions. A Christian affinity for al-Harith is also indicated by other details of his story as recorded by Ibn 'Asakir—Dhahabi. It is stated that his teaching at one time attracted Ghailan ak-Dimashqi, who, though of course a Muslim, was a Copt by extraction. This Ghailan, having been a 'Harithi' (the expression actually occurs) became one of the first Qadarites, the partisans of free-will in early Islam, and was made eventually put to death by the Caliph Hisham b. 'Abd al-Malik. The Qadarite school is usually said to have arisen under Christian Greek influence.

One of the first results of the Arab conquests was extensive conversion of Christians to Islam, striking cases of which were the father of Musa b. Nusair, the future conqueror of Spain, and the grandfather of Ibn Ishaq, who wrote the famous *Sirah* (Biography) of Muhammad—both of them captured in the church of 'Ain al-Tamar in Iraq, it is said, while they were studying the Gospels. Gradually the adherents of the two faiths came to be, so to say, sorted out. The existence of a fragment of the Palsms in Arabic written in Greek majuscules, found in the Umayyad mosque at Damascus and dated by the discoverer to the late 8th or 9th century, points already to a state of affairs in which the language of the conquerors has been adopted for religious purposes by the conquered, who here in Syria as elsewhere are permitted the exercise of their religion. But before this the religious situation was evidently one of confusion. Not all the converts of descendants of converts were, it seems, satisfied with the new religion. The appearance of al-Harith b. Sa'id as a prophet is no doubt to be regarded as a case in point.

REFERENCES

1. Mu'jam al-Buldan, ed. F Wustenfeld.
2. Al-Tarikh al-kabit, by Abd al-Qadir Badran, Damascus, AH. 1330. vol. III.
3. Al-Dhahabi, Tadhkirat al-Huffaz, Hyderabad Dn., 1375/1955, I, 303-304.
4. Al-Masudi, Muraj alDhahab, Paris, VII.
5. Ibn Qutaibah, Kitab, al-Maarif, ed. Wustenfeld, p. 244.

Revised and edited; originally published in Studies in Islam, JAn 1964.

10

The Book of Strife of Nuaim Ibn Hammad al-Marwazi

F KRENKOW

(Abstract: The book of Strife, or Kitab al Fitan, is a lesser known and heard source of Hadith literature. The author of this book was an inspirer and teacher of Imam Bukhari, Imam Muslim, and Imam Abu Dawud).

The great canonical books on Tradition, like that of Al-Bukhari and his successors, have been the chief cause for the disappearance of almost all earlier works which dealt with the same subjects; and manuscripts of the latter have become extremely scarce and, when discovered, are as a rule of great age. The cause for this is that later generations were more occupied with copying and commenting, or making extracts from, the great collections, often very idle work which never produced any valuable results.

We certainly possess in print the large Musnad of Ibn Hanbal and the Musnad of Abu Daud at-Tavalisi. Though the former, perhaps, contains most of the Hadith which has found its way into the canonical books, there existed a large quantity of works which were not fully utilised; and it is always interesting, nay important, to know the contents of such earlier books whenever they become accessible. I believe that we can get much nearer to a knowledge of the intellectual activity of the first two centuries of Islam if we know a little more concerning the works written at that time. It was a period full of activity in all branches of learning. Such books have always attracted my attention and I have always been on the look-out for manuscripts of this kind.

The free and democratic spirit of Islam under the dynasty of the Banu Omayyah had been crushed, never to be revived, by the advent of the 'Abbasid rule. The ancient despotism of the Sassanid Persian kings became the doctrine of the new dynasty which, in its lengthy career of over five hundred years, did not produce one single ruler equal to the talent of a Mu'awiya, 'Abdul-Malik or Al-Walid. The danger to the State and Religion from the fanatical Kharijis had passed away, but the Shi'ah, whose claims had been mainly political in the first century, now became a far greater peril as its work was carried on more secretly. The 'Abbasids had been greeted by the 'Alids as associates in trouble in times past and the latter hoped that they now could share with them the ruling of the destinies of the Muslim world. They were soon cheated and, when they protested, persecuted even more than under the Ommayads. With the 'Abbasids, also, two other phenomena are discerned for the first time, namely the outcrop of philosophical sectarians, the pre-decessors of the Sufis, with the invention of persons of earlier ages who had never existed, like Uwais al-Qarani etc.; and the search for heretics (Zindiqs). The times, in spite of the glamour of the Court, and the vast sums which couple be spent upon slave girls and singers, were looked upon with dismay by the pious of the old school. Though the rulers indulged in wine-drinking and all kinds of excesses, unfit as they were, they considered it their religious duty to punish other people who were accused, rightly or wrongly, for deviating from the right faith. This was surely the time for writing apocalypses, and pious people began to look for the promised Mahdi to appear and bring justice again into the wicked world.

Such a book in the "Book of Strife" of Nu'aim ibn Hammad. of which and excellent manuscript has been preserved. Nu'aim was one of the Shaikhs of Al-Bukhari, Muslim and Abu Da'ud. After collecting materials in various parts of the Muslim world he settled in Egypt. When the edict of the "Creation of the Qur'an" was promulgated he was one of the foremost in refusing to accept the official doctrine and was carried to Baghdad by order of the Cliph Al-Mu'tasim. As he persisted in his refusal he was cast into prison and died there on Sunday the 13th of Jumada I. 228 A.H.

Opinions as regards his trustworthiness as a traditionist differ according to the standards laid down by various critics; but it is generally asserted that he was a fierce antagonist of the Shi'ah—a statement borne out by the following tradition taken from the *Kitab al-Fitan* on the final authority of Safinah, a Maula of the Prophet (whom God bless): "When the Prophet, whom God bless, built the mosque at Al-Madinah, Abu Bakr came and placed a stone, then came 'Omar and placed a stone, then came 'Othman and placed a stone. Then the Prophet, whom God bless, said: "These are they who after me will carry on the succession (al-Khilafah)." No mention whatever is made of 'Ali. The author does not say that he will *not* carry on the succession, but simply passes him with silence, I am sure, intentionally.

In another passage, strangely on the final authority of 'Ali, from whom is was transmitted by Juwairiya daughter of Shammar, we get another political limit. "The realm of the people of Muhammad, upon whom be blessing, after his death will last one hundred and sixty-seven years and thirty-one days; after that God will cause weakness to rule over them.

As the author was able to prophesy retrospectively it would be interesting to find out what event is likely to be the one to which he desires the prophecy to refer. The Prophet, whom God bless, died on the 13th of Rabi'I in the year 11 and the required date consequently is the 14th of Rabi' II of the year 178 A.H. I believe this can only be brought into connection with a very brief statement made by Tabari (III. 631): "In this year (178) Ar-Rashid entrusted the whole of the affairs of State to Yahya the son of Khalid al Barmaki." Tabari does not give any more precise date, not does Ibn `Abdus al-Jahshiyari in his History of the Wazirs. The Barmakids are claimed, and probably rightly, but the Shi'ah as their own, and this may have been Nu'aim's reason for fixing such a date. Nevertheless Nu'aim, as if by intuition, was not far away from the truth because, from this time with sporadical interruptions due to the moods of the Caliphs, not on account of any political acumen on their part, the management of State-affairs got more and more into the hands of officials, most of whom were concerned principally with their personal greed, which was checked only by the intrigues of their adversaries.

The 'Abbasids had brought with them from Persia not only the luxury of the Persian Sassanid courts, which they emulated and imitated, but also the habitual dishonesty of their officials; and the contrary was rather the exception than the rule. Nearly all high his officers stole wholesale, though thieves for small amounts were still punished severely according to the Shari'ah—nay, very often far in excess of the legal punishment.

The time was certainly ripe for the appearance of the Mahdi and the author no doubt had this is mind: to prepare his hearers to make themselves ready for the longed-for appearance of the Saviour. This is principally reflected by the later chapters of the book; but another eleven centuries have rolled passed and the Mahdi has not appeared.

Al-Bukhari and his successors have special sections in their works dealing with the some subject, but nowhere is a dealt with so exhaustively nor so methodically, and for this reason I think it appropriate to give an index of the chapters at least. They are :

(1) What the Prophet, whom God bless, and his Companions foretold about the strife to come.
(2) How the people will lose their common-sense in the strife.
(3) Who gave licence to wish for death when trials and strife break out.
(4) The remorse of the Companions and others concerning the strife.
(5) How people wish they had few children and little property in the time of strife.
(6) Concerning the successors (*khulafa*) after the Prophet, whom God bless.
(7) How to differentiate between kings and successors (caliphs).

(8) Names of those who will rule after the Prophet, whom God bless.
(9) Concerning the rule of the Banu Omayya and their names after 'Omar.
(10) Another chapter about the Omayyads.
(11) Immunity from strife and what laudable in refraining from taking part in the strife.
(12) Signs concerning the end of the rule of the Omayyads.
(13) The rising of the 'Abbasids.
(14) The first sign of the termination of their realism and the rising of the Turks.
(15) Signs in the heavens portending the end of the rule of the 'Abbasids.
(16) Beginning of the strife of Syria.
(17) How mean and weak folk with gain the upper hand.
(18) The place of refuge in the strife.
(19) The first sign will be the rising the Berbers and people of the Maghrib.
(20) Events which will happen before the rising of the Berbers.
(21) Concerning the evil deeds of the Berbers and their fighting in Syria.
(22) The description of the Sufyani, his name and genealogy.
(23) First rising of the Sufyani.
(24) What will happen between the Sufyani, the people of Syria and the realm of the 'Abbasids near Raqqa.
(25) Concerning the acts of the Sufyani in the heart of Baghdad and the devastation of the 'Iraq.
(26) The entrance of the Sufyani and his followers into the city of Al-Kufah.
(27) The black standards of the Mahdi after the black standards of the 'Abbasids.
(28) End of the rule of the Sufyani and appearance of the Hashimi in Khorasan with black standards, and the battles between them till the cavalry of the Sufyani reaches the (Farthest) East.
(29) Armies sent to Al-Madinah and the slaughter there.

(30) Discomfiture of the army which the Sufyani sends against the Mahdi.
(31) Signs foreboding the appearance of the Mahdi.
(32) Further signs.
(33) Assembly of the people at Mecca to pay homage to the Mahdi.
(34) Rising of the Mahdi.
(35) The Mahdi leaves Mecca and marches to the Bait al-Maqdis.
(36) Description of the Mahdi and his gracious deeds.
(37) The extent of the Mahdi's dominion.
(38) What will happen after the Mahdi.
(39) The far-distant regions and the conquest of Constantinople.
(40) Concerning Alexandira, Misr and the frontiers towards the Rum.
(41) What will happen to the people when the Dajjal appears.
(42) Where the Dajjal will rise.
(43) The rising of the Dajjal and his evil deeds.
(44) How long the Dajjal will rule.
(45) Place of refuge from the Dajjal.
(46) The duration of the rule of 'Isa ibn Maryam after his coming down from heaven.
(47) The rising of Yajuj and Majuj.
(48) Eelipses, earth-quakes, trembling and transmutations.
(49) The fire which will flare up in Syria.
(50) The foreboding of the last hour.
(51) Signs about the last hour when the sun rises in the West.
(52) Rising of the sun in the West.
(53) Appearance of the Beast.
(54) The rising of the Habasha (Abyssinians).
(55) The Turks.

This is the last and longest chapter and with remarkable clearsightedness, amounting almost to prophecy, the author foresaw the danger to Islam from the quarter of the Turks (and Mongols), though he does not know the latter, because all nations towards the

North-east of the Muslim dominions were included in the name Turk, except China and the far-distant Yajuj and Majuj, about whom no very clear idea appears to have prevailed.

We have, as will be seen from the titles of the chapters in this work, a very systematic apocalypse in which every statement is traced back by a proper chain of authorities to its original source. While for the proper Sunnah these should go back to the Prophet himself we find here, as is also the case in the *Muwatta* of Malik, that frequently the author contents himself by citing only a statement of one of the companions. As I have pointed out earlier, the author does not refrain from letting his own tendencies influence the choice of the traditions which he records. The Hadith on the Caliphs already cited, if genuine, would certainly have included 'Ali also; and on this account I will examine his Isnad or chain of authorities. This runs: Ibn al-Mubarak after Khazraj b. Nubata, after Sa'id b. Jahman, after Safina, Maula of the Prophet whom God bless.

(1) Ibn al-Mubarak is 'Abd Allah b. al-Mubarak al-Marwazi who died in 181 A.H. at the age of 63. He is generally acknowledged as trustworthy.

(2) Khazraj b. Nubata is not mentioned in the biographies of traditionists, unless it is an error for Khazraj b. 'Othman al-Basri. The latter was *not* held in high estimation.

(3) Sa'id b. Jahman al-Aslami al-Basri is known to have handed down traditions which were recorded only by him. The date of his death is not known.

(4) Safina Muala of the Prophet, whose proper name is supposed to have been Mahran, was probably a Persian by birth as indicated by his supposed name. He handed tradition to Sa'id b. Jahman in other books of Hadith.

This tradition is weak on account of the mention of Khazraj ibn Nubata. Ibn Mubarak is one of the chief Shaikhs of Nu'aim.

The second tradition is even more suspicious. The authorities are: Ibn Lahi'ah, after an unnamed person, after Hajanna, after Ghalib b. Hudhail, after Juwairiya bint Shammar, after 'Ali.

(1) Ibn Lahi'a is a well-known Egyptian traditionist. He is 'Abd Allah b. Lahi'a al-Hadrami and died in 174 A.H. at the age of over 80 years.

(2) Al-Hajanna b. Qais al-Kufi. Daraqutni attached no value to him and stated that only two traditions were recorded on his authority; while Ibn Hibban, who is as a rule more lenient, declared him trustworthy and said that he transmitted often after Ibrahim an-Nakha'i.

(3 and 4) Both Ghalib ibn Hudhail and Juwairiya appear to be unknown as carries of Hadith.

Though the names may not be traceable in the works at out disposition it does not mean that such persons have not existed.

The only manuscripts of the work known to me is a recent acquisition of the Library of the British Museum Or. 9449 consisting of 201 leaves in quarto. The work is, after the method of ancient works, divided into Ajza'. The manuscript consists of ten such fascicula beginning respectively on fol. Ir, 25r, 45r, 66, 87, 119, 143, 157, 171 and 185; and the scribe tells us at the end that he completed his task on the slope of Qasiyun (Damascus) on the day of the 'Id al-Adha 760 A.H. He calls himself Muhammad b. Muhammad b. 'Ali as-Sairafi al-Ansari; he is not mentioned in the *Durar al-Kamina* as one of the scholars of Damascus.

A publication of this ancient work on tradition is highly desirable as it contributes considerably towards our knowledge of the mentality of Muslims at the time of a crisis in the history of Islam.

Revised and edited; originally published in Islamic Culture, Oct. 1929.

11

Muslim Creed According to the Traditionists and the Rationalists

MUHAMMAD ABDUL RAHMAN BISAR

(Abstract: An address dealing with human thought, and factors affecting Islamic thought; approach of both the traditionist (or Hadith specialists) and the rationalists are discussed in the light of the historic and Islamic sources).

Man, since olden times, has been steadily striving in considering the universe around him, and meditating on the Dominion of the Heavens and the Earth.

This pondering was given various moulds of representations and perceptions reflecting the image of this existence in man's soul, depicting its landmarks in his mind, conformably to the levels of culture and conceptual criteria that have been varying with every age, and keeping pace with the laws of progress and regress in accordance with the divers shades of thought and intellectual features.

More often than not did these divergent representations furnish the cultural legacy of a certain thinker or a group of men a particular view point entailing certain judgments, and urging the adoption of a certain line of behaviour.

Thus it was quite natural for intellectual problems to arise as an inevitable result caused by the adoption of various standpoints bearing on this existence with all its physical forces that can be perceived through the senses or the spiritual ones that can be no means be grasped save through deliberate meditation and sheer reflexion.

Since it had been beyond man's power to verify—with the exception of axiomatic statements—his judgements, respecting the intellectual propositions and metaphysical problems as accurately as he does in sensuous issues and empirical questions, it was quite natural that the conflict of ideas and the divergence of viewpoints be more intense and contradictory in the former than in the latter.

Hence had arisen serious problems in human thinking related to everything bearing on the unseen, and in particular to man's conception of God, throughout the various stages of his development and the cultural levels, as reflected in his systems of thought by the impact of these particular stages.

In this way originated the intellectual and dogmatic problems respecting the idea of God, and what is related to it within the sphere of Islamic thought.

Controversies dealing with these topics came to be so intense as to bring forth in our Islamic heritage a rich and varied corpus of doctrines and viewpoints coping with these problems, affording us a type of perception and meditation, and a wide range of mature thinking that have rendered Islamic culture a living example and a real model, demonstrating the flourishing of every doctrine that had been formulated, the viewpoint adopted, or the judgment reported.

Thus attained their prime a host of theologians, philosophers, mystics, traditionists, jurists, and empiricists together with other scholars who had been assimilated with the Muslim environment and whose views had been adjusted within the crucible of Islamic thought.

Gentlemen,

Hence had originated the divergences of men's approaches to everything related to metaphysical problems; an inevitable outcome due to man's nature and to his reasoning faculties with which he had been endowed to comprehend and to discern, and to gain a full grasp and to make exhaustive investigations.

This is undoubtedly one of the general intellectual features that are common to human thought.

As to Islamic thought and in particular to what is related to the articles of Faith there had arisen two other factors alongside of this general human feature. These will be briefly dealt with so as to demonstrate an important and essential fact bearing on the topic under discussion.

Its purport is that the divergences related to the problems of Muslim dogmatics had been the inevitable outcome of certain local conditions, respecting which it would have been unwise and contrary to the interests of the Islamic Call had Muslim thinkers ignored to cope with, or disregarded making attempts for their solution with all the possible means of inquire and ingenious methods of speculation.

Why There Had Been No Dogmatic Controversies During the Prophet's Life Time?

Nevertheless dogmatic dissensions bearing on the articles of the Muslim Faith as revealed in the Holy Quran had had no trace during the life-time of the Prophet (P.B.U.H.); a significant feature that was due to two main reasons:

First: Muslims during the advent of the Islamic Call had been (nearly) isolated non-Arab peoples.

Second: The Messenger (P.B.U.H.) had then still, been living in their midst. His relation with God, forceful and holy personality, and the attraction of the new Faith he called upon people to adopt, rendered his words as most conclusive and his judgements as positively decisive.

Whenever, he perceived in some of his Companions an inclination towards deep reflexion upon what is allegorical in the Holy Quran, or found them entertaining doubts in certain articles of the Faith, he used to forbid them from indulging in such unfathomable meditations. He never ceased to show them that holding a mystified sort of Faith would certainly lead to perdition. Most truthfully expressive, in this respect is a tradition reported to have been said by the Prophet (P.B.U.H.): "Do think over what had been created by God, but never meditate upon God's Essence, lest you should be lost."

Muslim (in his Sahih, canonical corpus of traditions) reported on the authority of Abu Hurairah that the Prophet (P.B.U.H.) had said: "People would ask you about everything until they say that God had brought into being His Whole Creation; but they would then ask: Who had created Him?"

In a further tradition, reported by Muslim, the Prophet (P.B.U.H.) had said: "The devil would come to anyone of you, asking who had created such and such a thing, until he asks who had created God. Once this issue had been reached, you should take refuge in God, and abstain (from pondering on such questions)."

Yet this attitude had not been indefinitely adhered to, owing to the occurrence of two factor that had been influential in stirring up a carving for explanations and the raising of equivocal points bearing on the problem of the Muslim creed.

The first was the death of the Prophet (P.B.U.H.) When his Holy Spirit had gone to God, Most High, Muslims found themselves missing the Personality that had been chosen by God, and sustained by His Infallible Revelations.

None of his Companions had had a distinction higher than that of any other, as to be accorded the position of primacy, since the Apostle (P.B.U.H.), considered all of them as equals in affording guidance, and that their viewpoints in matters of the Faith have to be adhered to by Muslims. In this connexion, he is reported to have said: "My Companions are like the stars: whomsoever you follow would certainly lead you to the right path."

According to the text of the above tradition, all the Prophet's Companions are worthy of being imitated, and, thereby, each one of them, is fit to be a religious leader. Therefore, it is admitted that all of them were competent in issuing fatwas in matters bearing on dogmatics or legislation; however unequal they might have been in the range of their learning, and the tenacity of their memory in reporting Prophetic traditions.

Thus each of them tended to reflect upon the Quran and the Sunna, according to his own particular approach, thereby causing a wide diversity of opinion.

The Second factor was the great Arab conquests that led the Arabs, as advocates of the Islamic Call, to be mixed with other peoples who had been converted to Islam, but retaining certain survivals from their ancient faiths that were to arouse subsequently doubtful and subtle issues.

The new converts had shown sincere or feigned eagerness to grasp the tenets of the new Faith, either for the sake of making a comparative study with other faiths, searching for points of criticise, or tending to have their beliefs confirmed.

But the style of the Holy Quran which is means to be an address to mankind at large, promoted a tendency for exhaustive study. It comprises clear and allegorical Revelations, in the latter sort of which are used a large variety of figures of speech, such as metaphors, kinayat, metonymies that by some converts as allegorical whilst others adopted the outward meaning they convey.

In this way, men had had recourse to their minds, indulging in raising question, after having used, during the Prophet's life-time to admit the texts of the Revelation, believing firmly in them without wavering or scepticism saying: "We believe in the Book; the whole of it is from our Lord". (III, 7).

What is the Right Method to Ascertain the Articles of Faith?

The diversity of opinion, as shown in the multiplicity of

doctrines, whether arising from the different ways of comprehending the creed by Muslims, or from endeavours to prove its truth in controversies with dissenters and renouncers, is largely due to a variety of methods in discerning the articles of the Muslim Faith, and the ways of making a full grasp of them.

People started to ask whether the method of knowing the creed and its tenets is "naql", tradition, as exemplified in the texts of the Holy Quran and what had been genuinely reported from the sayings and actions of the Prophet (P.B.U.H.), or that such knowledge can only be acquired through "aql," reason, as based on discernment, *reflexion*, and the methodology of proof and deduction, the rules of which had been laid be thinkers and scholars in the science of dialectics, aided by the laws of logic, and the art of thought.

No sooner had these questionings been raised than a practical answer emerged from the actual state of affairs of Muslims. The epistemology of ascertaining the article of Faith had already been classified into three methods, to be roughly stated as follows:

(1) The method of "multakallims", scholastic theologians who rely in the first place on the text, but they respect reason as well, together with the laws of thought. But if the text proved to be contrary to reason, they would adhere to the former and leave out the latter.

(2) The method of philosophers who depend, first and foremost, on reason, while they believe firmly in the authenticity of the text. Yet, once the text had run counter to reason, they resorted to interpret it in a way as to be in harmony with reason.

(3) The method of "sufis", mystics who rely on spiritual discipline and `mujahadah', psychological striving, so as to purify the heart from all the impediments that block up the way to true religious knowledge and well-attested proofs.

According to the viewpoint of the "sufis," such knowledge can never be attained save through constant striving in acting conformably to the tenets of the Quran and the Sunna, together with severing all relations with the material world, until knowledge of Divine Light is emanated to them from God, Most High, and the (hidden) meanings are revealed, leading then to absolute confidence and complete conviction in everything dealing with metaphysical questions as related to God, Glory be to Him.

Sufis called this sort of discernment as "Intuitive Knowledge", to which there is reference in the Holy Quran. God, the Almighty said: "And We taught him Knowledge from Our Own (min ladunna)" (XVIII, 66). That is to say knowledge acquired not through inquiry, inference, or any method of deductive reasoning formulated by others.

Reason as Reckoned with by Both Scholastic Theologians and Philosophers

In thinking over these three methods, we find that scholastic theologians whether they were Mu'tazilites or 'Ash'arites had not neglected reason in demonstrating the truth of the articles of Faith; neither did they disown it, nor did they lessen its worth. But they took it into account, to a great extent, though they assigned to it a second-rate degree after those who disown reason.

In fact, reason had not been neglected, nor its importance lessened, as a means to acquire knowledge and to ascertain the articles of Faith. The neglect had only been the attitude of certain sufis, and a group from amongst the anthropomorphists who had interpreted the allogorical expressions in the Quranic verses as to convey this outward sense, taking no heed whether these meanings beseemed or did not beseem God, Glory be to Him.

Some "salaf", pious predecessors who had had recourse to interpretation found that it was quite enough to disregard the outward sense of these expressions. So much did they distrust reason that they desisted from determining the intended exact meaning, since they felt they were incompetent to do so.

The attitude of these predecessors and others was adopted by some leading jurists and traditionists whose campaign against the advocates of the rational approach was not confined to philosophers, but was extended to scholastic theologians themselves, simply because the latter, after having relied upon tradition, accorded reason some limited trust and consideration.

They had applied in their theological systems the Aristotlian logic, certain parts thereof, or even a similar deductive method in their polemical discussions, and in confirming the truth of the Muslim creed.

In their campaign against scholastic theologians, these jurists and traditionists might have been influenced by certain extremist sufis who had gone beyond all limits in disowning reason and renouncing its methods.

The Vehement Confrontation Between the Traditionists and the Rationalists

Yet within the sphere of Muslim thought, and in particular in what is related to the artists of Faith, the opposition was not so intense and straight-forward as it had been between the traditionists and the rationalists. The former had never ceased denouncing the method of the rationalists and disdaining their conclusion.

They even went so far as to accuse the rationalists, sometimes, of heresy, and at others of unbelief and atheism, as was expressed in a saying that had, then, been current, claiming: "man tamantaq fa qad tazandaq", "He who comes to apply logic would fall into heresy". A poet from amongst the traditionists composed a couplet in the same strain, saying:

> "There has appeared in our age a sect, the emergence of which had been most inauspicious.
>
> "Its adherents never conform to the tenets of the Faith, save through what had been formulated by Avicenna and Abu Nasr"

Also is reported, in this connexion that, one of the leading fuqaha' Imam Al Haramayn, Abul-Ma'ali Al-Juwayni once said: "Had I been to know what speculative theology would lead me to, I would never have occupied myself with it."

Such an utterance—were it to be taken as genuine—indicates that Juwayni had passed through a stage in his life making exhaustive investigation in the doctrines of philosophers, the methods of the rationalists, and the inferences of logicians.

Tajul-Din Abdul-Wahhab Ibn Al-Subki, in his work entitled: "Tabaqat Al-Shaf'iyyah" (= Classes of Shaf'ite Scholars), quoted Juwayni as saying:

> "I have read a vast number of epistles, leaving out Muslims obediently adhering to the tenets of their Faith, and occupied in comprehending the outward meaning of Islamic disciplines. I attempted to plough the waves in a tempestuous sea, and in my eager search for truth, I plunged into what is forbidden by Islam."

"Formerly, I used to avoid "taqlid", the simple acceptance of truth on religious authority."

"But, at present, I have come back to the word of truth. Thus you have to follow the religious beliefs of old women."

> "If God did not save me through His Grace, so that I may die holding fast to the religious beliefs of old women, thereby making my end as good as that of the people of truth, reiterating the words of ikhlass, purity of Faith, then woe to the son of Juwayni".

If this quotation was accurately reported, it means that Juwayni had passed through an intellectual crisis, in which he could free himself from all the theological doctrines of former mutakallims especially the Ash'arites. Then, he examined each doctrine, according to the rules he had laid down, and made a basis for his theological method, to distinguish between genuine and false beliefs.

Juwayni's Attitude Towards Taqlid in the Articles of Faith

It would, now, be fitting to raise the question, whether Juwayni had really favoured the idea of admitting only the outward sense of religious texts without having recourse to reasoning, and that he had advised Muslims to base their Faith on sheer taqlid and not on inquiry and verification, or that he was an advocate of rational research and logical speculation.

Ibn Al-Subki gave the following comment on the above quotation: "This means that Imam al-Haramayn forbade dealing with the science of kalam, scholastic theology and its abstruse problems. Only should it be allowed to a few number of people. But, as to the masses, it is preferable that they base their beliefs on taqlid, admitting their truth, without ever making any inquiries and searching for proofs."

Ibn Al-subki, then, added: "Such is the conclusion as drawn from Juwani's saying: "Had I been to know what speculative theology would lead me to, I would never have occupied myself with it".

Yet Juwayni in the introductory chapter of his book entitled: "Al-Irshad Ila Qawati' Al-Adillah fi Usul al-I'tiqad" (= The Guidance to the Categorical Evidences to Sustain the Principles of Dogmatics), admitted the importance of applying the deductive method to prove the truth of religious beliefs; since, as he said: "it is the means to uphold the article of Faith, and to preserve them from heresy."

For the reason, the theological method should comprise categorical evidences and rational propositions. Evidences leading to the knowledge of the creed are classified by Juwayni into two sorts:

(a) Adillah 'Aqliyyah, evidences based on reason.
(b) Adillah sam'iyyah, evidence based on tradition.

Thus, Juwayni, in taking into account speculation and deduction went so far as to decide that it is incumbent upon every sound-minded adult, the moment he comes of age to have recourse to well-balanced reflexion which world lead him to accurate knowledge, or to most probable assumptions.

To adduce a proof for such an obligation, Juwáyni said: "The Muslim Community had commonly agreed that it is a binding duty to know the Creator, Most High. Yet reason has made it clear that the acquisitioner of knowledge can never be realized save through pondering and reflexion. Hence, *we conclude that the issue upon which the necessary is based in necessary.*"

It is obvious the Juwayni means by the evidence that is based on tradition, the texts of the Holy Quran and the authenticated Sunna. He intends by the evidence based on reason: "the thing indicating an attribute that is most requisite to quality it." He cited as an instance for that sort of evidence the Perfection that demonstrates the Omniscience of the Perfect.

Ghazali's Attitude

This is, Gentlemen, Juwayni's approach to the subject under discussion. If we turn to Ghazali's writing, we find fuller details and clearer explanations dealing with all the equivocal points of the problem, and providing incontestable conclusions and convincing solutions.

During the age of Ghazali, the methods that had been currently adopted for the comprehension of theological data were confined to three, as we have previously mentioned.

Yet Ghazali's method does not apply to any of these three. He often had recourse to a method in which logical speculations, juristic texts of the Shari'at, and Sufistic "dhawq", experience were inextricably mingled.

Ghazali passed through a phase in his life in which he had been ardently seeking for (religious) truth. Such a tendency required him, within the sphere of his investigations, to entertain doubts in everything considered as rationally necessary. The intellectual crisis lasted until Faith was restored to him through the Grace of God.

("At length", he said, "God healed me of that disease, and my soul returned to health and balance, and the necessary intellectual truths came back, accepted and certain").

"That was not by means of well-arranged proofs or by any elaborate form of sepculation; but by a light which God cast into my breast."

"That light is the key of the most of knowledge; and whoever believes that his "kashf", mystical unveiling is based upon abstract proofs narrows the wide Mercy of God."

It is obvious from the above quotation that Ghazali did not disown rational proofs "per se". He simply considered them to be quite unfitting to most people. They only apply to a particular group of them.

For this reason, he reviewed the rational trends of his age, studied the creeds of every group or sect, and the particular approaches they had adopted. He discussed their evidences, how far they proved to be appropriate to each individual, and the advantages occurring therefrom in confirming the Faith, or the harm these assumptions might cause in shaking it through raising doubt and confusion.

Ghazali criticises speculative theologians, because they assume that knowledge can never be sound and accurate, unless it be based on rational proofs and logical propositions. He considers their methodology to be defective. Its limitations render it quite incapable to realize what is aimed at from the science of speculative theology; that is to preserve the Greed from the muddled uncertainties of the innovators, and the destructive assumptions of atheists, together with showing the way for a true knowledge of God, or the gaining of a general grasp of well-attested theological facts.

In the introductory chapter of his book, entitled: "Maqasid Al-Falasifah" (= Philosophers' Aims), and in his Al-Munqidh Min Al-Dalal" (= Rescuer From Error), Ghazali emphasized the fact that a mutakallim should make an exhaustive study of that sort of discipline (philosophy), until he equals whomsoever is well-versed in it. Nay, he should dwell at length at further investigations that had not been done by scholars in that discipline.

Thus, according to this view, mutakallims had failed in engaging themselves wholeheartedly in studying the doctrines of philosophers and their methodology. In this connexion, Ghazali said, "Speculative theologians who had occupied themselves with the refutation of philosophers' assumptions failed in directing their efforts to study the ultimate scope of their disciplines. Hence, there is nothing in the works of these theologians but complicated terms and self-contradictory statements, supposed not to deceive the unlettered, as they equally to fall short of deluding the pretentions who presume to know thoroughly the intricate points of these disciplines."

It is abvious from the above that Ghazali urged speculative theologians to adopt the methods of their adversaries in dialectics and deductive reasonings, as they should also attain a through knowledge of what could be taken into account from amongst rationalistic propositions and logical proofs and conclusions.

Ghazali's work, in this connexion comprises two important trends:

First: A Negative and Critical Tendency Embodying two Main Attitudes

(a) *Ghazali's Attitude towards Philosophers*, which is fully depicted in his work, entitled: "Tahafut Al-Falasifah" (= The Inadvertent Precipitation of Philosophers), in which the author criticises philosophers' doctrines, refutes their evidences, and discusses their assumptions in accordance with their polemical rules and logical stipulations. Ghazali defies their equivocal points by reproducing similar arguments without making any attempt to solve the questions he had raised.

This means that did not adduce in his book reasons for what, he had assumed or believed in; but he simply engaged himself in opposing them saying that he started controversies with them to assert his chaims and to deny their assumptions and not to presume putting forward any proof.

(b) His Attitude Towards Speculative Theologians

This is depicted in his Al-Munqidh Min Al-Dalal (= Rescuer from Error), as it is also explained in his other works, such as Ihya 'Ulum Al-Din (= The Revivication of the Sciences of Religion), Al-Iqtisad fil-I'tiqad (= The Via Media in the Creed), and Iljam Al-Awamm An 'Ilm Al-Kalam (= Reining Back on the Commonalty from the Science of Speculative Theology).

Ghazali criticises the science of speculative theology and the method adopted by mutakallims. Also he forbids that everybody without discrimination be allowed the study of that science. He reproaches these theologians for having put a limit to knowledge where it can no longer be corroborated by rational and logical proofs.

Ghazali perceived that the aim of scholastic theology is to preserve the Creed from the confusion caused by innovators, and to show the way to acquire a true knowledge of God, or to grasp at least incontestable theological data.

But he held that the evidence put forward by these theologians turned up to be failing and insufficient to realize that aim. Though he admitted that they had done well in defending the Faith, yet they relied on premises they had borrowed from their adversaries, and were compelled either to adopt them through taqlid, or the mere quoting from the Quran and reported narratives.

"They had been chiefly engaged in picking up the contradictory arguments of their adversaries, and forcing them to admit what could be irrevocably concluded from their given facts. Yet this method proved scarcely availing, especially as regards those who recognized nothing but what is absolutely necessary. Thus to me was kalam inadequate, and to the ailment of which I complained, failing to offer any cure."

Moreover, Ghazali emphasized in his Munqidh that it would hardly be possible for anyone to find out the inconsistencies of these disciplines and to be able to discuss their evidences, unless he grasped their ultimate scope, and outmatched in learning the scholars who are known to be well-versed in them.

For this reason, he was not satisfied with the attitude of these scholastic theologians towards philosophers, nor was he persuaded by the evidences they had adduced, nor the method they had adopted in their discussions; since they failed to base their refutations on a comprehensive study of the evidences put forward by their opponents.

Ghazali said: "Those from amongst the scholastic theologians who had engaged themselves in refuting the views of the philosophers had not directed their efforts to grasp the ultimate scope of the latter's disciplines. Hence, there is nothing in the works of these theologians but complicated terms and self-contradictory statements, supposed not to deceive the unlettered, as they equally to fall short of deluding the pretentions who presume to know thoroughly the intricate points of these disciplines.

For all these reasons, the method of the scholastic, theologians failed to make the Muslim Creed firmly established in the hearts of the believers. Nay, it rendered their Faith seriously shaken, as a thread thrown into the air.

Here, Ghazali drew a comparison between the Faith of the unlettered and that of the mutakallims, and came to the conclusion that the former is more secure and well-established than the latter, that is mainly based on polemical methods, and, thereby, rendered like a thread that is subject to be shaken in different directions by the everblowing winds.

Only would be saved the mutakallim who admitted the evidence of the Creed, by simply accepting its truth on religious authority, as he had already done in believing in the selfsame Creed by way of taqlid.

It is because there is no difference between these two forms of admission: either in learning the evidence, or discerning the issue such an evidence tries to prove. To get acquainted with the evidence, and asking for indications through speculation, are two things that are quite remote from each other.

"The Shari'at, (at the advent of Islam), had simply required the rule Arabs to believe firmly in the Muslim Creed. Those Arabs had never been constrained to make inquiries and to build up an elaborate system of proofs (so as to demonstrate the truth of the articles of their Faith). He who wants to go through the way leading to the Here after should never cease performing the religious observances, and adhering to piety, until genuine guidance is bestowed upon him, and the certainty of these beliefs is unveiled to him through a Divine Light that would be cast into his heart.

Second: A Positive and Confirmatory Tendency

This tendency comprises, as well, two attitudes:

(a) After having refuted the viewpoints of philosophers and scholastic theologians, Ghazali could convince Muslims at large of man's failure to attain to certainties especially those related to theological data. Thus he could pave the way for their souls to be devoted to religion and to adopt the mystic way of life by going back to the heart which, with the purification of the soul by prayer and spiritual exercise, can perceive theological truth through dhawq and kashf.

Hence, we see Ghazali choosing the Sufi Path, because, after having experienced a spiritual crisis that lasted for years, he came to know for certain, "that the Sufis are the "salikoun', the journeyers who do journey in the Way of God, and that the quest they are undertaking and methodically pursuing would surely lead them to the rightest Path".

Ghazali believes that it one is wholeheartedly bent on going along this Why to God, he is apt to attain to the ultimate aim of religion that is the perception of the (major) theological truths reason can scarely comprehend through its premises and conclusions.

Therefore, "(he who believes in the Prophet and the Veritable Vision) should admit that the heart has two doorways: one from the outward through the senses, and the other from its inner depth. Yet the nearer of the two that leads to the Heavenly Kingdom, and from which emanate inspiration and intuition, fails to encompass the sciences through study and resorting to the common ways of acquiring knowledge. (Nevertheless, it is possible by way of "mujahadah", ceaseless spiritual striving to be adopted as a sure way leading to such enlightenment).

(b) The formulation of his theological doctrine and the laying down of his method of research in scholastic theology, which he intended to be well-adapted to various classes of people. Ghazali promised in his Tahafut to write a book entitled: Qawa'id Al-Aqa'id (= Rules for the Articles of Faith) in which he would be concerned with affirming the doctrine he had adopted as he had done in refuting the philosophers' viewpoints in his Tahafut.

The most important work of his, to be relied on, in studying his theological doctrine in the book, entitled: Al-Iqtisad Fil-I'tiqad which is intended for scholars. As regards the unlettered masses, he wrote al-Risalah Al-Qudsiyyah (= The Holy Epistle), and Ilgam al-Awamm 'An 'Ilm Al-Kalam (= Reining back of the Commonalty from the Science of Scholastic Theology).

Classification of the Dogmatic Problems from an Epistemological Standpoint

Ghazali holds that the theological method should be made up our of a combination of reason and Revelation. To make this method exclusively dependent on any of the two excluding the other, would obviously lead to erroneous inference and disregard to what is intended to be proved.

This is due to the fact that theological problems can be classified into three kinds according to the way adopted in discerning them:

1. What can be known through reason without Revelation.
2. What can be known through Revelation Without reason ('aql). (Here reason means intellect).
3. What can be known though both Revelation and reason.

First: As instances for the first kind, can be cited huduth Al' Alam, the origin of the world (its existence after non-existence), the Existence of the Muhdith, Originator, His Omnipotence, Omniscience, and Will These attributes are accorded a rank higher than Al-Kalam Al-Nafsi, Speech in the Mind (that is to say Thoughts in the Mind with which the Deity speaketh to Himself without letters or word—Tr).

This is due to the fact that the Deity's "Al-Kalam Al-Nafsi", Speech in the Mind can hardly be ascertained if we refrain from admitting the above mentioned Divine Attributes. Hence Divine Speech cannot be attested save through reason.

Second: As an instance for the second kind, is to admit the occurrence of two possible issues, such as the Hashr, Gathering, and Ba'th, Resurrection, Thawab, Reward and Jaza', Punishment, in the Hereafter, etc. These can never be known, save through Revelation from God.

Third: Everything lying within the scope of reason, but accorded a grade lower than attesting the Speech of God, Most High. Wc cite as instances the question of the "Beatific Vision", and believing that God is the Sole Creator of all movements and a'rad., accidents, together with everything that is characterized by a similar course.

The Attitude of Reason Towards Evidence Based on Sam', Tradition

Ghazali determined the attitude of reason towards traditional evidences, endeavouring, thereby, to avoid what had been considered by some thinkers as a conflict between reason and tradition. Thus what had been reported by tradition can be included in no more than three categories:

1. Anything reported through traditional evidence the belief in which is allowed by reason.
2. The reported traditional evidence which is ruled by reason to be impossible.
3. The traditional evidences respecting which reason suspends its judgment, thereby considering them as neither possible nor impossible.

In the first case, the traditional evidences may be well-authenticated in both "matn", text, and isnad, chain or narrators. Therefore, they become categorically convincing, and the truth of which, should be acknowledged. Or they may be defective in both matn and isnad; and hence they cannot be admitted.

In the second case, we have to interpret the evidence reported by tradition, since it is hardly rational to admit traditional evidences containing what is considered to be in flat contradiction with reason.

As to the third case, we have to recognize the traditional evidences. It is incumbent to believe in them, because reason has suspended its judgment, and refrained from deciding their impossibility.

Ghazali's Reckoning with the Rational Method

Ghazali's most important work for the study of his doctrine, theological attitude, and what he regards as an incumbent duty upon 'Ulemas to make deductive reasonings for the attestation of the Creed is his work entitled Al-I'qtisad Fil-I'tiqad, to Which he referred in his Ihya saying that he not gone beyond speculation on the principles of dogmatics and other topics dealt with by scholastic theologians.

The reading of the work, the allowed only to the intelligent. Who can find out where a question might be raised or an equivocal point might be stirred up.

His Campaign Against the Hashawiyyah:
For their Assumption that Taqlid is Incumbent

In the introductory chapter of his Iqtisad, Ghazali made a vigorous campaign against (the following):

(1) The Hashawiyyah who rendered obligatory the adoption of taqlid (= the simple acceptance of truth on religious authority) in matters related to the articles of Faith, and adherence to the outward sense of religious texts.

(2) Philosophers and extremists from amongst the Mu'tazilah who accorded an unlimited sway to reason, until it clashed with the fundamentals of the Shari'at.

"Thus we find" Ghazali said, "one group deviating towards "tafrit", failure, and the other inclined to "ifrat, excess. Both of them are remote from prudence and caution. But the abiding duty in the Creed is to cling to a middle course, and to rely on the right path, since the two extremes are blameworthy.

"How can anyone attaint to guidance through being content by following the reported traditions and narratives and renouncing the methods of inquiry and speculation? Does he hold the notion that there is no basis for the Shari'at but the utterances of the Prophet (P.B.U.H.), the best of mankind, while there is, as well, the evidence of reason with which was recognized the truthfulness of what he had said? Or how can anyone who had merely followed reason and who confined to it, be guided to truth?

The purport of this quotation is that deduction in dogmatics, according to Ghazali, should be based on both reason and Revelation. To the dependent exclusively on any of the two, apart from the other lead to erroneous deduction and disregard to what is intended to be proved.

What Ghazali Means by Reason Versus Revelation?

Such is the approach Ghazali adopted to determine the method that can be applied by reason and Revelation in dealing with the problems of scholastic theology and deducing the evidences corroborating theological data.

The term 'aql, reasons, mentioned by Ghazali, as versus Revelation is still vague. In other words, it is used by him as general term and given a variety of renderings in several occasion.

But what does he mean by 'aql? This perceptive faculty he variously called reason, "ruh", spirit, "nafs" soul, and qalb, heart? What is intended by those necessary and rational premises such as his asserting that existence and non-existence can never be attributed together to the self-same thing simultaneously? What about the logical speculation that had been used by philosophers and the Mu'tazilites in their dialectics?

It may be advisable to postpone the answers to these questions until we examine Ghazali's book, al-Iqtisad, to quote therefrom the deductive methods used in his work and which he preferred to make them a basis for his theological doctrine.

After having referred to the various deductive methods he had dealt with at length in his two works: "M'iyar Al-`Ilm" (= The Criterion of Knowledge), and "Mihakk al-Nazar" (= The Touch - stone of Speculation), Ghazali decided in his Iqtisad to avoid the ambigious ways (of drawing conclusions), and to be confined to three methods, possibly considered by him as the most important fundamentals in his theological doctrine.

First: Probing and Classification

It is restricting the proposition to two premises; then he refuting one of them, it becomes inevitable to deduce the truth of the second.

If we say, for instance, that the world is either originated or eternal; but its eternity is considered as impossible. Therefore, it must be originated. This necessary conclusion is drawn from two other premises, and cannot follow unless the proposition be arranged in a certain way so as to agree with the rules (of syllogism).

Second: Arranging two Premises in Another Way

As when we say: Everything affected by what is originated is hadith originated. The World is affected by what is originated Hence, it necessarily follows that the World is hadith, originated.

Third: Arguing that the Opponent's Assumption is Impossible

This is done by proving that the opponent's assumption will lead to an impossibility, and anything conducive to such an issue is categorically impossible. For instance:

> If philosophers were right in assuming that the Dawrat Al-Falak, the revolutions of the celestial bodies are interminable, they would have to admit that what is endless has ceased. And this necessary conclusion is an impossibility.

These are the three methods of deduction, out of which Ghazali could determine the meanings of "dalil", evidence, the madlul", the proposition to be proved, the "wajh al-dalalah", the reason for attention, and the haqiqat al-nazar", the reality of speculation. This is due to the fact that the conclusion that is necessarily inferred from the two premises is the proposition that has been proved. The construction of the two necessary premises is what would lead to the evidence. The process of thinking that has reproduced the two premises in the mind, and led to reflecting upon the conclusion that would necessarily follow, is speculation.

Ghazali went on reinforcing these methods, showing how far the differences characterizing them can be made of in speculative criteria, as he had demonstrated their value in carrying conviction.

He was sure that the conclusion would follow, once the opponent had admitted the premises of the evidence. But what would be the issue, were the opponent to reject the two premises altogether or one of them?

Ghazali would, then, turn the evidences into necessary premises, so much easy to understand that everybody would take them for granted. It is these premises out of which the evidence would have to be made up or to which the evidence would be due as regards the premises of the opponent, either directly or through other propositions. There are six kinds of these axiomatic evidences:

First: "Al-Hissiyyat", Sensuous Perceptions

That is to say things perceived through outward or inward observation. If we say, for instance:

(1) Everything originated has a cause.
(2) There are in the world originated things.

Conclusion

Therefore, these things must have a cause. The second premise can be perceived through the senses, because by direct observations we see the origination of animals, plants, clouds and rain. Also do we sense "a'rado", accidents, colours and voices which are transmitted from one place to another. Equally do we know through inward observation the occurrence of psychical phenomena such as pleasure and pain, etc. Hence, the opponent would be bound to take this premise for granted.

Second : Al-'Aqliyyat al-Mahdah", Sheer Intellectual Perception

If we say The World is either "qadim mu'akhar" lately prior, or "hadith muqaddam", formerly originated. Every sane, person would admit, thereby, that it is hadith, originated, since we deduce huduth, origination through a similar intellectual evidence. (When we say, for instance):

1. Everything that does *not* precede what is originated is originated.
2. The World does *not* precede what is originated. Conclusion: The World is originated.

The first premise is reasonable to which is sound-minded

person is bound to agree, because anything that does not precede the originated would either come into being before or after the originated. No third category does ever exist. Were the opponent to assume its existence, he would be rejecting what reason regards as axiomatic.

Third: "Al-Muqaddimat Al-Mutawatirah," Premises Identically Reported by Numerous Authorities

If we say: The Prophet was truthful, because he produce a miracle, Everything produced as such is conformable to fact, the opponent would, then, be quite unable to deny the occurrence of the miracle, since such a miracle had been testified by "tawatur", being identically reported by numerous authorities. Hence we take cognizance of it, as we did respecting the existence of Muhammad, Jesus, Moses and other Prophets.

Fourth: Premises to be Proved by other Syllogisms

These are based on evidence gained through sense perception, reasoning, or reported tradition of the sort called mutawatir. This would be realized, for instance, after having made accurate deduction testifying to the fact that the world is originated. Such conclusion would become in turn a premise the truth of which is taken for granted, and would, thereby, be used in a further inference, since it has acquired the validity of a sensous or a rational premise.

Fifth: Premises Based on "Sam", Tradition

If we assume that sins be committed through the Will of God, Most High, and establish the evidence corroborating such an assumption in the following way:

Everything that exists, owes its existence to God, Most High; but sins do exist.

We find that the truth of the second premise (the existence of sins) is proved through both the senses and the dictates of the Shari'at. It is because the existence of sins is certainly known by sense perception, as it is equally certain that the actions considered as sins are known by the Shari'at. Therefore, the opponent would not be able to reject the first premise (that sins are willed by God), if he were to take the Shari'at into account.

Sixth: Premises Borrowed from the Beliefs and the Date of the Opponent

Through there premises are not attested by evidences drawn from either sense perception of reason, they can be made use of in our argumentation with the opponent who assumes them to be true.

Thus, we can adopt any of these as a premise in our deductive reasoning. The opponent would, then be unable to reject it, since he would, thereby, be refuting his own doctrine.

These sorts of proofs vary in carrying conviction as they are unequal in the range of their use in deductive reasoning.

The first and second sorts are generally well-established, and could satisfy all kinds of people save those who are devoid of the faculty of reasoning and sense perception.

The third does only persuade those to whom the narratives were reported for numerous authorities. But mutawatir narratives might be considered as such by only a group of people with the exclusion of others.

Shafi'i's viewpoint, for instance, in the case of a Muslim who had killed a "dhimmi" (a Scripturary belonging to a people who have a Dhimma, covenant with Muslims) is commonly agreed upon as a mutawatir decision by Shafi'ite jurists from amongst the colleagues and disciples of Shafi'i. But such is not the case as regards the unlettered who adopt taqlid.

The fourth is only convincing to those who are well-versed in analogical reasoning, that is to say the making up of syllogisms, conforming to their rules and the methods of inferring conclusions from their premises.

The fifth persuades only those who consider tradition as

authoritative.

The sixth is unconvincing to the investigator himself, but it would be of use to him when engaged in a controversy with the opponent who believes in this sort of premises.

Reason According to Ghazali's Viewpoint

From the foregoing may have become clear the answer to the above-mentioned questions, together with what is intended by Ghazali as regards : reason versus Revelation.

Ghazali means by reason this reflective power in man which perceives factual data about things by speculation, through reproducing premises and finding out the conclusions that would necessarily be inferred from them.

This rational process is often confined to the Aristotelian syllogism as formed in a specific way, with its various kinds, rules, and conditions which lead to occurate inference. No less important are the axiomatic premises which should be relied upon to get binding and convincing conclusions.

It is as if the circumstances of Ghazali's life and his particular attitude towards strong opponents such as philosophers and Mu'tazilites, had forced him to introduce the Aristotelian system of deduction as a rational method to be used by him in solving dogmatic problems.

His adopted such a course after the orthodox theologians had remained for long shunning this sort of deduction; thus refraining from making use of it in dealing with theological questions. Nay they had gone so far as to forbid applying it to juristic disciplines in general, and to theology in particular.

Ghazali's Rational Method does not Fit all sorts of People

No sooner had Ghazali' elucidated his approach, than he did make a reservation, notifying that the method he had formulated ought not to be used by all sorts of people, nor should it be taught to everybody. It is because of the wide range of difference amongst kinds and classes of people in their ability and fitness either in adopting or avoiding it.

For this reason, Ghazali asserted that the evidences he had adduced in the science of scholastic theology should be looked upon as analogous to medicaments intended for the treatment of those who suffer from heart disease. The physician should be so prudent and cautious as to avoid worsening the case by failing to prescribe what is most specific to ensure a speedy recovery.

The populace are known to be so much fettered by their sense perceptions as to make their natural dispositions and minds utterly incapable to seek knowledge through rational speculation and logical inference.

Hence, they ought not to go beyond the Quranic texts, Prophetic traditions, and the bare study of "fiqh", since the evidences drawn from the Holy Quran are so much like nutritive food that is most wholesome to everybody. As to the proofs inferred by scholastic theologians, they are similar to medicine which would only be curative and salutary to a restricted number of people (who happen to be suffering from a certain ailment).

Hence, according to this method, people are classed by Ghazali into four groups:

(1) Those who had deviated from the true Faith, such as the unbelievers and the innovators who had tenaciously clung to the beliefs of their forefathers. Nothing did avail against these save through the use of force. For the majority of unbelievers had been converted to Islam by the sword. It has been ordained by God that the sword and spear-head can do what cannot be done by verbal expression and persuasion.

To prove that it was right to use force against the obstinate, Ghazali cited the conversion to Islam of many people from amongst the adherents of other faiths after desperate battles Muslims had won and heated controversies had availed nothing and had only made stubbornness much more intense.

Ghazali then added: "What we have mentioned should not be thought of as lessening our estimation of reasoning. The light of reason is a privilege that is only bestowed by God upon whom He singleth out from amongst His Saints. But the dominant feature characterizing the populace is incompetence and neglect. They fail to understand what is proved by reason. For they are just like bats which are incapable of beholding the light of the sun."

(2) Those who believed in truth through taqlid and tradition. But they are endowed with intelligence that enables them to find out certain equivocal points that caused them to entertain doubts about their beliefs. Or else, they might have heard some heretical views which made an impression on them.

Such a sort of people should be treated with moderation and mildness, so as to dispel doubts from their minds. Plausible and convincing proofs should be elucidated to them, either by the way of reciting Quranic verses and Prophetic traditions, or by quoting the sayings of a scholar noted for his acumen and wisdom, and whom they credit with authoritative learning.

If they were so intelligent and sharp-witted as to be only persuaded by evidences that can stand discussion and exhaustive investigation, then it would be advisable to provide them with the right proof. But this should only be given in case of need and agreeing particularly with the equivocal point under discussion.

(3) Those who had deviated from believing in truth; yet they show signs of intelligence. Since their former beliefs had been seriously shaken, or because of their innate disposition to entertain doubts, it is expected that they recognize and admit the true Faith. Such a sort of people should be mildly conciliated, but not through argumentation and fanatical controversies which would certainly incite them to persevere in stubbornness.

For this reason, the exhaustive study of scholastic theology and the total preoccupation with it are not a "fard' ain" an incumbent duty on every Muslim, but they are of a kind termed "fard kifayah", a duty that has only to be fulfilled by a sufficient number of Muslim, thereby relieving all others from having to fulfil it.

After having explained his assertions, Ghazali dealt with determining the value of scholastic theology and its standing in comparison with the science of Muslim jurisprudence as a religious discipline, and medicine as a secular one.

He adduced for reason to prove that scholastic theology is a fard kifayah the fact that doubts and uncertainties are rare phenomena, though it is not impossible that their propagation might take place. But once they have occurred, their banishment from the fundamentals of dogma becomes a binding duty. For this reason, the call to truth through self-evident inference is a matter of great significance in religious ussues.

Hence, there should be in every country someone who calls to truth and known to be well-versed in scholastic theology. He should be engaged in opposing the innovators and purifying the hearts of the Sunnites from yielding to heresies. If any country is ground to be lacking such a scholar, its whole inhabitants are bound to cover up such a deficiency.

Ghazali considered that "fiqh", Muslim jurisprudence is more important than 'Ilm Al-Kalam, scholastic theology. If it happens that there be in any country a scholar so competent as to master the two disciplines together, yet he has no time but to master only one of them, then he has to start with "fiqh" which is generally much more requistic than scholastic theology.

For the latter is just like the science of medicine; yet medicine is needed for the treatment of physical ailments, whilst scholastic theology is intended for the cure of those who suffer from certain indispositions in their hearts and minds.

Thus Ghazali accorded fiqh a standing much more higher than that assigned to scholastic theology, giving for reason the fact that the Prophet's Companions left out the latter, while they had been preoccupied with the former.

As to those who consider scholastic theology as more important because it is more closely related the fundamental of the Faith, whereas fiqh as compared to it, is rather subsidiary, Ghazali admitted their standpoint.

"But," he added, "it is rather of no avail, in this respect; because what is fundamental is the genuine belief which is gained through taqlid, whilst the need to logical reasonings, and dialactical methods are scarcely felt."

Such is Ghazali's classification of the various dispositions. His method is divided into small tables in which the different classes of people are distributed in a way conformable to their intellectual talents, power of apprehension, and the extent of the knowledge they had acquired.

It is to be remarked that Ghazali, in the method he had expounded in his Iqtisad, did not assign a place for the mystical approach the had chosen and adopted for himself as a path leading to true knowledge, especially to what is related to the article of Faith.

The Surest Path to the Knowledge of Facts

We have already referred to Ghazali's assertion as regards theoretical reasonings, considered to be inadequate in leading us to unquestionable truth. What would be his viewpoint, if his method failed to clarify any of the issues dealt with in scholastic theology? Are we to leave the believer plunged into grave doubts?" Or would there by a missing link or a next stage following Ghazali's rational method which would lead the Muslim to believe firmly in the Faith, if he had the chance to be initiated into it?

Ghazali, in his Iqtisad asserted that positive belief can be acquired through taqlid. But in his Ihya.' he classified Faith into three grades:

1. The Faith of the populace which is based on taqlid, the simple acceptance of truth on religious authority. This he calls in his Iqtisad: "traditional Faith".
2. The Faith of scholastics which he calls: "Faith by Inference". It is partly deductive and not far removed from that of the populace.
3. The Faith of those who know (out of spiritual experience) Their Faith is "mushahadah", beholding with the light of Reality. This he called : "Works added to Faith".

As an illustration of these three kinds of Faith, Ghazali likens the first to someone's knowledge drawn from what had been reported to him that such and such a man is in his house; so he believes in his presence. Secondly, he may hear the voice of that person in his house and will thereby make no doubt of his presence therein. Thirdly, when he enters his house and sees that person there, (thus gaining an assured knowledge of his presence).

It is possible, in the first grade of Faith, that the believers might have been mistaken in what they had heard. Ghazali placed them, on account of that, with the "Ashab al Yamin", the Fellows of the Right Hand, but would not, definitely, he grouped with "the Favoured".

The second grade Faith, acquired through study and deduction might equally be erroneous But the third grade Faith would never, in any case, be liable to error. The knowledge gained by the believers who had attained to the grade of Faith, is in the words of Ghazali, "Absolute Reality" and "Verit able Beholding."

Such is analogous to that of the Favoured and "Saints" whose Faith is based on "mushahadah", beholding which comprises the faith of both the populace and the scholastics, having a further distinction in accordance with Which their Faith is completely free from the possibility of failing into error.

Here we see Ghazali, assigning to the Faith based on taqlid the lowest grade. Nay, he considered it to be most exposed to error in questions of dogma. This is to be followed by Faith that is established on the method of logical deduction and rational speculation.

But the perfect Faith, Ghazali accorded to highest rank, is the one that can never be acquired through either taqlid or reasoning, but through a totally different path.

It is a path of mysticism that had already been chosen had adopted by him, considering it as the surest way to gain a well-certified knowledge of theological facts that in quite unblemished by any doubt of wavering.

Such facts as dealt with by the science of scholastic theology are closely identical with those embodied in mystical knowledge. If the speculative method failed to unravel these facts to the inquirer, and to banish any doubt or confusion that might have blurred them, this would be the final stage in the method of scholastic theology, (beyond which nothing would come of it).

The inquirer should then renounce everything and wait. "The door of guidance) might be opened to him to go through his path (of mysticism) which would dispel the bewilderment and perplexity he had met with".

Ghazali cited a considerable number of texts from the Quran and the Sunnah to prove the true guidance afforded by this path, and to demonstrate hat it would surely lead to a through grasp of the theological facts, reason with all its deductive inferences and proofs failed to reach.

This is amply explained in God's Saying: "And whosoever keepeth his duty to God, He will appoint a way our for him"(LXV, 2). That is to say God will guide him to an outlet which would relieve him from doubts and uncertainties.

God also said: "And He provideth for him from (sources) he never could imagine"(LXV, 3.). That is to say endowing him with knowledge, without requiring him to exercise and effort for its acquisition.

In this connexion, the Prophet (P.B.U.H.) is reported to have said: "He would acts in compliance with what he knows (of religion). God would enlighten him with knowledge he had never known."

To this sort of knowledge that comes through Divine Inspiration, God, Most High and referred in His Saying: "And We taught him Knowledge of Our Own (Min ladunna)". (XVIII, 65). By this is meant knowledge that can never be acquired in the familiar way that is through conscious reasoning and study.

In this way, Ghazali had introduced a sufistic approach into his scholastic method in order to supplement the latter with the former, either directly or indirectly, according to what can be gathered from the different trends of his thought.

(Such a standpoint Ghazali adopted), despite the fact that he refrained from assigning plainly, a place for his mystical element in his Iqtisad, when he attempted to determine the scope of his scholastic method.

Yet, it is possible to find traces of his sufistic tendency in the solutions of certain theological problems he had dealt with throughout the various aspects of his stupendous intellectual legacy and encyclopedic works.

Summing Up the Study

Gentleman,

After having reviewed the most important problems of Islamic thought, bearing on the subject of Divinity, and discerning the various currents that had arisen within its spacious scope; and after having examined the viewpoints of all parties in these dissensions, it would be possible for us to come to the following conclusions:

(1) It is to be remarked that, within the sphere of Islamic thought, the raising of questions, bearing on Divinity, especially from the philosophical standpoint, had never been a more a borrowing from other cultures and philosophies alien to the Muslim (intellectual) environment, as assumed by many orientalists and those who had followed them from amongst Muslim historians.

These problems had arisen on account of certain factors, the most important of which are the following:

(a) The great latitude in religious belief allowed by Islam to its adherents.

(b) The Quran urges Muslims to give themselves to serious through and meditation, requiring them to exercise their intellectual powers to discern the facts of the universe, to unravel its mysteries, and to determine man's place therein.

(c) Certain new-comers and neophytes made strong adverse criticism of Islamic tenets and beliefs in an attempt to shake the Muslim Faith, through the heated polemics they had stirred up, and the subtle objections they had devised the nature of which was liable to cause intense dissensions, and to break up the unity of Muslims.

(2) The first and foremost aim of Muslim who had held these divergent standpoints, bearing on are of the intricate theological problems they had been dealing with, was to exalt and dignify to the utmost the Essence of God, Most High, and to exert zealously every effort in "tanzih", excluding all human likeness from pronouncement regarding the Godhead.

Hence, it would not be fair to bring reproach upon one from amongst such and such a group, nor have we to accuse anyone of heresy or unbelief, though scholars and researchers are bound to refute groundless doctrines and to show the errors they embody Yet it is most likely that these mistaken views had never been intended by those to whom they were ascribed.

For this reason, it is possible to say of these doctrines what is generally said of any human (intellectual) attempt which is liable to be true or mistaken. Thus it may cause straying and deception, or it may lead to guidance and light.

(3) In fact, such problems originate only in our conceptions and the various endeavours we make to explain dogmatic questions bearing on Divinity. Yet the idea of God, acknowledging His Existence, and our need of Him are (instinctive) trends set in men's nature by Almighty God, since their first creation in the loins of Adam (P.B.U.H.).

"And (remember) when the Lord drew forth from the Children of Adam, from their loins, their descendants, and made them testify of themselves (saying): Am I not your Lord? They said: Yes, verily. We do testify". (VII, 172).

"So set thou thy face steadily and truly to the Faith as an Hanif, according to the fitrah constitution whereon God hath constituted men; there is no altering the Creation of God, that is the standard religion; but most men do not know".

It is to be remarked that Muslim philosophers and theologians had been in no need to assume such painful duties and to cope with these serious difficulties, whether in their commentaries and solutions of dogmatic problems, or in the methods they had devised for their discernment.

Only did they take such a course in order to remove any obstacles that might have intervened between Muslims and their sound nature according to which God had created them. They thought these impediments would vitiate the character of Muslims and tempt them to deviate from the sound nature with which they had been endowed.

For this reason, we have always to give due consideration to this obvious difference between:

1. Islam as had been ordained by God, be He Exalted, and expounded by Him in the Clear-Cut and Fundamental Revelations of His Book, together with the explanations embodied in the authenticated traditions of His Messenger Muhammad (P.B.U.H.).
2. Our own ways of understanding Islam, or the attempts we wake to explain its texts and interpret its tenets.

As regards the latter, they can possibly be considered as Islamic: but we cannot decide categorically that they do represent the true sense of Islam. Though these interpretations are related to Islam, they are too general to be exactly corresponding to its teachings, if not quite divergent.

But the former it contrast with the latter is never liable to error, nor does it cause any straying from the righ path. It is because: "No falsehood can approach it form before or behind it: it is sent down by One Full of Wisdom and Worthy of All Praise" (XLI, 42.).Failing to perceive such a difference between these two categories has been the source of a considerable number of mistakes made by orientalists in their judgements about Islam, of which Islam is quite clear.

O Lord! We pray Thee to guide us to Thine Right Path, and to favour us with the Bounty of rendering us fit to do what pleaseth Thee, and to act in conformity with Thine Shari'at and the Guidance of Thine Chosen Messenger, Muhammad (P.B.U.H.).

Verily, Thou art our Lord; over all thing Thou has Power; Thou art the Best to protect, and the Best to help.

Peace be upon you, God's Mercy, and His Blessing.

REFERENCES

1. Tabaqat al-Shafiyyah, vol. III, p. 260. Cairo, 1324 AH.
2. Macdonald, The religious attitude and life in Islam, Chicago, 1969, p. 190.

3. Al-Munqidh min al-Dalal, Cairo, 1329, AH. pp. 6,7.
4. Al-Ghazali, Maqasid al-falasefah,
5. Al-Ghazali, al-Iqtisad fil-I'tiqad..
5. Al-Ghazali, Ihya al-Uloom.
6. Al-Jili, al-Insan alKamil

12

The Meaning of 'Islam' in Hadith Literature

JANE I SMITH

(Abstract: Deals with the meaning and development of shades in understanding the term Islam and Muslim. While this discussion is not a complete compilation of every mention of *islam* in Traditions, it is considerably more than a random sampling and serves as the means whereby one is able to posit a number of categories into which particular traditions using the word *islam* can be placed. This an attempt at such a classification, based on more than one hundred listings from the significant collections).

Historically the religion of Islam with its theological foundations has been one of the least appreciated—perhaps because it has been one of the least understood—of the world faiths considered by Western theologians and writers. Over the past century, interest in studying Islam (to which as a religion the West has given a variety of names) has greatly increased often with an apparently corresponding increase in both sympathy and depth of appreciation for its constituent elements. Most orientalists include in their analyses some indication of how they understand the term *islam*, and some have gone into lengthy and detailed investigations of its origins and linguistic implications, generally within the Qur'anic usage.

Few Western writers, however, seem fully to have taken into account, for at least to have acknowledged by specific reference, the significance of the traditional usages of *islam* in the collections of *hadith* or the classical understanding of the term. One cannot but glance through the great Qur'an commentaries that have served as one of the principal vehicles of Muslim piety through the ages without finding oneself immersed in the sayings of what the Prophet said and did. This holds no less true for the exegesis of those verses containing the *masdar islam.* The following short survey. dealing specifically with those traditions in which *islam* is used or defined, is presented both to acquaint the reader with this basic source material and to attempt a general summary of the understanding (s) of *islam* as expressed in the *hadiths* of the first Islamic centuries.

It is clear that to a greater or lesser extent depending on the type of *hadiths* transmitted, the actual use o *islam* an the *masdar* from of *aslama* is often accidental. That is, in some cases two traditions are cited in a nearly identical way, except that one use *islam* and another uses of different form of the verb. This is an interesting illustration of what can also be noted in the Qur'an commentaries, that particularly in the early centuries of *masdar* form was so clearly understood as verbal rather than (or as well as) nominal that such an interchange of forms was possible. In many instances the general content is the same in several traditions except that some specifically mention *islam* and others use another from the very. In the survey we shall consider only those traditions using the *masdar islam* itself.

Here, then, are some of the categories into which the traditions seem naturally to fall. The largest grouping is that just mentioned which considers the duties (*fara'id*) prescribed by the Prophet.

The most commonly cited tradition of this type is that describing a man coming to the Messenger of God, very agitated, asking him about *al-islam.* The Prophet enumerates the duties and the men asks if more is required. No, says the Prophet, except that you be obedient. This sequence occurs several times with more duties cited, and ends with the man saying: I will not increase or decrease it, to which the Prophet replies: He is blessed if he is sincere (*aflaha'in sadaqa*).

In all of these narratives three duties specifically mentioned are five prayers day and night, fasting in the month of Ramadan, and paying the alms-tax (*al-zakat*). In four they are enumerated in answer to the Messenger of God's having been asked about *al-islam (yas'alu 'an al-islam).* In two instances (Bu. and Nas.) these three duties are referred to, but in answer to the question: What is the *fard Allah*? In discussing *zakat* the narrator says that the Messenger of God told the questioning man about the obligations of *islam (shara'i al-islam).*

Four other *hadiths* relate the duties of *islam*, all isolated examples in this sampling. In Nas. I, 330 we read that there are in the call to *al-islam* three essential elements: witnessing (that there is no God but He, *al-shahadah*), prayer *(al-salat)* and paying the alms-tax *(al-zakat).* And if after that anyting in necessary it is the duty of fasting (*al-saum*) and pilgrimage (*al-hajj*). The narrator goes on to say that the *arkan* are five. Then in an interesting passage he says that the first three pillars are credal (*i'tiqadi*), physical (*badoni*) and financial (*mali*), namely the *shahadah*, the *salat* and the *zakat*. It is in terms of these three that one really answers the call to *islam* and the other two, *saum* and *hajj*, are easy in comparison to these. "*Islam* is the basis (*asl*) and it is hard for the *kuffar* and prayer is hard because of its repetition and almsgiving is hard because of man's love of money." From this it appears that *islam*, as well as for the totality of the *arkan*, is used specifically for the *shahadah*, presumably because it designates "the act of" (whether becoming a Muslim, or committing oneself).

In A.b.H. IV, 200-201 we read that God commanded four things in *al-islam*; the performance of three of these does not suffice unless one observes them all: *salat* and *zakat* and *saum Ramadan* and *hajj al-bayt.* A.b.H. cites another tradition (I, 250), in which the Messenger of God says that the duties of *islam* are five with no increase. However he mentions only *zakat, saum Ramadan* and *hajj.* A final example is the instance cited by A.b.H. I, 264 of the mentioning of the duties of *islam* by the Messenger of God, specifically the *zakat* and *saum* and *hajj* and the obligations (*shara'i*) of *islam.*

If we tally up the results of these examples we find that the prayer have been mentioned nine times (both as simply *salat* and specifically as five prayers day and night), the fast Ramadan ten times, the *zakat* nine times, the *hajj* four times and the *shahadah* once. There is, of course, nothing absolute about these figures, given the fact that this sampling is not a complete listing of all references to *islam* in the traditions, nor do they necessarily indicate the importance put on the constituent elements of *islam* by either the Prophet or the *salaf*. Such an enumeration does, however, give a feeling for the proportionate emphasis put on these particulars, and provides an interesting illustration of how the various designations were actually used at this early period of Islam. It should also he reiterated that there are as many occasions in the *hadiths* literature, perhaps more, in which the pillar (*arkan*), or duties (*fara'id*) as they have been more frequently called in these examples, are listed with no mention of *islam* as there are cases in which the term *islam* is actually used. What is of interest for the purposes of this essay is not the specifics of the duties as much as the fact that the listing of them was the response of the Messenger of God, as recorded in the traditions, to his having been asked about *islam*. We shall consider the implications of this after having viewed other instances of the term *islam* as found in the *hadiths*.

Closely related to the above category is the group of traditions that relate the statement of the Messenger of God that *al-islam* is built on five (things). In only one instance out of twelve is this cited as an answer to a question, and here we know only that a group visiting the Messenger of God had previously been asking him about various matters. The results of these enumerations show more consistency that we saw above. All twelve mention that *islam* is built an *salat, zakat, saum Ramadan* and *hajj al-bayt*. It is only in regard to the first duty that there is some differentiation. Six mention the two *shahadahs*, four only the first *shahadah*, one says "to proclaim the unity of God" and one "to worship God and give the lie to all else." Two mention that the Messenger of God, having been asked about the *jihad*, indicates that it is good.

One of the most interesting groups of traditions mentioning

islam is that in which the Prophet defines *al-islam* as distinct from *al-iman.* The most popular version tells the story of a man who comes to the Prophet of God while he is seated with some of the Companions. The man has a beautiful face and black hair and a white robe. He is unknown to the assembled group, and bears no marks of travel. After placing one knee over the other and putting his palm on his thigh he asks the Prophet, What is *al-islam (ma-al-islam)*? or, Tell me about *al-islam (akhbirm 'an il-islam).* The circumstances of the story are altered somewhat in the different narrations, but the version in most common. Much to the surprise of the assemblage, after receiving the answer (which is that *islam* is the performance of certain duties, listed below) the man informs the Prophet that he, the Prophet, is correct. He then proceeds to inquire about *al-iman* (faith), *al-ihsan* (beneficence), and *al-sa'ah* (the hour or appointed time), indicating after each reply that the Messenger of God is correct. At the end of the narration it is revealed that the beautiful stranger is indeed the angel Jibril who says that he has come to teach the assembled group about their *din (atakum yu'allimukum dinakum).*

Summarising the sample of fourteen traditions we find that *islam* consist of the following elements (the number in brackets indicate frequency of mention in the various traditions) : witnessing that there is no God but God and the Muhammad is His messenger (eight); submitting to God with no association (*shirk*) of anything else (six); doing *salat* (fourteen); paying *zakat* (fourteen); *saum Ramadan* (thirteen); making the *hajj al-bayt* if it be possible (nine); and cleansing of the major ritual impurity (*janabah*) (one). *Imam,* on the other hand, means faith in the following: God (fourteen), His angels (fourteen), His Books (nine), His Book (three), His Messengers (twelve), His Messenger (one), the last day (seven), the decree (*al-qadr*) in its totality of good and evil (four), meeting Him (four), death and life after death (one), reckoning (*al-hisab*) (one), and the balance (*al-mizan*) (one). In several of the traditions cited the Messenger of God is asked after the recital of the elements of *islam* and *iman*: If I do that am I a *muslim/mu'min*? to which the reply is "yes".

In these traditions we seem to have a fairly distinct line drawn between *islam* and *iman*: the former consists almost exclusively of performance of the (five) specific duties prescribed by God through His Prophet for the *muslim*; the latter is faith in (acceptance and affirmation of) the various elements proclaimed through the word of the Prophet as real and valid. This distinction is further supported by such *hadiths* as the following: In A.b.H. III, 134-5 it is related that the Messenger of God asserted that *al-islam* is overt (*'alaniyah*) while *al-iman* is in the heart and pointing to his breast he said, piety (*al-taqwa*) is here. And in A.D. II, 523 a tradition is cited from al-Zuhri that the explanation of the Qur'an 49:14 is that *al-islam* is the word (*al-kalimah*) and *al-iman* is the deed (*al-amal*).

Such a clear distinction was not always made, however, and in several traditions we see that while *islam* and *iman* were generally gives different emphases, they were definitely seen as interrelated. In I.M. I, 34 occurs the only instance of a form of *amana* being use within the definition of *islam*. The Prophet tells 'Ade B. Hatim. If you submit you are preserved (*aslim taslam*). When 'Adi asks, What is *al-islam*? the Prophet replies: Witness that there is no God but God and that I am the Messenger of God, and have faith in all foreordinations (*al-aqdar kulliha*), their good and evil, their sweetness and bitterness.

Then there is a group of traditions in which the question, What (kind of) *islam* is best (*ayyu'l-islam khayr*)? is given the reply that it is giving food (feeding the poor and hungry) and offering peace (*salam*) to those whom one knows and does not know. To the question, Which *islam* is virtuous? We find the answer that the Muslim (the other members of the community) are safe from what one says and what one does (*'an yaslimu'l-muslimun min lisanika wa-yadika*), i.e., that the true Muslim is he from whom other Muslims are sage, and with whom they are secure. In one case the latter reply is given to the former question. However, there is one *hadiths* in which the Messenger of God is asked, What is *al-islam*? And to this question he replies that the *muslims* submit because of what one says and does. Then when asked which *islam* is more virtuous, he answers : *al-iman*, which consists of faith in God and His angels and His Books and His Messengers and the resurrection (*ba'th*). This progression continues so that the most virtuous *iman* is the emigration (*al-hijrah*), the most virtuous *hijrah* is *al-jihad.* and so on. Here *iman* is a kind of subdivision of *islam*, and understanding which also may may apply to the above-mentioned narratives in which Jibril inquires progressively about *al-islam, al-iman, al-ihsan* and *al-sa'ah.*

Al-Bukhari himself in introducing a *hadiths* concerning which *islam* is good says: The spreading out of peace (*al-salam*) is from *al-islam*; and 'Umar said, There are three things which when gathered constitute *iman* for the gatherer: being fair, giving peace to the world, and being generous (I, 30). Here again there seems to be no clear indication of where *islam* seems to consist of *iman* plus works, as the Messenger of God upon being asked to discuss *al-islam* answers that one should say, "I have faith" and should walk the straight path.

Thus far we have been considering those *hadiths* that are generally concerned with definite *al-islam.* Several more traditions are relevant here. One group deals with the signs of *islam.* A man comes to the Messenger of God and asks him: With what has you Lord sent you to us? The Prophet replies: With *al-islam* Asked what are the signs of *al-islam*, he answers: *Al-Salat* (six), *al-zakat* (six), submitting one a face to God and being sincere (four), two *shahadahs* (one), and submitting one's heart to God and turning one's face to Him (one). In several cases it is added that God will not accept the one who does *shirk* after one's *islam.*

A final *hadiths* on the defining of *islam*, of which this collection has a single example, says that *al-islam* is a eighteen portions. The narrator, who does not claim an *isnad* direct from the Prophet, lists some of the portions, of which *al-islam* itself is one. The other portions mentioned are *al-salat, al-zakat, al-hajj, saum Ramadan, al-jihad,* and command to what is fitting (*al-amr bi'l-ma'ruj*) and prohibition of the forbidden. If this tradition is seen in the light of others dealing with the *arkan* it would appear that *islam* in the larger sense consists of the usual elements, including *jihad*, and in the narrower sense probably refers to the act of submission itself in which is included the saying of the two *shahadahs*.

The traditions thus far considered, and they make up the great majority of those in which the term *islam* is used, have been concerned primarily with the elements that comprise the act of submission of are connected with it. And it is clear that by *islam* has been intended individual submission,. regardless of how this was seen in relation to *iman*. The rest of the *hadiths* in our collection are not dealing directly with the constituent elements of the act, but in a number of them it is still quite apparent that the act, rather than the group of community, is intended.

Three traditions discuss what God will do if the servant submits and his *islam* is good. One says He will forgive all the evil done before, one that *al-islam* will be written ten-fold for him, and one that it will be increased ten to seven hundred times and the evil wiped away.

Islam as *din* is mentioned specifically in several traditions. In A.b.H. I, 318 it is related in reference to those whom a *muslim* may marry that all are forbidden to have a *din* other than the *din al-islam*. And the relationship of *iman* and *islam* is again touched on in Tir. II, 103 where we read: He tastes the food of *al-iman* who Prophet. In a reference to 49:14 of the Qur'an, while not dealing specifically with *iman*, al-Bukhari himself discusses true *islam*. (I, 30). He says that *al-islam* out of fear of being killed is not true or real (*haqqan*), but is *istislam* (i.e., *islam* not because they are sincere but merely out of physical surrender). This accord with God's having said, "The Arabs say 'We believe.' Say: You do not believe, but say 'We have submitted'. And if it be true, says al-Bukhari, it is in accordance with His having said, "Truly *al-din* with God is *al-islam*." (Qur'an 3 : 19).

One interesting *hadiths* refers to the bonds (*'urwah,* pl. *'ura*) of *islam*. The Messenger of God said, Let them destroy (pick apart) these bonds of *islam* one by one. Each time one bond is removed people cling to the remaining one (the one next to it). And the first of these likely to be destroyed is judgment (*al-hukm*) and the last is *al-salat.*

On another occasion, the Messenger of God in discussing the Day of Resurrection says that the *salat* will come and say, Oh Lord, I am the *salat* and He will say, You are correct. This sequence continues with the coming of the truth (*al-haqq*) and the fast. Then the Messenger of God says: Then *al-islam* will come and say, Oh Lord, you are the *salam* and I am the *islam.* And God will say: You are right: today I accept you and by you this day I will give recompense. A.b.H. follows this by citing, "Whoever chooses other than *al-islam* as (a) *din* will not have it accepted from him and he will be a loser in the Hereafter." (Qur'an 3:85). This is varied slightly in Tay, where it is the Lord who says: You are the *islam* and I am the *salam.* This interesting tradition, in which we may find an echo of Zarathustrian lore, lends itself to a variety of possible interpretations and frequently is referred to in the Qur'an commentaries.

While there is certainly room for more than one understanding of some of these last traditions, it is, as has been said, quite clear that the intention of *al-islam* is the individual act of submission. There are a few *hadiths*, however, in which it is less easy to understand just what is meant by *islam*; in some cases they seem to suggest an interpretation of the term as communal rather than as individual, although their metaphorical nature makes it difficult to determine this with any certainly. Centuries of Muslim scholars have debated the exegesis of some of these more ambiguous traditions.

One group contains the familiar reference to *islam* as strange (*gharib*) All of these centre on the phrase: *al-islam* began strange and it will return (as it began) strange, and blessed are the strangers. Several ask the question: Who are the strangers? The answers comes that they are those who are righteous when the people are corrupt. What seems to be implied by *gharib* here is that (sincere) *islam* is rare and will become rare, apparently another indication of personal submission. Finally we have the interesting assurance that *islam* will join (or seek shelter in) (*ya'rizu*) the two mosque (probably referring to those at Mecca and Medina) as the snake shrinks in its hole.

Related to this eschatological prediction are the narratives that discuss the revolution of *al-islam.* These are essentially the same in content and tell that the Messenger of God said that the millstone of *islam* will turn in a circle (*tadawwara*) for thirty-five or thirty-six or thirty-seven years, and those destroyed will have gone the way of destruction while the remaining will have their *din* set up for them for seventy years. In two of the narratives (A.h.H. I, 395, 451) the word "disappear" (*tazulu*) is used instead of *tadawwara.*

One story related by A.b.H. (III. 463) tells of 'umar b. al-Khattab in a mosque in Medina. Asked about *al-islam* he said that he had heard the Messenger of God saying that *al-islam* begins as a stem, then doubles, then quadruples, then is made six-fold, then splits into many branches. And 'Umar said, There is nothing after the branching (*al-buzul*) except decrease.

In the most general terms, then, we see *islam* is the traditions interpreted primarily by means of its constituent requirements or duties, sometimes as these are compared with the elements that made up *iman.* The various ways in which *islam* and *iman* can be understood in relation to each other were later to be spelled out with great specificity by those such as al-Baqillani, Ibn Taymiyah, al-Taftazani commenting on the Creed of al-Nasafi and many others. The attempt to base these precise formulations on the detailed of the *hadiths* materials, however, seems probably to have been a labour of some real frustration, as the seeds of a variety of interpretations concerning this *islam iman* relationship are present in the traditions, but without the structure of a clear and absolute definition. It also seems apparent from the above body of materials that by *islam* is meant the personal element of submission rather than the community of Muslims. From the perspective of the modern understanding one can say that the intent of *islam* in these traditions is primarily the act of the individual person in his or her response to God rather than the religion itself (as for example, Hinduism, Christianity, Islam). In some cases the *hadiths* present a metaphorical or allegorical picture, often with an eschatological intent.

There are more isolated instances of the mention of *al-islam* in this collection of traditions, but their inclusion would not alter or particularly augment the understanding of the intention of the term as already outlined. Let two last examples here suffice to illustrate the significance of *islam* in the eyes of the ancestors. In the first we see that three are those things found in the sweetness of *islam*: that one loves God and His Prophet more than anyone else, that he who loves a human being loves him for God's sake, and that one avoids returning to faithlessness (*al-kufr*) as one would hate being thrown into the fire. And in the second a man is talking with the Messenger of God, saying: I have not prepared for the hour with great works, but truly I love God and His Prophet. To this the Prophet replies: You are with him whom you love. And the narrator concludes: Nothing else brings joy to the *muslimun* as great as their joy in *al-islam*.

REFERENCES

1. For a collection of relevants traditions, the following sources have been consulted: al-Bukhari (Bu). *Sahih* Muslim (Mu), *Sahih*; Abu Da'ud (A.D.), *Sunan*; al-Tirmidhi (Tir.). *Sahin*; al-Nasa'i (Nas.), *Sunan;* Ibn Majah (I.M.), *Sunan*: al-Darimi (Da.), *Sunan*; Malik Ibn Anas (Ma.), *Muwatta'*; Zayd Ibn 'Ali (Z.), *Majmu al-fiqh*; Ahmad ibn Hanbal (A.b.H.), *Musnad*; and al-Tayalisi (Tay.), *Musnad.*
2. W C Smith, Meaning and end of religion, New York, 1963.
3. The author's "Continuity and change in the understanding of 'Islam'", Islamic Quarterly, 1972, Vol. XVI.
4. A J Weinsinck, A handbook of early Muhammadan Traditions, Leiden, 1960.

Revised and edited; originally published in Islamic Culture July 1974.

13

Al-Ghazali's on Islamic Piety

MUHAMMAD ABUL QUASEM

(Abstract: Deals with the concept of outward piety, pre-requisites of this piety, methods of its preservation, consequences of this preservation, etc. And highlights: "It is the view of the goal of the pious life that makes Islamic piety individualistic in nature").

Introduction

Every revealed religion, whether Islam or Christianity or Judaism or any other, prescribes piety as man's religious ideal in life. Religions such as Hinduism, Jainism and Buddhism also prescribe piety as the religious ideal which man should realize in life. Even some of the contemporary atheistic philosophies of the West, (e.g. naturalism, logical positivism, and later pragmatism) despite rejecting belief in the supernatural, appreciate man's observance of piety, even though this appreciation is only based on social and ethical grounds. Apart from appreciating piety in a general way, religions, and also many philosophies, differ among themselves on several specific aspects of the problem of piety, such as its nature and spirit, its scope, the source of its obligation, its requirements and its goal and consequence. Thus piety in Hinduism, for instance, is to a great extent different from piety in Christianity when compared in respect of these specific aspects. This article aims at giving a brief account of some aspects of a theory of Islamic piety *(taqwa)* presented very systematically and elaborately in the works of Imam al-Ghazali (d. 505/1111) and followed by numerous pious Muslims from his time till now. This account needs to be preceded by mention of the factors which led al-Ghazali to take an intense interest in the formulation of a theory of piety, for this will throw additional light on that account.

Islamic religious teachings on piety in all its aspects are set forth in the Qur'an briefly—briefly because brevity and conciseness form the basis of exposition in the Qur'an—and in Tradition (*hadith*) somewhat elaborately because Tradition is an explanation of the Qur'an. In the thoughts and practices of the early Muslim ascetics is to be found a concept of piety which is primarily ascetic in nature—ascetic because, as a reaction to the worldliness which crept into the Islamic society of the time, these ascetics emphasized those Qur'anic verses and prophetic traditions which are predominantly otherworldly in character. These ascetics were followed by a series of sufis, most of whom were orthodox in their thoughts and practices, and the last of those who were orthodox was Imam al-Ghazali, who is certainly one of the greatest authorities of Islam after the Prophet (may peace be upon him!). These orthodox sufis, especially al-Muhasibi, al-Makki, and al-Ghazali, presented theories of Islamic piety which, though containing asceticism as only an element, may, on the whole, be characterized as moderate in nature but very comprehensive in scope—moderate because these theories are based on both the more other-worldly and the less otherworldly teachings of the Qur'an and Tradition, and comprehensive because they concern many aspects of human life.

Among these orthodox sufis, however, it was al-Ghazali who took the most intense interest in the formulation of a theory of Islamic piety, because in his time there was so great deterioration in people's faith and observance of the *Shari'ah* that they "reached thc verge of destruction" The deterioration, according to al-Ghazali, was due to the influence of four factors, namely, the contemporary philosophy of al-farabi and Ibn Sina, false brand of sufism, Batinism and corrupt religious scholars. The renewer (*Mujaddid*) of the sixth Islamic century, al-Ghazali, very carefully examined all these forces, exposed their errors and set forth the truths of Islam in his numerous works. In an effort to bring the people back to pious life, he worked out a theory of piety, mostly in the light of the *Shari'ah* and *Tariqah*. The theory was much deeper and far more systematic and elaborate than those presented by other sufis, and has had lasting influence upon Muslim intellectuals as well as common men. It has an outward part and an inward, and it is the former which is more within the reach of ordinary Muslims. A few aspects of this outward part of al-Ghazali's conception of piety we propose to discuss in the article very briefly; this may be useful in this age of slackness in Islamic faith and practice.

The Concept of Outward Piety

The aim of Islamic religious knowledge, al-Ghazali says, is neither wordly gain sought by evil religious scholars, nor knowledge for the sake of knowledge as thought by some Muslim and Greek philosophers, but receiving guidance (*hidayah*) in order to obtain the pleasure of God and consequently happiness in the hereafter. Guidance is identical with piety (*taqwa*) and the guided are the same as the pious (*muttaqiyyun*)—only the pious are guided. Thus it is piety which is the aim of Islamic religious knowledge. Guidance is also identical with practice of religion, and hence the terms 'guidance,' 'practice of religion' and 'piety' have the some connotation according to al-Ghazali.

Piety, al-Ghazali says, consist in obedience to God's command and avoidance of His prohibition. God's commands and prohibitions include those of His Messenger Muhammad (may peace be upon him!) who is His representative on earth. The command of God concern both faith and action, as do His prohibitions. The pious man, then, is one who accepts the faith prescribed by god and His Messenger, rejecting the faith not approvable by them, and who performs the acts commanded by god and His Messenger and leaves undone the acts they have prohibited. This is identical with the assertion that the pious man is one who follows the Qur'an and Tradition, for these two contain the commands and prohibitions of God and His Messenger involving faith and action.

God's commands and prohibitions relating to action concern man's outward aspect or body as well as his inward aspect or soul, i.e. his whole being. Obedience to the commands and prohibitions of God concerning action related to man's outward aspect is what al-Ghazali calls outward piety or the beginning of piety, and obedience to God's commands and prohibitions relating to man's inward aspect he calls inward piety or the end of piety (with which this article is not concerned). Outward piety, precedes the inward piety in practice. Some commands of god are obligatory, while others are supererogatory. Likewise, some prohibitions are very serious in nature, while others are less serious.

Outward piety is of two levels, lower and higher. The former is attained by obeying all obligatory commands of God concerning man's outward aspect, and the latter by obeying, in addition, all supererogatory commands related to the same respect. To fall short of the lower level is impiety, wickedness and wrongdoing, terms used in the Qur'an. The higher level of piety includes the lower and something more: it requires the performance of *both* obligatory and supererogatory acts falling under the scope of outward piety. Similar is the case concerning the prohibition of god related to man's outward aspect: the lower level of piety necessitates the avoidance of more serious sins, while the higher level requires avoidance of these sins as well as those which are less serious. It also requires the avoidance of those things or acts concerning the sinfulness of which there is doubt (*shubahat*). Further, it requires one to keep away from the things or acts which are clearly lawful according to the Islamic law but from which one may slip into unlawful things or acts. The higher level of piety demands extreme caution about all matters.

Faith (*iman*) required at both lower and higher levels of outward piety (and also inward piety) is the faith of the people of Sunnah and Jama'ah which is the same as faith prescribed in the Qur'an and Tradition and which was the faith of the Companions of the Prophet. At the higher level, however, this faith is stronger than at the lower. This article does not deal with the 'faith aspect' of outward piety. What is deals with is the 'action aspect' in its three parts, namely, acts of obedience to God, avoidance of sins, and association with people. The requirements of piety (at its both levels) in these parts can only be stated here very briefly.

Requirements of Outward Piety

1. *Acts of Obedience to God*: The requirement of piety in acts of obedience to God (*ta'at*), al-Ghazali states, is in force from the time of a man's waking up from sleep until the time of his return to bed. A brief account can only be attempted here by dividing it into three parts: (a) piety in waking up from sleep and returning to bed, (b) piety in the five obligatory ritual prayers and ritual cleanliness, and (c) piety in the time between obligatory ritual prayers.

(a) Piety requires waking up from sleep at midnight for the *tahajjud* prayer and waking at dawn for the dawn prayer. The first thing that comes to the mind of the pious man is the remembrance of God and praise of Him for raising him up a live from sleep. (There are also detailed directions regarding hygienic requirements and the ritual to be observed on such occasions.)

(b) Piety requires perfection of cleanliness, whether in the form of ablution or bathing, and this perfection consists in the performance of all supererogatory parts of ablution or bathing in addition to all obligatory parts. Al-Ghazali gives the detail of these parts together with an emphasis upon the use of a tooth-stick just before starting an ablution. The pious man sits facing the direction of Ka'bah for ablution, and in the course of ablution reads fourteen supererogatory supplication formulae. One who neglects the supererogatory acts in cleanliness is the loser; such a man endangers his basic, obligatory activities, for the supererogatory parts add to the obligatory ones.

Similar is the requirement of piety in the case of five obligatory ritual prayers. With the obligatory *rak'at* of these ritual prayers are associated certain supererogatory *rak'at* and these are necessarily performed by the pious man, even though he is in a hurry or has other business. Again, every *rak'at* whether obligatory or supererogatory, has obligatory as well as supererogatory parts, and the pious man diligently performs both. Further, ritual prayer has on outward aspect as well as an inward aspect consisting in humility and submission to God, and attention of mind, and the pious man is very particular about this inward aspect, for this aspect constitutes the life of ritual prayer, while the outward aspect is its body.

Piety requires the performance of obligatory ritual prayers in the mosque in congregation and supererogatory ritual prayers at home alone. The pious man's walk to the mosque, his intention and his mental states are all for God alone. Wherever he may be physically, his mind remains attached to the mosque. At the approach of the time for a ritual prayer, he hastens to the mosque, and when and after entering it, performs certain prescribed supererogatory acts.

(c) This pious man utilizes the time between every two ritual prayers in the best way possible. To him, time is extremely important, for he knows that by making the best use of it he can achieve happiness in his eternal life in the hereafter.

(A detailed timetable is prescribed for the pious man for the whole day so that he may spend it in prayers, both the obligatory and the supererogatory, recitation of the Qur'an, praise (adhkar) and glorification (tasbihat) of God, meditation, acquisition of knowledge, service to fellow Muslims or procuring necessities of life for himself and his family.)

As for Friday, the best day of the week in Islam, the pious man devotes it entirely to the hereafter, by performing different forms of devotional acts as well as all sorts of good deeds directed to human beings.

He fasts on Friday with either Saturday or Thursday and gives alms to the poor. As preparation for the Assembly Prayer, he cleanses his body thoroughly, takes a bath, arrays himself in white clothes, and uses the best perfume he has. He tries to go to the mosque in the early hours and, on entering it, makes for the first now. After the Assembly Prayer is over, he supplicates to God earnestly, reads the two Qur'anic suras about seeking protection with God, and prays many times for blessing upon the Prophet. From this time until sunset he remembers God very much, since this is commanded in the Qur'an. On Friday he supplicates to God at sunrise, sun decline and sunset, at the *iqamah* of the Assembly Prayer, at the imam's ascending to the pulpit, at the moment when the devotees stand for the Assembly Prayer, and between the two addresses.

In regard to Ramadan fasting, piety requires more than mere abstention from food, drink and sexual activity. The pious man perfects his fasting by restraining all parts of his body from all that God dislikes. He breaks his fast with *halal* (lawful) food and drink. He observes supererogatory fasts on great days of the week, of the month, and of the year.

Concerning pilgrimage to Mecca (*Hajj*) and divine tax (*Zakat*), piety requires their performance with full attention to both their obligatory and supererogatory parts. When these two devotional acts are not obligatory upon the pious man, he tries his best to perform them as supererogatory acts. All devotional acts he performs sincerely for God, and not for social approval, show off or any other wordly gain.

2. *Avoidance of Sins of the Body*: The second requirement of piety is to avoid all that God has forbidden. The prohibition of certain acts by God is not through His arbitrary will, but through a consideration of their evil consequences, whether to their agents or to persons to whom these acts are directed. Thus, as in the case of acts of obedience, so in the case of prohibited acts, al-Ghazali holds the consequence theory of value. By leaving undone all that which God his prohibited, the pious man guards himself as well as others against their evil consequences.

The leaving undone of forbidden acts is more difficult than the performance of acts of obedience to God, because the former involves the setting aside of desires which is a difficult task, for all desires have their roots in a faculty produced in the soul before all other faculties, and are strengthened by their repeated satisfaction. Nevertheless, the pious man succeeds in his effort to set aside his desires.

Leaving undone of forbidden acts is identical with the avoidance of sins. The parts of the body are the tools for commission of sins, and hence piety necessitates constant watch over these parts. The body is God's gift to man and a trust committed to him so that it may serve as a means of his success in this life and the Hereafter. The pious man knows that to betray the trust committed to him is the highest degree of impiety.

The parts of the body required by piety to be guarded against sins are seven in number : the eyes, the ears, the tongue, the stomach, the genitals, the hand, and the feet. The sins of the eyes are: looking at women other than those whom it is unlawful to marry according to Islamic law, looking lusfully at a beautiful form, looking at a Muslim with a look of contempt, and finding faults with a Muslim. The sins of the ears are: listening to hearsay, backbiting, obscenity, vain conversation, and the mention of man's evil deeds. The sins of the tongue are eight in number: lying, breaking promises, backbiting, disputing, self-glorification, cursing, invoking evil towards others and mocking. The sins of the stomach are: to make the food forbidden by Islamic law and to eat that concerning the lawfulness of which there is doubt. The sin of the genitals is sexual intercourse with anyone other than one's wives and slave women. The sins of the hands are: beating a man unjustly, receiving wealth acquired by unlawful means, harming any creature, betraying a trust of deposit, and writing words the utterance of which is forbidden by the *Shari'ah*. The sins of the feet are to go to places forbidden by the *Shari'ah* and to oppressors in order to acquire worldly gain without necessity or compulsion. Al-Ghazali discusses these sins in great detail and suggests the methods for their avoidance.

The requirement of piety to avoid these sins of the seven parts of the body is very comprehensive inasmuch as it concerns all prohibited deeds done by the body in all aspects of life. The pious man, wherever he may be and whatever work he may be engaged in, keeps every part of his body under control so that it cannot commit sins.

3. *Avoidance of Sins of the Soul*: In accordance with Islamic teachings as well as philosophic tradition, al-ghazali says that the sins of the body proceed from the sins of the soul, i.e. from the evil qualities or vices of the soul, a view which forms part of his theory of interaction between the soul and the body. Therefore, the requirement of piety with regard to the body can only be fulfilled if vices of the soul are removed. However, since these vices are numerous and since their removal is a lengthy and painstaking process it is not necessary, at the stage of outward piety, to purify the soul from all vices. What is necessary is only to get rid of three root vices—envy (*hasad*), ostentation (*riya'*) and pride (*kibr*)—which are destructive in themselves and the roots of all other destructive qualities. Guarding against these three vices will enable the pious man to guard against other vices.

Envy is defined by al-Ghazali as man's displeasure when another man achieves something good and his desire for the removal of that thing even though he himself is not benefited by that removal. This is the depth of evil and destroys, as the Prophet warned, all good deeds just as fire destroys all dried things. The pious man is not envious; he is one whose mental state remains the same in people's weal and woe. Ostentation is defined as a man's desire to show off his devotional acts in order to impress others. This is a hidden polytheism and renders the acts not only invalid but also sinful. The pious man is nor ostentatious; he performs devotional acts for God alone. Pride consists in a man's consideration of himself as superior and others contemptible. It is the worst of all vice, and its opposite, humility, is the greatest of all the virtues of the pious. The pious man is neither proud nor lowly, but polite and humble. Al-Ghazali discusses envy, ostentation and pride in great detail and suggests the methods of their removal from the soul.

These three root vices originate from a more basic vice, namely, love of the evil aspect of the world which is described in Tradition as "the fountain-head of all sins." The mind of the pious man is free from this love; it is filled with the love of the good aspect of the world, since this aspect serves as means of preparation for the eternal life in the Hereafter.

4. *Observance of Good Manners of Companionship with God and Man:* The pious man, al-Ghazali says, lives a family life and a life is a community. He has not ascended to the stage of an ascetic, so that he does not withdraw himself from social life even for a limited period of time; nor does he adopt celibacy even temporarily without any absolutely compelling reason. In his day-to-day life, wherever he may be, he is aware that God is with him and He sees everything he is doing and hears every word he is uttering. His mind is sometimes filled with grief over his shortcomings in religious duties caused by his engagement in household an social affairs. To compensate for these short-comings he reserves part of his day or night to be alone with his Master and enjoys the pleasure of secret converse with Him, and this special devotion is accomplished by observing certain good manners (*adab*) which al-Ghazali calls 'the good manners of companionship with God.'

In his social life when the pious man comes in the company of different categories of people, he observes the good manners of companionship with them. Thus if he is a teacher or a student, piety requires him to observe the good manners of association with students and teachers, respectively. The pious man is very particular in the observance of good manners of association with his parents and other relatives. All such good manners described by al-Ghazali follow the Qur'an and the Sunnah very closely.

Concerning other people, al-Ghazali says that they can be considered under three categories: intimate friends, those who are known but not intimately, and those who are unknown, i.e. other men. Intimate friends are made some-times for otherworldly benefits, sometimes for the worldly gains, and sometimes simply for fellowship. The pious man befriends those who can give him or receive from him any religious assistance in the widest sense. Once friend-ship is established he does not fail to fulfil the duties of friendship which are discussed in detail by al-Ghazali and in brief by Muslim philosophers and sufis. When dealing with people who are known but not intimately and with people who are unknown, the pious man is very cautious and reserved lest his religious nature suffers.

It is not possible to mention here different sets of good manners of companionship with people worked out by al-Ghazali in detail. What is possible is only to mention the general principle of pious behaviour to them. This principle al-Ghazali states thus: "... in all your dealings with people, treat them as you would be pleased to be treated by them, because the faith of the worshipper is not complete until he loves for others what he loves for himself." This maxim includes two principles, namely, the principle of justice and the principle of beneficence. The lower level of piety requires justice to others which is identical with abstention from causing harm to them. To do injustice or to cause harm to anyone is impiety. The higher level of piety consists no in merely doing justice, but in rising to the stage of beneficence to other Muslim in various forms.

The maxim just mentioned is linked by al-Ghazali with another principle which states that; Muslims, wherever they may be, form a unity, an organic whole: they are like a body so that if one part suffers, the rest of the body also suffers; or they are like a building one part of which supports and strengthens the others. Fully conscious of this principle, the pious man considers the interests of other Muslim like those of his own. He considers all other Muslims as his brother in respect of religion and tries to fulfil the duties of Islamic brotherhood. When admonishing others to do good and to refrain from evil, he is compassionate and polite; if admonition is not possible, he only hates evil with his mind, for this is the lowest grade of faith. Al-Ghazali derives all these principles of social behaviour from the Qur'an and Tradition. and is aware that his predecessors among sufis and Muslim philosophers also recognized these principles.

Methods of Perseverance in Piety

Following the Qur'an and Tradition, al-Ghazali asserts that perseverance in piety is necessary throughout one's life. There is no holiday in pious life, just as the Greeks said that there is no holiday in moral life. Continuance in piety is a difficult task, but al-Ghazali suggests certain methods which will facilitate this continuance.

The first is to secure full control over the carnal soul (*nafs*) and to repeal Satan, for these two—one from man's inside and one from his outside—are the main obstacles to perseverance in piety. The carnal soul is very reluctant to perform devotions act; by nature it tends to exceed the limit set by the *Shri'ah* and thus to commit sins. Satan, a being from man's outside, incites the carnal soul to exceed that limit; he gives evil suggestions to the human mind. Al-Ghazali suggests that in order to make the carnal soul amenable to devotional acts it should that in order to make the carnal soul amenable to devotional acts it should be reproached by pointing out its ignorance and stupidity. To stop its tendency to exceed the proper limit, severe punishment should be inflicted upon it for any sin it has committed. Its strength can be reduced by reducing the amount of one's food to the extent of one-third one one's capacity. Satan can be repelled by often reading the two Qur'anic suras about seeking protection with God.

The second method is to remove reliance upon divine generosity and forgiveness. Man should realize that the statement 'God is generous,' is true in general, but false in the context of piety. The Lord of this world and the next is the same; just as in this world He does not provide man with a harvest unless one cultivates the land nor knowledge unless one acquires it through hard efforts, so He will not grant happiness in the Hereafter unless one practises piety in this life. Divine generosity consists in facilitating piety only. In the Qur'an, salvation is made dependent upon faith and pious deeds. Realization of all this will remove the difficulties of pious life to a great extent.

The third method is the abandonment of hope of a long life. Once's feeling that one may die soon, perhaps tomorrow or even earlier, will impel one to persist in piety, however difficult this may be. This suggestion of al-Ghazali is in accord with the Qur'an and Tradition and is emphasized by other sufis as well.

These three methods concern human effort to persevere in piety. This effort, however, can only be successful if it is coupled with a supernatural element, namely, divine grace (*tawfiq*) for continuance in piety. A means of drawing forth this grace is supplication to God for it—a reason why numerous prayer-formulae for facilitating different aspects of pious life are set forth in the Qur'an and Tradition. The need for divine grace was also recognized by other sufis as well as by Muslim philosophers, but not by Aristotle who believed that man can achieve virtue by his efforts alone.

The human effort and divine grace together make cultivation of piety possible. However, perfection of piety can only be attained by the Prophet whose effort was the utmost, in whose case divine grace was of the highest degree, and who, like all other prophets, possessed piety naturally as something given to him by God at the time of his birth. Other people can only approach him in piety.

Consequences of Perseverance in Piety

Perseverance in piety facilitated by the methods mentioned above has consequences both in this life and the Hereafter. Following the Qur'an, al-Ghazali maintains that peace and tranquillity of mind, contentment and other similar spiritual states are among the mental consequences of piety in this life. Material prosperity also accrues from piety through blessings of God who is pleased with the pious man for living a pious life. The effects of piety towards other people in this world appear in the form of harmony and concord, love and fellow-feeling, justice and beneficence, and many other religious values that operate in society. Al-Ghazali believes that all effects of piety in this world, whether in the life of the pious individual or in that of others, accrue from it as necessary consequence, and not as its aim as some of his contemporary Muslim philosophers maintained.

The main consequence of piety is that which is obtainable in the Here-after. Indeed it is that which is the aim of piety. The Hereafter for an individual starts immediately after his death and continues eternally. Its major stages are those of the grave, the resurrection, crossing of the bridge-like path to be suspended over Hell, and finally Paradise or Hell. At each of these stages the effect of piety is obtained in the form of freedom from misery and experience of happiness. Happiness and misery are both physical and spiritual and have innumerable grades according to innumerable variations in the strength of men's faith and the quality of their righteous deeds. The innumerable grades in paradise are, however, subsumed under two broad levels, lower and higher. The former consists in the sensuous pleasures of food, drinks, company of houris and so on, while the latter consists in nearness to God and gazing upon the glorious face of God forevermore. The effect of the lower grade of piety is freedom from misery and experience of happiness in the lower level of paradise, and the effect of the higher grade of piety is the experience of happiness in the higher level of paradise. All these views of al-Ghazali on the consequence of piety are in accord with the Qur'an and Tradition which he quoted frequently. He regards as infidelity the view of his contemporary Muslim philosophers that the effect of piety in the world to come is only spiritual in nature.

Islamic piety, al-Ghazali says, is individualistic in nature inasmuch as its basic motive or *goal* is the good of the individual (taking the form of happiness in the world to come). What makes a religious system individualistic or universalistic or altruistic is not so much its laying down an individualistic or universalistic or altruistic set of rules for daily conduct, but its view of the *goal* of religious life. For the individualist it is the individual's own good, for the universalist it is the good of all, and for the altruist it is the good of others alone. Islamic piety includes many universalistic and altruistic acts and forms of behaviour, but in each of these an individual is urged to have the basic, *ultimate* motive of benefit to *himself* in the life to come. Although the basic motive of piety is individualistic, a man is not permitted by Islam to show any trace of selfishness in his character, for (consistent with individualism) it is in the service of others that an individual realizes his own good. Abandonment of self-interest for the sake of other people means attainment by the self of greater good in the next life, for by this the self has done something towards the improvement of character. Thus, it is the view of the *goal* of pious life that makes Islamic piety individualistic in nature.

REFERENCES

1. Muhammad Fuad Abd al-Baqi, al-Mu`jam al-Mufahras, Egypt, 1378 AH.(provides Quranic verses on piety).
2. Al-Ghazlai, al-qistas al-mustaqim, ed. al-Yasui, Beirut, 1959.
3. Al-Ghazali, Bidayat al-Hidayah, Egypt, n.d.,
4. Al-Ghazali, Ihya ulum ad-din, Beirut, n.d.,
5. See my book, The ethics of al-Ghazali, New York, 1978.and Al-Ghazali on Islamic guidance, Kuala Lampur, 1980.

Revised and edited; originally published in *Islamic Culture*, April 1982.

14

Muhammad and World Unity

KHALID SHELDRAKE

(Abstract: The unity of humanity is not a dream, rather is a reality, ushered in the life and the system of the Noble Prophet Muhammad).

Historically, it seems that, unity of mankind is impossible. People of the East and West rose and fell, being succeeded by others. Looking upon the great empires of the world despite their glories, something indeed was lacking. Each of the great civilizations came and departed as separate entities. Looking upon themselves as the salt of the earth, they despoiled and enslaved others, regarding them as legitimate prey. The legends we read of the Hebrew race are just the same. All outside their own nationality were to be enslaved or exterminated. Studying the religions and philosophies of these tribes, we find them purely national, having no conception of the idea of common humanity, or toleration for others outside their own particular people. Their idea of gods who fought for them alone reflects their mentality. When beaten they considered that their deity was offended, or had deserted them. In the scope of the present paper it is impossible to dwell at length upon the different religious systems of these peoples, but it suffices that each had their great men, their religious teachers, their Prophets who brought guidance, but unfortunately these beautiful moralities, divine precepts, stopped short at their frontiers. When reading the Bible one is struck with the peculiarly narrow view of the writers who gave us the biographies of the great man of the Hebrew race. Philistines, Ammonites, Moabites, Jebusites, etc., were regarded as outside the influence or care of the Hebrew divinity Jehovah, whom they considered was the special deity of their own. According to the Biblical account, the Israelites were ordered to "Slay ye every one of them; take not one of them alive." Such a policy naturally reacted upon themselves, and they found captivity their portion time after time. Even these severe lessons taught this people little. Every page of their literature we find full of anathemas hurled at the heads of surrounding nations. Then came the advent of Jesus. Unfortunately we know but little of him. We read varied stories of his birth, lose sight of him until he is twelve, again not hearing of him until he reaches manhood. Let us be quite fair and say that from the meagre records we possess it is impossible to do justice to this great Teacher. We read that he said this and that, but so great is the doubt attached to the authenticity of these records that it behoves us to remember that it is quite possible that the unknown authors of the different Gospels, of which so many exist, may have put into the mouth of Jesus sayings which were not his. We cannot, after the lapse of all these centuries, do more than glimpse the mind of the Prophet of Palestine, being only able to utilize the material at hand, which is admittedly faulty. Jesus preached (after his baptism by John the Baptist, when the Holy Ghost is said to have descended upon him in the form of a dove) to a handful of fishermen. These became his disciples, poor and ignorant men, who time after time failed to grasp the meaning of his words. Gaining other disciples we read that he sent them out with the instructions, "Go not into any city of the Gentiles, and into any city of the Samaritans enter ye not: but go rather to the lost sheep of the house of Israel." On a woman of Caanan—a Syro—Phoenician—coming to him and asking that her daughter be healed it is written that he said: "I am not sent but unto the lost sheep of the house of Israel"; and further: "It is not meet to take the children's bread and cast it to dogs" Let these extracts be sufficient. It should be intelligible to all that Jesus regarded himself as a Hebrew, as seemingly shared the hatred of non-Jews common to his people, his mission being to Israel alone. An objection might be raised that after the alleged resurrection it is reported that he sent his disciples to preach to others. Let us say first of all that the Church itself regards the final portion of St. Mark (itself often quoted as the source from which the other Gospels were compiled) as spurious. It we carefully examine this, are we to believe that Jesus, who had preached only to the Jews, and had forbidden his disciples intercourse with other nations, suddenly received a revelation or message whilst in the tomb? If this command to preach abroad were genuine, it would stamp Jesus as one who was unaware of the compassion and love of the Divine Being for all His creatures, that he was neither broad-minded nor filled with love for his fellow-men, but confined his sympathies to a handful of Hebrews, making his teaching that of a narrow—minded Rabb. It is an ugly picture, my friends, for which we must thank the authors of the Gospels. There seems to be nothing in the lifetime of Jesus to make us think that his mission was to other than the Jews, and we must bear in mind that the early Christians were but a Jewish sect conforming to every ritual of the Mosaic creed. Again we are face to face with this tribal deity, that being who had a "chosen race." How necessary it was that God, in His infinite mercy, should reveal Himself to humanity clearly and distinctly.

Lonely and solemn, brooding over the desert waste rose the Hill of Hira. There, lying wrapped in his mantle, was one who had earned the title of "Ameen"—the Faithful, the Trustworthy. Moses climbed Sinai to speak with the Lord, the North-American Indians pour out their hearts to the Great Spirit on the highest peak. Verily beaten seems nearer when lifted above the surging mass of humanity, in city and plain, and one is alone to meditate upon the beauties of creation. Man, living always amidst bricks and mortal, is apt to forget all except that immediately around him, but one who is in touch with Nature becomes in tune with the Infinite. Oh! happy Hira! from you was to pour a flood of Light which was to illumine the uttermost parts of this planet. To him, lonely there, came the Vision Beautiful, through his sonl coursed the Divire stream, and he was called to the service of the Most High. The Message was given to Muhammad of blessed memory, and he became the vehicle of the Word of Allah to humanity, sent as "a blessing to mankind" to call them to the right path. From this blessed day a new note came into being a new idea implanted upon the mind of man. For the first time men were compelled to leave their old narrow conceptions and join the Brotherhood of Humanity. The Holy Qur'-an shows clearly for all time that Allah is the Creator, Sustainer and Cherisher of all—not of a petty race or tribe, but of mankind. What a glorious ideal was thus presented to the world by Our Holy Prophet. In his lifetime how beautifully he showed his regard for others. One cannot forget the Christian delegation coming to him and wishing to hold their service, he bade them use the Mosque. Thirteen hundred years have passed, but I have never heard that this nobility of spirit has been shown by a Christian community. We have no Mosque in London, but would any Christian ask us to celebrate prayer in a church? I fear not. Still the old exclusive spirit! How needful it is to show the beauties of Islamic action to these people. When a coffin passes the Holy Prophet he rises to his feet, and on being told that it was the body of a Jew speaks thus: "Was it not the holder of a soul?" He further tells them: "Should the bier of anyone pass by you whether of a Jew, a Christian or a Muslim, rise to your feet."

He gave the death-blow to arrogance when he said: "A community must desist from boasting of their ancestors Mankind are all the sons of Adam, and he was from earth." This cuts at the root of class or caste distinction. A noble criterion is established: "The best of men is he from whom most good accrueth to humanity." Again: "All God's creatures are His family; and he is the most beloved of God who trieth to do most good to God's creatures." Can one find a nobler doctrine than this? Humanity!—the broad ideal swept aside geographical, tribal, caste and other distinctions, and directed men to look upon their fellows with a new interest as "God's creatures." What a wonderful change this wrought! And its practical development was shown when students from all parts of the world came to study at the feet of the Muslim teachers in the glorious colleges in Muslim lands. All speaking the same tongue, studying together, the black and white and yellow men all brothers under the sacred banner of Islam, yet were Jews, Christians, Buddhists side by side with Muslims of all nations. A writer, speaking of the degradation of Europe, points out that contact with the Muslims at the time of the Crusades began to civilize the barbarous nations of the West. He says: "It was during the later Crusades that a spirit of humanity was first introduced into war, and leniency to the captive and the fallen ranked in the number of military virtues." In peace and in war the Muslims brought with them that great feeling for humanity which gradually changed the mentality of men. To-day we find a League of Nations, Leagues of this and that, which show that even now the West seeks the ideal of peace and brotherhood. Let us show to them the life of Our Holy Prophet, his deeds and his words. Let us teach them to study the Holy Qur'-an, and divest themselves of all those false ideas foisted upon them by corrupt and degraded doctrines. The very existence of these Leagues is sufficient evidence that the Church has completely failed to produce unity, so we must infuse them with the spirit of toleration and brotherhood brought into existence by Islam through the medium of Our Holy Prophet. The Holy Qur'-an says:

"Verily the true believers are brethren," and a Christian writer: "There is another Christian idea suggested by a study of Islam, which emerges from the last, the idea of the Brotherhood of the Father's children. This is of the very essence of Christianity as it is of Islam, but has never been carried into effect in the same magnificent way. There are many illustrations of this. The absence of all caste distinctions in Muslim society, the kindly relations which exist between master and servant, rich and poor, Mussulmans of various races. Christianity has much to learn in these directions." Most significant is the title, "The Failure of Christianity," appended to a chapter of the book. Allah, in His infinite wisdom, knew that the time would come when the truth revealed by other Prophets would be perverted or lost, and sent His Messenger with the final and complete revelation.

Muhammad (on whom be peace) is the Prophet of Humanity, sent as a blessing from the Lord of Worlds. All know the wonderful benefits mankind has derived from him. Study at his feet these Divine precepts, cease to quibble, and you will find that the Unity of Mankind is not a dream, but a living reality ushered in by the noble Prophet.

Revised and edited; originally published in Islamic Review.

15

Muhammad the Prophet

K S RAMAKRISHNA RAO

(Abstract: When I thought of writing on Muhammad the Prophet, I was a bit hesitant because it was to write about a religion I do not profess and it is a delicate matter to do so for there are many persons professing various religions and belonging to diverse schools of thought and denominations even in the same religion).

In the desert of Arabia was Muhammad born on April 20, 571. The name means "highly praised." He is to me the greatest mind among all the sons of Arbia. He means so much more than all the poets and kings that preceded and succeeded him in that impenetrable desert of red sand.

When he appeared, Arabia was a desert—a nothing. Out of nothing a new world was fashioned by the mighty spirit of Muhammad—a new life, a new culture, a new civilisation, a new kingdom which extended from Morocco to Indies and influenced the thought and life of three continents—Asia, Africa and Europe.

Though it is sometimes, claimed that a religion is entirely personal yet it cannot be gainsaid that it has a tendency to envelop the whole universe seen as well as unseen. It somehow permeates sometime or other our hearts, our souls, our minds their conscious as well as sub-conscious levels and unconscious levels too. The problem assumes overwhelming importance when there is a deep conviction that our past, present and future all hang by the soft delicate, tender-silked cord. If we further happen to be highly sensitive, the centre of gravity is very likely to be always in a state of extreme tension. Looked at from this point of view, the less said about others religion the better. Let our religions be deeply hidden and embedded in the resistance of our innermost hearts fortified by unbroken seals on our lips.

But there is another aspect of this problem. Man lives in society. Our lives are bound with the lives of others willingly or unwillingly, directly or indirectly. We eat the food grown in the same soil, drink water from the same spring and breathe the same air. Even while staunchly holding our own views, it would be helpful, if we try to adjust ourselves to our surroundings, if we also know to some extent, how the mind of our neighbour moves and what the main springs of his actions are. From this angle of vision, it is highly desirable that one should try to know all religions of the world, in the proper spirit, to promote mutual understanding and better appreciation of our neighbourhood, immediate and remote.

Further, our thoughts are not scattered as they appear to be on the surface. They have got themselves crystallised around a few nuclii in the form of great world religions and living faiths that guide and motivate the lives of millions that inhabit this earth of ours. It is our duty, in one sense, if we have the ideal of ever becoming a citizen of the world before us, to make a little attempt to know the great religions an systems of philosophy that have ruled mankind.

Inspite of these preliminary remarks, the ground in this field of religion, where there is often a conflict between intellect and emotion is so slippery that one is constantly reminded of 'fools that rush in where angels fear to tread.' It is also not so complex from another point of view. The subject of my writing is about the tenets of a religion which is historic and its prophet who is also a historic personality. Even a hostile critic like Sir William Muir speaking about the holy Quran says that. "There is probably in the world no other book which has remained twelve centuries with so pure a text." I may also add Prophet Muhammad is also a historic personality, every event of whose life has been most carefully recorded and even the minutest details preserved intact for the posterity. His life and works are not wrapt in mystery. One need not hunt for the accurate information and embark on arduous expeditions to sift the chaff and husk from the grain of truth.

My work to-day is further lightened because those days are fast disappearing when Islam was highly misrepresented by some of its critics for reasons political and otherwise. Prof. Bevan writes in Cambridge Medieval History, "Those accounts of Muhammad and Islam which were published in Europe before the beginning to the 19th century are now to be regarded as literary curiosities." My problem to write this monograph is easier because we are now not generally fed on this kind of history and much time need be spent on pointing out our misrepresentations of Islam.

The theory of Islam and Sword for instance is not heard now frequently in any quarter worth the name. The principle of islam that there is no compulsion in religion is well-known. Gibbon, a historian of world repute, says, "A pernecious tenet has been imputed to the Mohammadans, the duty of extirpating all the religions by the sword." This charge based on ignorance and bigotry, says the eminent historian, is refuted by the Quran, by the history of musalman conquerors and by their public and legal toleration of Christian worship. The greatest success of Muhammad's life had been effected by sheer moral force, without a stroke of a sword.

But in pure self-defence, after repeated efforts of conciliation had utterly failed, circumstances dragged him into the battlefield. But the Prophet of Islam changed the whole strategy of the battlefield. The total number of casualities in all the wars that took place during his lifetime when the whole Arabian Peninsula came under his banner, does not exceed a few hundreds in all. But even on the battlefield he taught the Arab barabarians to pray, to pray not individually, but in congregation, to God the Almighty. During the dust and storm of warfare whenever the time for prayer came, and it comes five times everyday, the Congregational prayer had not to be postponed even on the battlefield. A party had to be engaged in bowing their heads before God while another was engaged with the enemy. After finishing the prayers, the two parties had to exchange their positions. To the Arabs, who would fight for forty years on the slight provocation that a camel belonging to the guest of one tribe had strayed into the grazing land belonging to another tribe and both sides had fought till they lost 70,000 lives in all, threatening the extinction of both the tribes to such furious Arabs, the Prophet of Islam taught self-control and discipline to the extent of praying even on the battle-field. In an age of barbarism, the Battlefield itself was humanised and strict instructions were issued not to cheat, not to break trust, not to mutilate, not to kill a minor child or a woman or an old man, not to hew down date palm nor burn it not to cut down a fruit tree, not to molest any person engaged in worship. His own treatment with his bitterest enemies is the noblest example for his followers. At the conquest of Mecca, he stood at the zenith of his power. The city which had refused to listen to his mission, which had tortured him and his followers, which had driven him and his people into exile and which had unrelentingly persecute and boycotted him even when he had taken refuge in a place more than 200 miles away, that city now lay at his feet. By the laws of war he could have justly avenged all the cruelties inflicted on him and his people. But what treatment did he accord to them? Mahammad's heart over-flowed with affection and he declared "This day, there is no *reproof* against you and you are all free. "This day he proclaimed." I trample under my feet all distinctions between man and man, all hatred between man and man."

This was one of the chief objects why he permitted war in self defense, that is to unite human beings. And when once this object was achieved, even his worst enemies were pardoned. Even those who had killed his beloved uncle, Hamzah, mangled his body, ripped it open, even chewed a piece of his liver.

The principles of universal brotherhood and the doctrine of the equality of mankind which he proclaimed represents one very great contribution of Mahammad to the social uplift of humanity. All great religions have also preached the same doctrine but the Prophet of Islam had put this theory into actual practice and its value will be fully recognized, perhaps centuries hence, when international consciousness being awakened, racial prejudices may disappear and a greater brotherhood of humanity come into existence.

Miss. Sarojini Naidu speaking about this aspect of Islam says, "It was the first religion that preached and practised democracy' for in the mosque, when the minaret is sounded and the worshippers are gathered together, the democracy of Islam is embodied five times a day when the peasant and the king kneel side by side and proclaim, "God alone is great". The great poetess of India continues "I have been struck over and over again by this indivisible unity of Islam that makes a man instinctively a brother. When you meet an Egyptian, an Algerian and India and a Turk in London, what matters is that Egypt is the motherland of one and India is the motherland of another."

Mahatma Gandhi, in his inimitble style, says "some one has said that European in South Africa dread the advent of Islam-Islam that civilized Spain, Islam that took the torch light to Morocco and preached to the world the Gospel of Brotherhood. The Europeans of South Africa dread the advent of Islam. They may claim equality with the white races. They may well dread it, if brotherhood is a sin. If it is equality of the coloured races that they dread, then their dread is well-founded."

Every year, during the Haj, the world witnesses the wonderful spectacle of this international Exhibition of Islam in levelling all distinctions of race, colour and rank. Not only the Europeans, the African, the Arabian, the Persian, the Indians, the Chinese all meet together in Medina as members of one divine family, but they are all clad in one dress-every person in two simple pieces of white seamless cloth, one piece round the loin and the other piece over the shoulders, bare-headed without pomp or ceremony, repeating "Here am I O God: at thy command; thou art One and alone; Here am I." Thus there remains nothing to differenciate the high from the low and every pilgrim carries home the impression of the international significance of Islam.

In the opinion of Prof. Hurgronje "the League of Nations

founded by the Prophet of Islam put the principle of international unity and human brotherhood on such Universal foundations as to show candle to other nations." In the words of the same Professor "the fact is that no nation of the world can show a parallel to what Islam has done towards the realisation of the idea of the league of Nations."

The Prophet of Islam brought the reign of democracy in its best form. The Caliph Umar, the Caliph Ali and the son-in-law of the Prophet, the Caliph Mansur, Abbas, the son of the Caliph, Mamun and many other caliphs and kings had to appear before the judge as ordinary men in Islamic courts. Even today we all know how the black Negroes are treated by the civilized white races. Consider the state of BIAL, a Negro slave, in the days of the Prophet of Islam nearly 14 centuries ago. The office of calling muslims to prayer was considered to be of status in the early days of Islam and it was offered to this Negro slave. After the conquest of Mecca, the Prophet ordered him to call for prayer and the Negro slave, with his black colour and his thick lips, stood over the roof of the holy mosque at Mecca called, the Ka'ba the most historic and the holiest mosque in the Islamic world, when some proud Arabs painfully cried aloud, "Oh, this black Negro Slave woe be to him. He stands on the roof of holy Ka'ba to call for prayer." At that moment, the prophet announced to the world, this verse of the holy Quran for the first time.

> "O mankind, Surely, we have created you,
> families and tribes, so you may know one
> another. Surely, the most honourable of you with God
> is the most righteous among you.
> Surely God is Knowing, Aware."

and these words of the holy Quran created such a mighty transformation that the Caliph of Islam, the puirest of Arabs by birth, offered their daughters in marriage to this Negro slave, and whenever, the second Caliph of Islam, known to history as Umar the great, the commander of the faithful, saw this Negro slave, he immediately stood in reverence and welcomed him by "Here comes our master; Here comes our lord." What a tremendous change was brought by Quran in the Arabs, the proudest people at that time on earth. This is the reason why Goethe, the greatest of German poets, speaking about the holy Quran declared that. "This book will go on exercising through all ages a most potent influence." This is also the reason why George Barnard shaw says, "If any religion has a chance of ruling over England, say, Europe, within the next 100 years, it is Islam."

It is this same democratic spirit of Islam that emancipated women from the bondage of man. Sir Charles Edward Archibald Hamilton says "Islam teaches the inherent sinlesseness of man. It teaches that man and woman have come from the same essence, possess the same soul and have been equipped with equal capabilities for intellectual, spiritual and moral attainments."

The Arabs had a very strong tradition that one who can smite with the spear and can wield the sword would inherit. But Islam came as the defender of the weaker sex and entitled women to share the inheritance of their parents. It gave women, centuries ago, the right of owing property, yet it was only 12 centuries later, in 1881, that England, supposed to be the cradle of democracy adopted this institution of Islam and an Act was passed called "the Married Women's Act." But centuries earlier, the Prophet of Islam had poclaimed that" Women are the twin halves of men. The rights of women are sacred. See that women are maintained in the rights granted to them."

Islam is not directly concerned with political and economic systems, but indirectly and in so far as political and economic affairs influence man's conduct, it does lay down some very important principles to govern economic life. According to Prof. Massighon, it maintains the balance between exaggerated opposites and has always in view the building of character which is the basis of civilization. This is secured by its law of inheritance, by an organised an not an arbitrary system of charity known as Zakat, and by regarding as illegal all anti-social practices in the economic field like monopoly, usury, securing of pre-determined unearned incomes and increments, cornering markets, creating an artificial scarcity of any commodity in order to force the price to rise. Gambling is illegal. Contribution to schools, to places of worship, hospitals, digging of wells, opening of orphanages are highest acts of virtue. Orphanages have sprung for the first time, it is said, under the teaching of the Prophet of Islam. The world owes its orphanages to this Prophet who was himself born an orphan. "Good all this" says Carlyle about Muhammed. "The natural voice of humanity, of pity and equity, dwelling in the heart of this wild son of nature, speaks."

A historian once said a great man should be judged by three tests: Was he found to be of true metal by his contemporaries ? Was he great enough to rise above the standards of his age ? Did he leave anything as permanent legacy to the world at large ? This list may be further extended but all these three tests of greatness are eminently satisfied to the highest degree in the case of Prophet Muhammed. Some illustrations of the last two have already been mentioned.

The first is: was the Prophet of Islam found to be of true metal by his contemporaries ?

Historical records show that all contemporaries of Muhammed both friends and foes, acknowledged the sterling qualities, the spotless honesty, the noble virtues, the absolute sincerity and the trustworthiness of the apostle of Islam in all walks of life and in every sphere of human activity. Even the Jews and those who did not believe in his message, adopted him as the arbitrator in their personal disputes by virtue of his perfect impartiality. Even those who did not believe in his message were forced to say "O Muhammed, we do not call you a liar, but we deny him who has given you a book and inspired you with a message." They thought he was one possessed. They tried violence to cure him. But the best of them saw that a new light had dawned on him and they hastened to seek that enlightenment. It is a notable feature in the history of the Prophet of Islam that his nearest relation, his beloved cousin and his bosom friends, who knew him most intimately, were not thoroughly imbued with the truth of his mission and were convinced of the genuineness of his divine inspiration. If these men and women, noble, intelligent, educated and intimately acquainted with him private life had perceived the slightest signs of deception, fraud, earthliness or lack of faith in him, Muhammed's moral hope of regeneration, spiritual awakening, and social reform would all have been foredoomed to a failure and the whole edifice would have crumbled to pieces in a moment. On the contrary, we find that the devotion of his followers was such that he was voluntarily acknowledged as dictator of their lives. They braved for him persecutions and danger; they trused, obeyed and honoured him even in the most excruciating torture and severest mental agony caused by excommunication even unto death. Would this have been so, had they noticed the slightest backsliding in their master ?

Read the history of the early converts to Islam, and every heart would melt at the sight of the brutal treatment of innocent men and women.

Sumayya, an innocent woman, is cruelly torn into pieces with spears. An example is made of "Yasir whose legs are tied to two camels and the beasts are driven in the opposite directions", "Khabbab Bin Arth is made to lie down on a bed of burning coal with the brutal legs of their merciless tyrant on his breast so that he may not move and this makes even the fat beneath his skin melt". "Khabban Bin Adi is put to death in a cruel manner by mutilation and cutting off his flesh piece—meal." In the midst of his tortures, being asked whether he did not wish Muhammad in his place while he was in his house with his family, the sufferer cried out that he was gladly prepared to sacrifice himself, his family and children and all to save Muhammad from the prick of a thorn.

Hundreds of heart-rending incidents of this type may be narrated. But what do all these incidents show ? Why was it that these sons and daughters of Islam not only surrendered to their prophet their allegience but also made a gift of their hearts and souls to their master ?Is not the intense faith and conviction on the part of the immediate followers of Muhammad, the noblest testimony to his sincerity and to his utter self-absorption in his appointed task ?

And these men were not of low station or inferior mental calibre. Arround him in quite early days, gathered what was best and noblest in Mecca, its flower and cream, men of position, rank, wealth and culture, and from his own kith and kin, those who knew all about his life. All the first four Caliphs, with their towering personalities, were converts of this period.

The Encyclopaedia Britannica says that "Muhammad is the most successful of all Prophets and religious personalities."

But this success was not the result of mere accident. It was not a hit of fortune. It was a recognition of the fact that he was found to be of true metal by his contemporaries. It was the result of his admirable and all compelling personality.

The personality of Muhammad! it is most difficult to get into the truth of it. Only a glimpse of it I can catch. What a dramatic succession of picturesque scenes." There is Muhammad, the Phophet. There is Muhammad the General; Muhammad the King; Muhammad the Warrior; Muhammad the businessman; Muhammad the preacher; Muhammad the Philosopher; Muhammad the Statesman; Muhammad the Orator; Muhammad the reformer, Muhammad the refuge of orphans; Muhammad the Protector of Slaves; Muhammad the emancipator of women; Muhammad the Law-giver: Muhammad the Judge; Muhammad the Saint.

And in all these magnificent roles, in all these departments of human activities, he is alike, a hero.

Orphanhood is the extreme of helplessness and his life upon this earth began with it; Kingship is the height of the material power and it ended with it. From an orphan boy to a persecuted refugee and then to an overlord, spiritual as well as temporal, of a whole nation and Aribter of its destinies, with all its trials and temptations, with all its vicissitudes and changes, its lights and shades, its ups and downs, its terror and splendour, he has stood the fire of the world and come out unscathed to serve as a model in every face of life. His achievements are not limited to one aspect of life, but cover the whole field of human conditions.

If for instance, greatness consists in the purification of a nation, steeped in barbarism and immersed in absolute moral darkness, that dynamic personality who has transformed, refined and uplifted an entire nation, sunk low as the Arabs were, and made them the torch-bearer of civilization and learning, has every claim to that greatness. If greatness lies in unifying the discordant elements of society by the ties of brotherhood and charity, the Prophet of the desert has got every title to this distinction. If greatness consists in reforming those wrapt in a degrading and blind superstition an pernicious practices of every kind, the Prophet of Islam has wiped out superstitions and irrational fear from the hearts of millions. If it lies in displaying high morals, Muhammad has been admitted by friend and foe as Al Amin, or the faithful. If a conqueror is a great man, here is a person who rose from a helpless orphan and an humable creature to be the ruler of Arabia, the equal and of Chosroes and Caesers, one who founded a great empire that has survived all these 14 centuries. If the devotion that a leader commands is the criterion of greatness, the Prophet's name even to-day exerts a magic charm over millions of souls, spread all over the world.

He had not studied philosophy in the school of Athens of Rome, Persia, India or China. Yet, he could proclaim the highest truths of eternal value to mankind. Illiterate himself, he could yet speak with an eloquence and fervour which moved men to tears, to tears of ecatacy. Born an orphan and blessed with no worldly goods, he was loved by all. He had studied at no military academy; yet, he could organise his forces against tremendous odds and gained victories through the moral forces which he marshalled. Gifted men with a genius for preaching are rare. Descartes included the perfect preacher among the rarest kind in the world. Hitler in his Mein Kamp has expressed a similar view. He says "A great theorist is seldom a great leader. An agitator is far more likely to possess these qualities. He will always be a better leader. For leadership means ability to move masses of men. The talents to produce ideas has nothing in common with capacity for leadership." "But" he says, "The Union of the theorists, organiser and leader in one man, is the rarest phenomenon on this earth; Therein consist greatness."

In the person of the Prophet of Islam the world has seen this rarest phenomenan on the earth, walking in flesh and blood.

And more wonderful still is what the Reverned Bosworth Smith remarks, "Head of the state as well as the Church, he was Caeser and Pope in one; but, he was pope without the Pope's claims, and Caeser without the legions of Caeser , without an standing Army, without a bodyguard, without a palace, without a fixed revenue. If ever any man had the right to say that he ruled by a right divine, it was Mohammad, for he had all power without its instruments and without its support. He cared not for the dressings of power. The simplicity of his private life was in keeping with his public life.

After the fall of Mecca, more than one million square miles of land lay at his feet, Lord of Arabia, he mended his own shoes and coarse woollen garments, milked the goats, swept the hearth kindled the fire and attended to other menial offices of the family. The entire town of Madina where he lived grew wealthy in the later days of his life. Everywhere there was gold and silver in plenty and yet in those days of prosperity many weeks would elapse without a fire being kindled in the hearth of the king of Arabia, his food being dates and water. His family would go hungry many nights successively because they could not get anything to eat in the evening. He slept on no soften bed but on a palm mat, after a long busy day to spend most of his night in prayer, often bursting with tears before his creator to grant him strength to discharge his duties. As the reports go, his voice would get choked with weeping and it would appear as if a cooking pot was on fire and boiling had commenced. On the very day of his death his only assets were a few coins a part of which went to satisfy a debt and the rest was given to a needy person who came to his house for charity. The clothes in which he breathed his last had many patches. The house from where light had spread to the world was in darkness because there was no oil in the lamp.

Circumstances changed, but the Prophet of God did not. In victory or in defeat, in power or in adversity, in affluence or in indigence, he is the same man, disclosed the same character. Like all the ways and laws of God, Prophets of God are unchangeable.

An honest man, as the saying goes, is the noblest work of God. Muhammad was more than honest. He was human to the marrow of his bones. Human sympathy, human love was the music of his soul. To serve man, to elevate man, to purify man, to educate man, in a word to humanise man-this was the object of his mission, the be-all and end all of his life. In thought, in word, in action he had the good of humanity as his sole inspiration, his sole guiding principle.

He was most unostentatious and selfless to the core. What were the titles he assumed? Only true Servant of God and His Messenger. Servant first, and then a messenger. A messenger and Prophet like many other prophets in every part of the world, some known to you, many not known to you. If one does not believe in any of these truths one ceases to be a Muslim. It is an article of faith.

"Looking at the circumstances of the time and the unbounded reverence of his followers" says a Western writer "the most miraculous thing about Muhammad is, that he never claimed the power of working miracles". Miracles were performed but not to propogate his faith and were attributed entirely to God and his inscruitable ways. He would plainly say that he was a man like others. He had no treasures of earth or heaven. Nor did he claim to know the secrets that lie in the womb of future. All this was in an age when miracles were supposed to be ordinary occurances, at the back and call of the commonest saint, when the whole atmosphere was surcharged with supernaturalism in Arabia and outside Arabia.

He turned the attention of his followers towards the study of nature and its laws, to understand them and appreciate the Glory of God. The Quran says "God did not create the heavens and the earth and all that is between them in play. He did not create them all but with truth. But most men do not know." The world is not an illusion, nor without purpose. It has been created with truth. The number of verses in the Quran inviting close observation of nature are several times more than those that relate to prayer, fasting pilgrimage etc., all put together. The Muslims under its influence began to observe nature closely and this gives birth to the scientific spirit of observation and experiments which was unknown to the Greeks. While the Muslim Botanist IBn Baitar wrote on Botany after collecting plants from all parts of the world, described by Mayer in his Gesch. der Botanikaa-s, a monument of industry, while Al Byruni travelled for forty years to collect mineralogical specimens, and Muslim Astronomers made some observations extending even over twelve years. Aristotle wrote on Physics without performing a single experiment, wrote on natural history, carelessly stating without taking the trouble to ascertain the most evil verifiable fact that men have more teeth than animal. Galen, the greatest authority on classical anatomy informed that the lower jaw consists of two bones, a statement which is accepted unchallenged for centuries till Abdul Lateef takes the trouble to examine a human skeleton. After enumerating several such instances, Robert Priffault concludes in his well-known book "The making of humanity", "The debt of our science to the Arabs does not consist in startling discoveries or revolutionary theories. Science owes a great deal more to Arab culture; it owes its existence." The same writer says "The Greeks systematised, generalised and theorised but the patient ways of investigation, the accumulation of positive knowledge, the minute methods of science, detailed and prolonged observation, experimental enquiry, were altogether alien to Greek temperament. What we call science arose in Europe as a result of new methods of investigation, of the method of experiment, observation, measurement, of the development of Mathematica in a form unknown to the Greeks. That spirit and these methods. concludes the same author, were introduced into the European world by the Arabs.

It is the same practical character of the teaching of Prophet Muhammad that gave birth to the scientific spirit, that has also sanctified the daily labours and the so-called mundane affairs. The Quran says that God has created man to worship him but the word worship has a connotation of its own. God's worship is not confined to prayer alone, but every act that is done with the purpose of winning the approval of God and is for the benefit of the humanity comes under its purview. Islam sanctifies life and all its pursuits provided they are performed with honesty, justice and pure intents. It obliterates the age-long distinction between the sacred and profane. The Quran says if you eat clean things and thank God for it, it is an act of worship. It is a saying of the Prophet of Islam that a Morsel of food that one places in the mouth of his wife is an act of virtue to be rewarded by God. Another tradition of the Prophet says "He who is satisfying the desire of his heart will be rewarded by God provided the methods adopted are permissible. A person who was listening to him exclaimed `O Prophet of God, he is answering the calls of passions, is only satisfying the cravings of his heart. Forthwith came the reply, "Had he adopted an awful method for the satisfaction of this urge, he would have been punished; then, why should he not be rewarded for following the right course."

This new conception of religion that it should also devote itself to the betterment of this life rather than concern itself exclusively with the super mundane affairs, has led to a new orientation of moral values. Its abiding influence on the common relations of mankind in the affairs of every day life, its deep power over the masses, its regulation of their conceptions of rights and duty, its suitability to the ignorant savage and the wise philosopher are characteristic features of the teachings of the Prophet of Islam.

But it should be most carefully born in mind that this stress on good actions is not at the sacrifice of correctness of faith. While there are various schools of thought, one praising faith at the expense of deeds, another exhausting various acts to the detriment of correct belief, Islam is based on correct faith and righteous actions. Means are as important as the end and ends are as important as the means. It is an organic Unity. Together they live and thrive. Separate them and they both decay and die. In Islam, faith cannot be divorced from action. Right knowledge should be transferred into right action to produce the right results. How often the words come in the Quran—Those who believe and do good, they alone shall enter paradise. Again and again, not less than fifty times these words are repeated as if too much stress cannot be laid on them. Contemplation is encouraged but mere contemplation is not the goal. Those who believe and do nothing cannot exist in Islam. Those who believe and do wrong are inconceivable. Divine law is the l;law of effort and not of ideals. It chalks out for the men the path of eternal Progress from knowledge to action an from action to satisfaction.

But what is the correct faith from which right action spontaneously proceeds resulting in complete satisfaction. Here the central doctrine of Islam is the Unity of God. There is no god but one God is the pivot from which hangs the whole teaching and practice of Islam. He is unique not only as regards his divine being but also as regards his divine attributes.

As regards the attributes of God, Islam adopts here as in other things too, the law of the golden mean. It avoids on the one hand, the view of God which divests the divine being of every attribute and rejects, on the other, the view which likens him to things material. The Quran says, on the one hand, there is nothing which is like him, on the other, it affirms that he is Seeing, Hearing, Knowing. He is the King who is without a stain of fault or deficiency, the mighty ship of His power floats upon the ocean of justice and equity. He is the beneficent, th merciful. He is the guardian over all. Islam does not stop wit this positive statement. It adds further which is its most special characteristics, the negative aspect of the problem. There is also no one else who is guardian over anything. He is the mender of every breakage, and no one else is the mender of any breakage. He is the restorer of every loss and no one else is the restorer of any loss what-so-ever. There is not

God but one God, above any need, the maker of bodies, creator of souls, the lord of the day of judgement, and in short, in the words of Quran, to him belong all the excellent qualities.

Regarding the position of man in relation to the Universe, the Quran says "God has made subservient to you whatever is on the earth or in the universe. You are destined to rule over the Universe. But in relation to God, the Quran says `O man God has bestowed on you excellant faculties and has created life and death to put you to test in order to see whose actions are good and who has deviated from the right path.'

Inspite of free will which he enjoys, to some extent, every man is born under certain circumstances and continues to live under certain circumstances beyond his control. With regard to this God says, according to Islam, it is my will to create any man under conditions that seem best to me. Cosmic plans finite mortals cannot fully comprehend. But I will certainly test you in prosperity as well as in adversity, in health as well as in sickness, in heights as well as in depths, My ways of testing differ from man to man. from hour to hour. In adversity do not despair and do not resort to unlawful means. It is but a passing phase. In prosperity do not forget God. God-gifts are given only as trusts. You are always on trial, every moment on test. In this sphere of life there is not to reason why, there is but to do and die. If you live, live in accordance with God; and if you die, die in the path of God. You may call it fatalism. But this type of fatalism is a condition of vigorous increasing effort, keeping you ever on the alert. Do not consider this temporal life on earth as the end of human existence. There is a life after death and it is eternal. Life after death is only a connection link, a door that opens up hidden reality of life. Every action in life however insignificant, produces a lasting effect. It is correctly recorded somehow. Some of the ways of God are known to you but many of his ways are hidden from you. What is hidden in you and from you in this world will be unrolled and laid open before you in the next. The virtuous will enjoy the blessings of God which the eye has not seen, nor has the ear heard, nor has it entered into the hearts of men to conceive of them. They will march onward reaching higher and higher stages of evolution. Those who have wasted opportunity in this life shall under the inevitable law, which makes every man taste of what he has done, be subjected to a course of treatment of the spiritual diseases which they have brought about with their own hands. Beware, it is a terrible ordeal. Bodily pain is torture, you can bear somehow. Spiritual pain is hell, you will find it almost unbearable. Fight in this life itself the tendencies of the spirit prone to evil, tempting to lead you into iniquitious ways. Reach the next stage when the self-accusing spirit in your conscience is a wakened and the soul is anxious to attain moral excellence and revolts against disobedience. This will lead you to the final stage of the soul at rest, contented with God, finding its happiness and delight in Him alone. The soul no more stumbles. The stage of struggle passes away. Truth is victorious and falsehood lays down its arms. All complexes will then be resolved. Your house will not be divided against itself. Your personality will get integrated round the central core of submission to the will of God and complete surrender to his divine purpose. All hidden energies will then be released. The soul then will have peace. God will then address you 'O Thou soul that art at rest, and restest fully contented with thy Lord return to thy Lord. He pleased with thee and thou pleased with Him; So enter among my servants and enter into my paradise. This is the final goal for man; to become, on the, one hand, the master of the universe and, on the other, to see that his soul finds rest in his Lord, that not only his Lord will be pleased with him but that he is also pleased with his Lord. Contentment, complete contentment, satisfaction, complete satisfaction, peace, complete peace. The love of God is his food at this stage and he drinks deep at the fountain of life. Sorrow and defeat do not overwhelm him and success does not find him vain and exuslting.

The western nations are only trying to become the masters of the Universe, but their souls have not found peace and rest.

Thomas Carlyle, struck by this philosophy of life writes "and then also Islam—that we must submit to God; that our whole strength lies in resigned submission to Him, whatsoever he does to us, the thing he sends to us, even if death and worse than death, shall be good, shall be best; we resign ourselves to God." The same author continues "If this be Islam, says Goethe, do we not all live in Islam? Carlyle himself answers this question of Goethe and says "Yes, all of us that have any moral life, we all live so. This is yet the highest wisdom that heaven has revealed to our earth."

Revised and edited; originally published in *Islam and the Modern Age*, Vol. IX, no. 1.